The Paths We Choose

ThePaths WeChoose

A Memoir

SULLY ERNA

Bartleby Press
Washington • Baltimore

Printed in the United States of America

Published and distributed by:

Bartleby Press
8600 Foundry Street
Savage Mill Box 2043
Savage, Maryland 20763
1-800-953-9529

Library of Congress Cataloging-in-Publication Data

Erna, Sully.
  The paths we choose : a memoir / Sully Erna.
    p. cm.
  ISBN-13: 978-0-910155-98-4 (Paperback)
  1. Erna, Sully. 2. Rock musicians—United States—Biography. 3.
Godsmack (Musical group) I. Title.

ML420.E74A3 2007
782.42166092—dc22
[B]
                                        2006033507

To Mom
Thank you for raising me the way you did. I know you feel guilty about the way things were, but this is the one time I can say you're wrong. Believe me, I wouldn't change anything.

CONTENTS

ACKNOWLEDGMENTS

Who would believe that the best teacher I've ever had is only five years old? But my daughter Skylar has changed my life in ways she'll never know. I now understand the true meaning of unconditional love. She has helped me grow from a boy into a man, and every day I learn a little bit more about being a better dad. She will always be my little girl, and I will always try to give her the best life that I can. And when I make mistakes, as I know I will, I hope she can forgive me from time to time. Because I'll never be as perfect as she is in my eyes.

Skylar's mom, Jennifer Cabezon, has inspired me in different ways. Watching her give birth to an angel made me realize that I had a new hero in my life. I will continue to try to learn from her honesty, loyalty and love.

I'm also very proud to mention that Jen was responsible for getting me and my father to start rehabilitating our relationship. These days me and Dad are doing just fine.

Thanks to my band, Robbie Merrill, Tony Rombola and Shannon Larkin, for being my musical soul-mates and brothers at heart. You *are* my path. Also, thanks to my dearest friends, Jimmy Mustapha, Jeff St.Hilaire, Freddy Cristaldi, Kevin Sheehy, Marsha McManus, and my manager, Paul Geary.

I need to recognize Michael Azerrad for taking the time to help me with this book early on and Lydia Wills for her advice and direction (you said you might kick yourself in the ass if you let this one go—I hope you don't bruise too easily).

Finally, I want to express my appreciation to John Branigan of the William Morris Agency for his assistance, and of course Jeremy Kay of Bartleby Press for all his hard work and guidance.

As for the rest of my family, friends and those who have touched my heart, I honor them for the wisdom that they've given me, and I thank them for the education I've acquired through our experiences together.

Peaceful journeys to all!

PROLOGUE

It was the summer of 1984, and nighttime had fallen over the town of Lawrence, Massachusetts. It was a clear cool evening and the streets were dry, so driving from the north side of town to the south side wasn't a problem. It was nothing like during the winter months. I was with my two best friends, Jimmy Mustapha and Freddy Cristaldi. We decided to jump in Freddy's Mercury Cougar and check out a party that we'd been told about. We were the kind of kids that were always looking for a good time. If we could smoke a little dope, drink some beers, and hopefully find some girls to play with, well, that was a good enough reason to throw on our jackets and head out for the evening.

When we arrived, we noticed that there weren't many cars parked in front of the two-story house. Our first thought was that this party could be pretty lame. But we could see that there was definitely *something* going on through the second floor windows and decided it was worth investigating.

Getting out of the car, Freddy popped the trunk open and called me and Jimmy over to show us something. There next to the spare tire was a sawed-off shotgun that Freddy was "babysitting" for his sister's boyfriend. He pulled it out and handed it over to me. I remember feeling excited when I held it. My dad had started me hunting at a very young age so I'd always had a passion for guns. But after a few moments, Freddy insisted that since we were on a main road we should put it away before any cops drove by. Reluctantly, I handed it back. Freddy locked it back into the trunk and we made our way upstairs.

Once we got inside, two words were enough to describe this party—sausage festival! There were *maybe* two girls out of the twenty some odd people that were there. Way too much testosterone for us in most cases. Still, being underage and all, it was nevertheless a place to catch a buzz.

We schmoozed for awhile, drinking and huddling up in the corner to gossip about the muscle-headed idiots that laced the room trying to out-do each other's egos. But we weren't tight with any of these people, and after a couple hours of boredom, we'd had more than enough. On our way out, I realized that I had forgotten my jacket. I'd told Jimmy and Freddy to go downstairs and get the car and I would catch up with them in a second.

I headed back into the party, nudged my way through the room and grabbed my jacket off of the couch. On my way back to the door, me and this other kid unintentionally slammed into each other. Our beers went crashing to the floor and we both just looked at each other wondering who should apologize first. Then he peered at me with this unfocused look in his eyes and mumbled some smart-ass remark. Next thing I know, push comes to shove. We hit the beer-soaked floor and started going punch for punch.

At the same time, I begin to feel people kicking me in the

ribs and in the back of the head. I thought at first that it might have been people from the party just trying to break us up and being rough. But it only took a few more boots to the back of the head before it clicked that I was in the wrong place at the wrong time. I began thinking, "Shit! These fuckers are all his friends. This is *not* good. I gotta get the fuck out of here." It was just my luck, though, that the only two people that I knew could help me out of this mess had already gone downstairs to get the car. Finally, the kid who was throwing this party made his way over to us and broke up the fight, giving me the chance to get to my feet and out of the house.

As I walked across the front yard, I could see Jimmy and Freddy waiting for me in the car. I could tell they had no clue what had been going on by the way they were banging their heads and playing air drums to the tunes that they were cranking on the stereo. When I finally got close enough to catch Freddy's eye, he was able to see that something was wrong by the way I was huffing and puffing. My shirt was ripped, my face was red from getting punched and kicked and I was cussing up a storm!

They jumped out of the car and approached me.

"What the fuck happened to you?" they said, confused.

"Those motherfuckers just jumped me upstairs! This dude slammed into me with a beer and blah, blah, blah."

I started spitting out the whole story. As I babbled away and worked Jimmy and Freddy up into an ass-kicking mood, I saw Jimmy look over my shoulder and across the yard. I turned around and saw the same guy that I had just fought come stumbling out of the house with four or five of his buddies behind him. He was walking right towards me with his eyes locked onto mine. All I thought to myself was, "Here we go!"

Freddy and Jimmy immediately began heading in their direction to see if they could calm the posse down. I walked right behind them waiting to see if this shit was going to explode again (of course, feeling a lot more confident about it now that my bro's were by my side). It looked like something out of "The Warriors"; both parties heading towards each other with leather jackets on, ready to rumble.

Just as everyone started yelling at each other about what happened, I saw this dude pull out one of those huge-ass Rambo knives from his jacket. And with his eyes still locked on to mine, he broke away from the rest of the bunch and started heading in my direction.

Of course no one else saw this because they were all too busy arguing and trying to calm each other down. But I saw it clear as day. I began thinking, "Fuck this! I am *not* getting stabbed with that thing." I turned my ass around and ran back to Freddy's car, snatched the keys from the ignition, popped the trunk open, and pulled out the shotgun that he had stored away earlier. My adrenaline was so high that if I were a horse, I could have won the Kentucky derby that night.

I didn't hesitate for a second. I walked right back at this dude, who at this point was being held back by some of his own friends as they tried talking him out of using the knife. Well, that is, at least up until they saw me with a sawed-off shotgun in my hands. At that point they let him go and everyone seemed to have taken a step back. Could you blame them? It didn't seem to bother Rambo, though. He kept on coming right at me with this insane look on his face. I remember thinking, "Wow! Either this dude is really wasted, or he's really crazy. He has no idea that I'm holding a shotgun in my hands." He was on a mission. He had red in his eyes, and no matter what, he was going to stab me. Showtime!

As he got within feet of me, he raised the knife above his head in a stabbing position, only seconds away from plunging it into me. I pulled the shotgun up, pumped it once to load the chamber and pointed it directly into his face. I remember feeling nothing for this person at that point. My insides were filled with fear, kicking my survival instincts into full-force. And I knew as I braced my finger firmly on the trigger, if I hesitated for a second it could cost me my life.

But how did it come to this? How did my life get to this point? At the age of 16, I was about to throw away my future and risk spending the rest of my life in prison over a bad night and some spilled beer. Maybe I should just start from the beginning...

PART ONE

CHAPTER 1
WELCOME TO LAWRENCE

Lawrence, Massachusetts is an old industrial town filled with mills, factories, and aging machine shops. Railroad tracks surround the city's outskirts, and to this day trains still make their local runs to deliver cargo and other supplies from Haverhill all the way to Boston, twenty-six miles to the south. When you drive into the downtown area and cross the rusty iron bridges that lead to cobblestone roads, you can see the smoke stacks filling the air as if they were cloud factories.

Back in the 1930s, areas like Tower Hill and Prospect Hill were where the wealthy lived, and you can see that the homes that still stand there were mansions at one time— massive single-family colonials stand tall at the top of every street, surrounded by hand-laid stone walls. Now each of those once-gorgeous houses has been broken down into several different apartments. But I'm sure these neighborhoods were quite a sight to see in their heyday.

Most of my knowledge about Lawrence's history comes from my mother and her parents. They would tell me how

7

beautiful Lawrence still was even in the 1950s. The public fountains were so clean, my grandparents were able to bring their children down to the local park and actually swim in them. Or for five cents they could cool off in a movie theatre on Broadway and watch whatever flick was playing as many times as they could stand it.

But as time went on, as they tell it, Lawrence's main industries began to fail and what once was a beautiful, prosperous, and safe city evolved into a montage of darker realities: the streets which are now flooded with gangs, hookers, junkies, guns, and drug dealers, make Lawrence a pretty tough sale in the real estate market these days.

In August of 1984, the lower section of Tower Hill erupted into three days of racial rioting. It all started when a gang of Hispanics started beating some Frenchman's dogs with baseball bats because they thought the Frenchman had broken a windshield on one of their cars. Eventually, hundreds of people poured through the streets, firebombing houses, throwing rocks at passing cars, fighting anyone they came in contact with, looting stores, and even shooting people. One poor lady was partially scalped.

I remember when me and my friends got down to the area, there were people on the roof tops of three-story houses throwing Molotov cocktails and television sets down onto the police cars. Helicopters from the National Guard were circling the area like vultures. Hispanics and Whites were separated by barricades that the riot squads tried to keep up while the two groups fired rocks and bricks at each other from across the street. Some people were being pulled over the wooden horses and beaten by police while other sections of the crowd were tear-gassed to control the vulgar display of hostility. The whole event made national news, and papers as far away as Japan headlined it.

This memory makes it hard for me to grasp the reality of how beautiful Lawrence could've been at one time. For me, I've only known Lawrence as a place that makes the South Bronx look like a tropical resort. More than anything, I feel blessed knowing that I just survived it. The Lawrence I remember was full of murderers, thieves, and rapists, and half the time those people were your next-door neighbors. I've known young girls who got raped on the railroad tracks and watched them turn from wholesome schoolgirls into junkies. I've seen people smash through windows just to grab television sets for crack money, or a local gang bash someone's face in with a brick because they were wearing a certain color that the gang had claimed to be *their* color for that day. There were times when even me and some of my friends would occasionally threaten the life of a store clerk to keep his mouth shut when we needed to steal a box of frozen chicken patties from the local Store 24 so we could eat that day. Growing up on food stamps and powdered milk wasn't exactly our idea of nourishment.

Yep! Lawrence was about as ghetto as it gets, and it was as big an influence on me as it would be any person who's lived there.

My father Salvatore was raised in a small town called Melilli, on the island of Sicily, by his parents Mariano Erna and Carmela Carta. Interestingly enough, I'd found out that Carmela's brother, my great uncle Emanuele Carta, was a famous composer in Melilli. And still to this day they honor him once a year by having a festival in the streets where people dance, eat food, and listen to the local marching bands play the music that he composed. I guess with that in my blood-line it was inevitable that I was going to be a musician.

In 1961, at the age of 17, several years after Carmela passed away, my dad and his father came to America through an arranged marriage to try and make a better life for them-selves. Working in a shoe shop in Lawrence, they struggled.

When my mom met my dad he was living at the YMCA in Lawrence. She told me that when she would go over there to visit him, the entire room, which was all of 8' by 12', would be covered in empty Coca-Cola bottles and Marlboro cigarette packs. Somehow she still stomached the thought of having a life with this man and married him in 1964. By May 1, 1965, their first child was born, my older sister Maria. Three years after that, on February 7, guess who arrived? Yours truly!

My mother Constance and her sister Barbara were also raised in Lawrence by my grandparents Peter and Sally Peluso. Good ol' Peter. I could write a whole book on him alone. My grandfather was a real-deal barber, just like his dad. And until the day he died, in his mid eighties, I remember him whip-ping up his own shaving lather, sharpening up that straight edge razor on his leather belt, and shaving himself old-school style. It's something I was never quite brave enough to try.

Since the day I was born my mom always said I was a pain in the ass. Literally, since I was born breech! I almost died at birth choking on my umbilical cord as I tried to slide my way out feet first. I guess I was in a hurry to get the hell out of there and get the show rolling.

I was named Salvatore Paul Erna after my father. So why

do they call me Sully? "Sully" is usually short for Sullivan, an Irish name. And Irish I am definitely not. I am 100% pure Italiano!

Well, there are two answers to that question. For one, my dad tells me that he didn't want me to be a "junior." He says he's always hated that nickname. And secondly, you have to remember that my dad was straight off the boat from Italy and was very naive about this country. So when someone told him that Sully *was* the nickname for Salvatore, he bought it hook, line and sinker. So, I got the name Sully. Go figure!

We grew up on the ground floor of a brown three-story home on the corner of Arlington Street and Basswood Street. My aunt Barbara and my uncle Bill lived above us and my grandparents occupied the third floor.

But because our house sat on the corner, we were always a magnet for trouble. Center Street dead-ended at my house, so when any cars were speeding up that street and had to make the turn at the end, if they didn't crash straight into us they would either swerve left to avoid our house and crash into the antique store that was on one side of us, or they would swerve right and crash through the house that was on the other side of us. Either way, we always had the best views of many good accidents.

When I was around ten, my sister Maria and I were sitting on the living room couch watching TV. It must have been around noon when we heard sirens coming up the road, getting closer and closer, until they were right outside our window. Maria and I jumped up off the couch and looked out the window to see this car come *flying* up Center Street with two or three police cruisers right up its ass. Well, sure enough, they came speeding up the street so fast that they couldn't make the turn and crashed straight into the house to our left. BANG!

My sister and I ran out onto the porch to see the crash, and before you knew what was happening, this guy climbs out the driver's-side window of his smashed-up car, stumbles around, and starts shooting at the cops. The cops are hiding behind their doors shooting back at him as he's running up the street. My mom runs out and grabs me and my sister and shoves us to the floor. We were so riveted that we didn't realize we were standing twenty or thirty feet away from all these bullets flying around. When the shooting finally stopped we got up and I saw the guy lying dead on the sidewalk in a pool of blood. Nice thing for a ten year old kid to see, right? Like I said, that's the Lawrence I remember.

It wasn't always car crashes and gun fights that became close calls for us either. There were all kinds of reasons why our house was a target for trouble because it sat on the corner. Another time when me and my sister were in the living

*With sister Maria
on Christmas Day*

room watching television (I think "Lassie" was on), we kept hearing someone throwing rocks or something at the house. So we would look out the window to see what it was, but every time we'd open the curtains and look, there was not a soul on the street. We started to get freaked out because it was plain as day that something was hitting the house. This went on for over an hour. Every ten seconds or so we would hear this knock sound, but there was never anyone there.

Then, out of nowhere, SMASH! A fucking *arrow* comes screaming through our window and misses my sister's head by about six inches. She dives on the floor and I go running out of the living room yelling for my mother.

She says to me, "Sully! What the hell are you doing in there?"

"Nothing—that wasn't us! Someone shot an arrow through the living room window!"

So she goes running into the living room, and sure as shit, there's an arrow lying on the carpet, and a couple more stuck in the curtains! My mom calls up to my Aunt Barbara and Uncle Bill and tells them what happened.

It turns out they were hearing the same noises and couldn't figure it out either. So we all met outside and looked around to see who was doing this. Then we noticed that there were over 150 arrows stuck in the side of our house. My Uncle Bill goes back upstairs and pulled out one of his rifles with a high-powered scope and started scanning the area looking for the shooter. Finally he spotted the guy a few houses up from us. The man would peek his head out every so often when he felt the coast was clear and fire off another round from his porch, so my uncle called the cops.

When the police arrived, not only did they arrest him right out of his house, but they also confiscated several dozen compound bows, crossbows, and thousands of arrows. It turned

out he had robbed some weapons supply store in the area
and decided to brush up on his archery skills. I have no idea
what this guy was thinking, but I'm sure glad they got him
before he got us.

That's just a small taste of some the wonderful memories
that Lawrence has supplied me with. But as hard as it was
growing up on the streets and constantly watching your back,
it still had its advantages.

For one, it really helped me acquire the attitude I needed
to become a successful rock musician. Knowing what I know
today about the business and realizing how tough you need
to be to get somewhere in this life, I'm grateful to the streets
for toughening me up in that way.

My dad has also played a very big role in inspiring me to
become a musician. Being a trumpet player his whole life he
would have jazz bands that played in our basement when I
was a child. They called themselves the "Salvatore Erna Band."
I remember this because the initials "S.E." were on the front
of the music podiums that would hold their sheet music. It
all looked just like Lawrence Welk to me. I would stay up so
late watching them rehearse that I would fall asleep in the
acoustic guitar cases. I suppose that's how I first became interested in music.

I started taking drum lessons at the age of three and a
half. I'd been driving my mom nuts banging on everything in
the house, from pots and pans to my high chair. I begged her
to get me drum lessons, and although she had no problem
with that, no one would teach me. They would just tell her,
"The kid is three years old, how serious can he be? It's just
a phase he's going through. He'll get over it."

Finally my mom went to Consentino's Music in Lawrence. The instructor there was a Berklee College of Music graduate named Dave Vose. My mom said to Dave, "Please teach my son how to play the drums. He's hounding us every day. If I see he isn't taking it seriously, or that it's just a phase he's going through, I'll put a stop to it immediately, but either way you'll get paid for your time." Dave agreed with no problem, and finally I was in.

After about six months of lessons, I began begging my parents for a drum set, so on my fourth Christmas Santa gave me a brand new toy drum set—it was some kind of Muppet drums or something. Little did they realize that I would know the difference. You have to remember, I had been watching my dad's band for at least a year and knew the difference between a real drum set and a toy drum set. So I just put my foot through the bass drum and sent it out the window.

Santa didn't make the same mistake twice. The following Christmas I got my first real drum set and man, was I psyched!

Five years old with his "blue sparkled beauty"

I was five years old and I got a four-piece, blue-sparkled beauty! I was so small that my dad would have to sit me on his knee and lower me down just so I could reach the foot pedal. And I'm sure I drove my mom and dad up the wall with all the noise, banging on these things night and day, but I was determined to be a drummer. Me and my mom still joke about how much money she could've saved shipping my drums around the country as I joined different bands, and more importantly, how much sanity she could've retained if I would have only chosen to play the harmonica instead.

Right around the time I got my first drums, my parents got divorced. I was still a little young to really know what had happened between the two of them and why they decided to call it quits. But for whatever reason, they decided that they'd be better off separating. And I know at that point times got real tough for the both of them. My dad struggled going through several different kinds of jobs while my mom was left to raise two children on her own, busting her ass working double shifts as an x-ray technician. Somehow my mom always found a way to make it work though. She'd never let us see when she wasn't doing so well. She always kept a smile on her face so we wouldn't feel her desperation. She always sacrificed for us so we could be happy children.

Years went by before my dad was able to pay her a dime for child support, and even then he could only throw her $30.00 a week. When they eventually worked things out so that he would have visitation rights, I still remember him only being a weekend dad. If there was any major drama between them, most of it is just a blur to me. But then again, why would I remember? I was only five years old. As I see it, children have this built in ability to block out drama. Arguments and violence, whether verbal or physical are not what children should be subject to. That's the beauty of being a child. It's all about the innocence. We, as adults, should try and relearn that every now and then. It would save us a lot of stress not sweating the small stuff.

Children haven't been corrupted by society's ways yet. *We're* the ones who expose them to that through religion and politics. They haven't been influenced by the big bad wolves of the world yet. *We* introduce them to those creatures from lack of discipline and through certain movies and books. Children aren't interested in drama or confrontation. *We're* the ones who teach them that through our own personal confrontations which they have nothing to do with. They just want to be kids and play. So, our responsibilities as parents and guardians are to shelter them from these negative entities and allow them to just be kids. Their only responsibilities should be figuring out how to get those damn square blocks in that round hole. *They're just kids. Let them be kids!*

As for me, I was all about playing. Only building blocks and puzzles weren't really my thing. It was all about drums for me. Beating the skins baby! A lot of people spend their lives trying to figure out what they want to be in life, but for some reason, even though I was only five, I just knew what I wanted to do—*play music!* By the time I was seven years old, I'd already learned how to play the classic surf-rock instrumental "Wipeout." When I was eight, I remember sitting in the hallway of the music store, patiently waiting for the eighteen-year-old student before me to finish his lesson so I could begin mine. Finally the door opens, and anxiously I jump off my seat thinking his time is up, but instead Dave pokes his head out all aggravated and says, "Sully, can you come in here for five minutes?" So I throw my sticks under one arm, my book under the other arm, and head into the room.

There was this giant teenager with a very unpleasant look on his face staring down at all three feet of me as if to say, "Who the fuck are you?" Dave said, "Read this piece of music and play it for this gentleman." So I did, and it was obvious this kid was really pissed off watching me blast right through it with no problem whatsoever. I guess it was Dave's way of releasing his own stress.

I stopped taking lessons when I was eleven or twelve years old. I just didn't feel satisfied with reading music anymore. It felt really restraining to me. I wanted to just go off like the drummers I began listening to. After going through several instructors, I finally met up with a guy who confirmed my instincts by telling me it was easier for me to hear something and play it than it was for me to read it. So I quit taking lessons and just started to listen to records and play along.

John Bonham of Led Zeppelin was, and still is, my ultimate hero and you can hear a lot of Bonham in my playing today. I never saw anyone hit the drums harder and faster than Bonzo, and his footwork is still some of the best. His grooves were solid and very friendly to the ear. He was the ultimate caveman drummer.

Like a lot of Massachusetts rock fans, I was also very inspired by Aerosmith, "the Boston bad boys." They were the coolest! I got a lot of my blues edge from their drummer Joey Kramer. But believe it or not, their guitarist Joe Perry was the guy that made me come to an important realization. It was the *Live Bootleg* record that did it for me. I saw the picture of Joe holding up his B.C. Rich guitar, hair covering his face, standing in front of a stadium full of people and I said, "That's it! That's what I want to be! I'm going to grow my hair long and become a rock star!"

Then it was on to Neil Peart from Rush. Holy shit! When I heard "Tom Sawyer" for the first time, I nearly came in my pants. I remember thinking, "Who the fuck *is* this guy and what the fuck is with this drum set?" I never saw anything like it. I was used to a four-piece Ludwig set with three cymbals, and this guy comes out with a 200-piece drum set, three million cymbals and who knows what else was in there. He would play shit that most people couldn't even air drum to. But not me; I just saw it all as a challenge for me. I got albums like *2112, Moving Pictures* and *Exit…Stage Left*, strapped on my headphones, and sat in my room playing those records every day for years. Now that I think of it, I would have to say that Neil is probably the one responsible for me becoming such a perfectionist. I was so intrigued by his playing that if I didn't learn every little nook and cranny of his music, I wasn't satisfied.

That was the beginning of the end for me. After that, I would skip school every day to go home and practice, steal money out of my mom's coat pocket to buy another record, and blow off hanging out with anyone just to be able to play my drums. All I did was play, play, play! I remember needing woodblocks for my drums because there was a part in a song called "The Trees" off Rush's *Exit…Stage Left* album that had woodblocks on it. So I went to school that day and stole a set of woodblocks out of the music room. I folded up the stand, wrapped them in a blanket and dodged my way around teachers and through the corridors until I was out the back door.

I'm not sure who saw me and who didn't, but thinking about it, if you were a school teacher and seen some long haired dude scurrying through the hallways with some long object wrapped in a blanket, wouldn't you be just a little curious?

Music always came pretty easy for me. From a very young age I was determined to be successful. I had always fantasized about being a rock star and my family truly supported my dream. Well, let me correct that; my mother and my sister supported me. My dad wasn't so cool with it, which fucked me up real bad for a while. As a matter of fact, it was what started the downward spiral in our relationship as father and son. I found it ironic that he had such a problem with me taking my playing so seriously, when he's the one who'd been a musician his entire life and started me playing drums in the first place. It never made any sense to me when he would say, "music is not supposed to be a full-time thing. It doesn't lead to anything. You have to have some kind of a real job to fall back on. Music is just a hobby."

Something to fall back on? Music's just a hobby? If I thought I needed something to fall back on, then that would mean I had a doubt somewhere in my mind about succeeding as a musician. Why would I want to think that way? And as far as it being a hobby, fuck that! Music is the one thing I did and did well. I'd be a musician first and everything *else* would be a hobby.

Now, I may not know everything about being a dad yet, but I do know what *not* to do through the experiences I've had with my father. You don't tell your kid things like, "You're gonna be a bum for the rest of your life," or "If I don't see you do well in school, I'll crack you over the head with a two-by-four." His temper was way too intense for a small child to handle and the verbal abuse and lack of support became an ongoing issue between my father and me. As the years went by I grew to hate him more and more because of it.

And although I became very distanced from him, I also became a little hot-head like him. What do you expect when that's your only role model? You eventually go into the real world and you handle tough situations with violence, not intellect. Those are the tools I was given to raise myself to become my own man, or whatever I thought my version of a man was.

At that time I didn't even realize that he had no clue on how to be a dad. I mean for Christ's sake, his own father would tie him to the table and whip him with extension cords if he brought home a bad report card. Or he'd get the old knuckle sandwich for rolling his eyes at the dinner table. Gee, I wonder where he got his temper from.

Several years later my dad re-married, to a wonderful Central American lady named Zoila Azucena, who we all call Carol. And eventually they had my half-brother Carlo and my half-sister Elizabeth. Although me and my dad never really had a great relationship, my mom would still ship me off to live with him once in awhile when I became too out of control running around the streets being a juvenile delinquent. She knew I feared him so she figured that she could calm me down by sending me to live with him.

But it really never worked. I would still come and go as I pleased, even knowing I would get a beating for it. I'm sure I tested my father's patience every day. But what can I say—when I wasn't playing music, I loved hanging out on the streets.

In some ways, the street life is great. You learn how to defend yourself and survive; it motivates you and teaches you

to get off your ass and hunt for the things you need to get
to the next step. But in other ways it sucks. It conditions you
to be uncaring and cold. It hardens your personality to the
point where sometimes you feel no remorse for anything.

   From when I was very young, until I was in my early
twenties, the streets had molded me into someone who wasn't
so sensitive to other people's feelings, not to mention my own.
It didn't bother me to watch someone get a beating. It was
actually exciting for me. It didn't affect me when I broke
some girl's heart, or when I heard shootouts or sirens in the
neighborhood. It was just another of the everyday things that
happened. Like I said, it toughens your soul. Even the things
that frightened me as a young child I'm sure later on contributed to hardening my shell as an adult.

   When I was about eleven years old, I was hanging upstairs at my grandparents' house after dinner. At about 8:00
that evening I headed back downstairs to get settled in for
the night. When I got to the bottom of the stairs I noticed
our kitchen door was already opened a little bit, but I don't
remember thinking anything of it. So I pushed the door open
and walked into the house. When I did, I remember the door
didn't open all the way. It was as if something stopped it
from hitting the wall. When I looked back to see what it was,
I'll never forget the cold chill that rushed through my body
when I saw this Hispanic man standing there hiding behind
the door. He stood about five-foot ten wearing these dirty
ripped clothes and was as skinny as a junkie. He just stood
there starring at me with these dead eyes as if he was frozen.

   I screamed at the top of my lungs and ran as fast as I
could toward the light in the bathroom, where my mother
was putting her hair up in curlers before going to bed. When

she stepped out of the doorway in her bathrobe to see what the hell I was yelling about, she sees this guy just standing there starring at us like some kind of zombie. My mom getting scared began to yell at the guy, "What do you want?" But between the both of us being in a state of panic we scared the guy off and he ran out the door and down the street.

To this day I'm still not really sure what his intention was, but something tells me that my timing that evening probably saved my mom from being raped or killed. Whether or not that was one of those situations that toughened me up internally, I can't say. I'm not a psychologist. My guess is, it more than anything taught me subconsciously to be prepared for the unexpected at any time.

I remember feeling disappointed that I wasn't able to defend my mother. I was supposed to be the man of the house. The only problem was, I was only eleven years old. I wasn't old enough to have to go through that kind of experience yet, and sure as hell wasn't strong enough to protect her. It's not like I couldn't fight or anything. Hell, I'd been in plenty of fights by that age and had no problem holding my own. I was always a small kid with something to prove so I wouldn't back out of a fight for any reason. But when I'd been thrown into my first real situation, I felt like I'd failed. That bothered me, even then.

CHAPTER 2
THE FIGHTING YEARS

When I was around eleven years old, I witnessed the most unbelievable thing I'd ever seen.

It was a beautiful, sunny afternoon in May and the park was full of people. Two adult softball leagues battled each other while innocent children played in the sand boxes and on the swing sets at the other end. It was everything you would see in a perfect scene from a movie.

After school, me and a couple of my friends decided to go down to the Playstead Park to throw the football around and kill some time.

The park was so crowded that the only spot we could find was behind the homerun fence. So we hung out there and tossed the football around for an hour or so. Suddenly, we heard this huge BANG above our heads. The sound was so loud and scary that at first we thought someone had lit off a stick of dynamite.

As we looked up, all we could see was a lot of grey smoke and this silver-like glitter coming down, like confetti falling from the sky. I don't think anybody had the slightest idea what it was, but I remember the whole park came to a standstill and you could almost hear everyone take a breath.

Then, from through the smoke cloud, we saw these huge pieces of airplane coming down right on us. Two small planes that were circling each other had crashed into one another. Everyone in the park started screaming and running, scattering anywhere they could to get out of harm's way. I don't think I've ever run so fast in my life. You'd be surprised how fast you can run when there's an airplane heading right for you.

In an instant we heard the loudest crashes that I have ever experienced. It was like God shook the earth for a few seconds, and those seconds felt like forever.

Big hunks of plane were crashing down everywhere. The dust that had been kicked up on the ground had barely settled when I saw the most horrific thing I have ever witnessed: small and large body parts began to fall all over the park. It was unbelievable. Three blocks away, outside an elementary school, there was a leg stuck in a tree. An engine from one of the planes crashed about four or five blocks away from the park. It went right through someone's second-floor kitchen wall and demolished their house. A piece of wing landed in some phone wires and leaked jet fuel all over the street. A bloody piece of flesh landed on a girl's windshield and she was so horrified she drove into the side of a bridge.

I remember seeing this girl on the swing set eating a bag of chips and a half of a head fell right next to her. That poor girl got up and ran so fast screaming, I don't think that her feet even touched the ground. There were parts of bodies and pieces of flesh that you couldn't even tell what they were scattered all over the place. Some kids were just standing around screaming. Some of them started throwing up.

By this time there were people everywhere sprinting to

the park to see what had happened. A kid named Freddy, who I met years later and became good friends with, was there as well. Freddy told me that while he was standing around looking at all this insanity, he saw a human finger on the ground. He picked up the finger, stuffed it in his pocket and ran home to his house. He busted through the door and began telling his mother what he had just witnessed. When he saw that she wasn't buying into the story, he pulled out the finger and showed it to her. She freaked out and told him that not only was it disgusting, but it was bad karma to take it and to bring it back immediately. So he did.

It turned out that one of the planes was coming back from the airport in Bedford Mass. The other one had just taken off from the Lawrence airport—the pilot was getting tested for his license. Somehow they got on a head-on collision course; when they tried to take evasive action, they both turned the same way and crashed only about 1,000 feet above the ground. Everyone in the two planes were killed. It was a miracle that nobody on the ground was even injured.

You might say that a lot of my childhood was like that plane crash, with me always running head-on into trouble and not being able or even trying to get out of the way. As far back as I can remember, I've always reacted by throwing punches. I've *really* fought my way through life. I'm not exaggerating when I say that I've been thrown out of almost every single school I ever went to. Would you believe I even got thrown out of daycare? Most kids there never do anything except color books, eat graham crackers, and take naps. Not me, though. I guess I was just what you'd call...*overactive.*

My aunt Barbara told me about the times she had to pick me up from daycare because my mom was working a double shift at the hospital. Almost every time she would get there, her first question to the adults in charge would be, "Is he really that bad? Isn't there anyone else in the classroom that acts up besides him?" Apparently I'd always be standing in the corner with a dunce cap on for some stupid reason or another.

I personally don't remember this, but I know I was a little troublemaker so it doesn't surprise me. I do have a few memories from back then, though. Once, I was sitting at a table one day coloring away and this kid started taunting me. I don't remember why or how it started, or if I had done anything to instigate him. With me who knows. Maybe I could've started the whole thing and just conveniently forgot. But what I do remember is this kid throwing and hitting me in the face with one of those beanbags that you toss through the clown's mouth. Boy, did it sting like a son of a bitch! So I got up and punched him dead in the face. That, my first fist fight, I remember, clear as day. And I guess that was that! They called my mom, told her to come and get me and kicked me out—out of *daycare center!*

In first grade at Holy Rosary School, some girl named Lynn kept aggravating me while we were standing in line for something or other. She was doing stupid shit to me just to rile me up. You know, pulling my hair, poking me, flicking my ears, shit like that. So finally I turned around and socked her one, breaking all the blood vessels in her nose. She dropped to the ground on one knee as the blood poured out of her face. I just stood there in shock, knowing my ass was dead-meat. When my father got to the school he was so upset that he dragged me down the school stairs by my hair and threw me in the car to take me home. I don't remember too much after that. I guess he was a little upset.

Following that little incident, my parents didn't know

what to do with me. Only a first grader and I'd already been
expelled twice. But they just thought that Catholic school
was the only answer to a good education and good discipline,
so they shipped me off to another one. My destination: St.
Mary's Elementary School. My sister Maria hated the idea
because she'd been going there for years and did really well.
They all loved her because she was such a great student: well-
mannered, smart, punctual, honest. And then there was me:
a complete horror show! Maria knew what was in store for
that school when I got there, and even tried to warn them
about me. It didn't work though, because I still got in. And
it wasn't long before all hell broke loose.

Things were fine until the fourth grade, where I'm in the
schoolyard and this kid decides to challenge me to a wrestling
match. Of course I accept, and we start going at it right there
on the asphalt. I end up getting him in my death-grip headlock and I begin cranking down on his head pretty hard trying
to get him to say "uncle." My arms were strong for my age
because I'd been a drummer my whole life so there was no
breaking free. After a while he stopped saying anything—no
groaning, squawking, nothing. So I let him go expecting him
to come at me again. But instead he just lay there crying,
holding his neck. Next thing I know an ambulance shows up,
his parents show up, my parents show up and I'm in this
world of shit at nine years old. I had sprained his neck so bad
that they had to take him to the hospital in a neck-brace. I
felt horrible. I was being competitive, that's all. I thought we
were just playing.

Man, I thought my dad was going to kill me right there
on the school grounds, but I also think that, in a sick way,
being his son and all, he was happy that I won the fight. I

tried to explain to him what happened but he didn't want to hear it, and I wasn't about to push my luck by trying to explain. All I really wanted to tell my dad was, "I would've let him off the hook a lot sooner, but the son of a bitch wouldn't say 'uncle!'"

When I returned from my suspension a couple of days later, I went about my business as usual; goofing off and being the class clown as I always did. No big deal. What, did people expect that I should be on my best behavior or pay attention trying to learn something?

Well, apparently, Sister Maloof saw it that way. She came over to me right at the beginning of class and smashed my hands with one of those big fucking rulers that nuns carry around like samurai swords. Man, I stood up and freaked. I picked up my table and threw it at her so violently that the table actually hit and broke the blackboard. The look on her face was priceless. She was horrified. And the class was even more horrified that I had just thrown a desk at a nun. I could tell that even though she was too scared to approach me, she wanted to kill me. I stormed out of the room and walked home. That little outburst got me expelled from St. Mary's forever! The only good news was that my days in a Catholic school were finally at an end.

I skated my way through the rest of fourth and fifth grade without too many problems in a public school called the "Tarbox," right down the street from my house. I don't re-member too much excitement there except for the time I learned how to sell penny candy and pixie sticks to my class-mates for ten cents more than what they were worth. After the principal caught me a few times and called my mother down to school to take my ass home, she had had enough.

She called my father and shipped me off to live with him up on Prospect Hill.

Luckily for us there was a school called the Rollins right down the street from his house that would take me. But it didn't take long for things to go wrong again. Within the first few months of the sixth grade, this big-ass Hispanic bitch and her friends got some hair across their asses about me, and she decided that she wanted to fight me. At first I just ignored her, thinking that it was ridiculous to even entertain the thought of actually planning a fight with a girl (my fight in first grade notwithstanding). But she just kept at it, continually egging me on into fighting her. I knew it was wimpy to scrap with a chick and I really felt like I was doing my job by ignoring her, but this girl who looked like a linebacker for the New England Patriots just would not let up on me.

One day we had our showdown. She came at me, determined to get me to fight. A couple of slaps here and a punch there and I'd taken all I could take—it was on! I can't honestly say that I kicked her ass either—this bitch gave me a run for my money. Probably one of the better matches I'd ever had. But nevertheless, it ended the same as all the other fights. I was tossed out of school again.

Proudly, at the age of eleven, I decided that my woman battering days were over. And thank God for that. I would've hated to be known as a woman beater. I don't remember ever having to get into it with another girl from that point on. Except for my sister of course, but that doesn't count, right?

You see, Maria and I were very different growing up. We rarely got along, not until I was about eighteen anyway. She had this prissy, disco queen-like attitude, and I was always a wise-ass little punk. We would constantly be at each other's

*Eleven years old
and ready to hunt
with Dad's 30/30*

throats for no reason whatsoever. If she were in a mood some day and I even glanced in her direction, pots and pans would be flying across the house. I guess you could say we had some very "special moments together."

Just to give you an idea, on my tenth Christmas I got up at around 6AM like any ten year old would, all excited to open my presents. I went into my Mom's room and jumped on the bed. "Mom? Time to get up and open presents." My Mom looks over at me and patiently says, "Okay, sweetie, give me a second to make some coffee and I'll be right there."

Then I go running into my sister's room to wake her up. Still excited, I fling the door open and yell, "Maria, it's Christmas morning! Get up so we can open our presents!"

She yells back at me, "Get the fuck out of my room, I'm sleeping until noon today!"

I said, "No, you're not! It's time to open presents. NOW GET UP!" Boy, was I was pissed. She had never slept in before, but for some reason she thought that because she was thirteen now, a big teenager, she needed to sleep late all of a sudden.

So I did what any normal 10-year-old might. I began probing and poking at her, trying to pull the covers off of the bed. At least, until she yelled again, "If you don't get out of my room I'm gonna beat you!"

Disappointed, I stomped back into the kitchen to find my mother so she could tell Maria to get her lazy ass up. But Mom wasn't there. I peeked my head in her bedroom and there she was, sound asleep. She had never even gotten up to make her coffee. I started to get real mad, thinking, "This can't be happening! Its Christmas morning and I need to open my presents!"

To make things worse, I was still stewing about my sister yelling at me earlier and throwing me out of her room. A single thought went through my mind: "I'll fix her ass!"

I ran into the bathroom, opened up the medicine cabinet and made a cup of Alka-Seltzer. I snuck back in my sister's room, crept up next to her and poured the whole cup in her ear.

Now I had heard about people being startled in their sleep before, but this was more like a convulsion. She thought I'd poured acid in her ear. She flew out of that bed screaming and swatting at her ears yelling, "Ma! He poured acid in my ear. It burns, IT BURNS!"

She knew damn well it wasn't burning her. As far as I was concerned, it was just high teenage drama. I was laughing so hard I practically pissed myself. Then I saw my mom come out of her room. All Maria's yelling and dancing around woke her up too.

Of course, I was overjoyed. Now that everyone was up we could open presents. I really wasn't paying attention to how upset my Mom was, and I was most likely about to get a slap from her. But more importantly, I also wasn't paying any attention to the fact that my sister had snuck up behind me first. As I turned around to see if she was still whining about her ear, she delivered a brutal kick to my balls and I went down hard.

My Mom ran over and slapped my sister. My aunt, uncle and grandparents all came running downstairs to see what the hell all the hollering was about. I was lying on the floor trying to catch my breath. My Mom was trying to regain control of the house. And everything just became one big fucking mess.

Needless to say, me and my sister didn't get to open any gifts that morning. We were both sent to our rooms and didn't get to open our gifts for a few days. At least I got everyone up, even if it was a total backfire.

It was always something with me. At school or in the house was one thing, but when I was on my own it was even worse. My first run in with the law was at the age of eleven. I had known this kid that was a paperboy in my neighborhood. So one day when no one was home, I climbed through the window of his bedroom and stole eighty dollars of his paper route money. Not knowing that someone had recognized me breaking in, I walked to a store up the street where they had all kinds of video games and went crazy on Pac-Man and Space Invaders for several hours. By the time my mother had been tipped off and found me, I had about seventeen dollars left. Space Invaders and french fries aren't cheap, you know.

I remember being completely freaked out when my mother grabbed me and told me that the police were looking for me and that she had to turn me in. I was begging her not to take me there. But she knew that the signs of the streets were already starting. Breaking and entering at the age of eleven ought to have any parent concerned.

What I didn't know was my Uncle Paul who had been on the Lawrence police force for years had been contacted by my mother to set up a scare tactic for me. You know, show me some tough love. A couple of detectives took me into a room where they questioned me while I cried my eyes out. "We'll have to fingerprint him before we take his mug shots" the two detectives said to each other firmly. Then they pulled out a Polaroid camera, wrote up some fake inmate number on a piece of cardboard with a black magic marker and made me hold it up to my chest while they snapped a picture of me. I was a mess at that point. This was the big time. I was going to prison for life as far as I knew. I was balling my eyes out begging my mother to take me out of there. Boy, I would I love to know where that picture is today.

After my photo-shoot, I was taken down to the jail cells. I remember hearing the sounds of criminals yelling and moaning from down the corridor. It was so fucking creepy to me. The floors were wet from who knows what, and it smelled even worse than it looked.

As I stood there looking into the dark empty jail cell, the detective's voice echoed through the halls as he instructed me to get in. "Go on son. This is your new home." I was petrified! My body was frozen with fear. But as I looked around the room, I realized something very peculiar. There was no toilet paper in there. I looked up to the detective with my best puppy dog eyes and said, "How do you wipe yourself?" He lashed back, "You wipe yourself with your hands. Now go on!" They slammed the door behind me and walked out of sight. I began crying and apologizing, begging them to let me out and promising them that I would never do anything like that again. But all I got for a response was the eerie hollow sounds of the inmate's voices mocking me from their cells. I was so scared my body was trembling.

After about fifteen minutes or so they took me out and told me they were going to cut me a break. But if I was arrested again, they would lock me up for good. Then they let my mom take me home.

On the ride back to the house I was still trying to catch my breath from being hysterical. Even though my mom needed to show me some tough love, I could tell that she felt bad for me by the way she gently asked if I had learned my lesson. I reassured her that I would never do something that bad again and that I would be an angel from that point on. My halo was shining bright. The only problem was, no one could see that there was a set of horns holding the damn thing up.

One thing that did scare me straight for a little while was some advice I got from my Mom's boyfriend at the time. She was dating this guy named Eddie who was a pretty nice guy from what I can remember. But he had also gotten himself into some trouble one day when the pressures of the streets had gotten to him.

It was tough out there in the hood trying to make a buck or two. A lot of people struggled for months at a time trying to find work to support their families. And when you don't have money or food after so long, survival takes over. Sometimes in the wrong way.

For Eddie, this kind of stress led him into getting together with some men one day and robbing a bank. He was caught immediately and sentenced to 30 years in Walpole prison. That's how I remember him best. We went to visit him every week in prison.

I remember the ride taking forever to get there. And when we would finally arrive, it was scary as hell seeing those big prison walls, and barb-wired fences. Then we would have to go through iron barred doors and into a room to be searched with prison guards up on cat walks overlooking everyone with machine guns.

After being searched and cleared, we would finally be allowed to enter a room where we could all sit together and talk for a half hour or so. Every time I went there I would think, "I don't ever want to go to prison. Ever!"

One afternoon in prison, when Eddie was asleep, a man who didn't like him for whatever reason had entered his cell and stabbed him fifteen times in the back. Miraculously, he survived. When he was finally paroled, he would come to our house and visit my mom, and when he heard about me getting into little bits of trouble, he would take off his shirt and show me the scars on his back.

"Stay outta trouble Sully," he'd say. "You're a bright kid and I don't want to see this happen to you. Prison is no joke!" Seeing those scars on his back and hearing his stories from inside those prison walls would always scare the shit out of me enough for me to want to behave. But as you all know by now, kids have short memory spans. So it wasn't long before those stories and images faded from my mind and I was getting into trouble again.

Right around the same age, I smoked pot for the first time. My mother asked my sister Maria to baby-sit me one night so that my mom could go out to dinner with some friends. Maria wasn't very thrilled about the idea because she wanted to go to a party that same night with her new boy-friend. But my mom told her that she needed to stay home and take care of me instead. So after my mom left, Maria took me with her. But not without me promising to her that I'd behave and not tell mom. When we got to this person's house, there were only about fifteen to twenty people there. Maria introduced me to her friends then made her way around the room to say hi to some people. A couple of her male friends said they would keep an eye on me while she mingled. As Maria drifted off into the kitchen with her boyfriend, the guys took me into a bedroom.

They pulled out a bong that was as tall as me. I had no clue what it was when I saw it. But I remember it looked really cool to me; a big red see-through tube that smoke would travel up through when they would smoke from it. Of course only being eleven I was very curious and kept asking them what it was and why they smoked like that. It just looked fun.

They offered me a hit and I took them up on it. They showed me how to hold the "shot gun hole" with my finger and where to put my mouth at the top of the tube. The only problem was, I could barely reach the top of the tube with my mouth and hold the carburetor at the same time. I was too short. So they manned the carburetor for me as they lit the bowl.

After my first pull off the bong, I coughed my brains out choking on the smoke I had just inhaled. They sat there and laughed; kind of like you would when you throw a ball to a dog on a slick hardwood floor and watch him slide into the cabinets as he chases it.

Once my coughing fit was over, I asked for more. But they immediately shut me down and told me not to say a word to my sister. Then they left leaving the bag of weed and the bong in the room with me. I didn't remember feeling any different as I sat there in the bedroom by myself. So I took some more pot from the baggie and stuffed it into the bong, just as they had showed me. I stood on a couple of books and managed to get my finger on the hole as I fired up the three-footer again. I had no idea what I was doing, nor did I really know what I was smoking—all I knew was it smelled different than tobacco.

When my sister was finally told by her friends what I had been up to with the other guys, she snapped on all of them. "What the fuck are you doing?" She yelled at the guys. "He's *eleven* years old! You can't get him stoned!" Then she ripped me out of the bedroom and took me home.

I don't remember feeling high as much as I did just being dizzy and feeling a little weird. But then again, at that age, what would I know about feeling high? I was probably baked for all I know.

The first time I remember actually knowing that I was stoned was when I was twelve years old and I was hanging out with this kid Keith who was the same age as me. Me and Keith always had this love-hate kind of relationship. We lived right around the corner from each other and went to the same schools. We were punks of the same kind I guess you could say; strong minded and stubborn, the kind of kids who didn't want to be pushed around by anyone. But that worked against us as well. Some days we would act like best friends and other days (depending on our moods) we would be beating the shit out of each other. Keith also had a rough upbringing and was toughened up at an early age by his older brothers. So he was a tough kid to deal with; angry at the world most of the time. He's also the one responsible for getting me to start smoking cigarettes at that age.

* * * *

One afternoon when we were hanging out at the Playstead Park, the same park where I saw the plane crash, I was sharing a joint with Keith and some of his friends. We were sitting on a wall behind the softball field listening to *Aerosmith Rocks* on a boombox. I remember hearing the riff from "Last Child" playing over and over again and I just went into this trance. That's when I knew I was high. I was in a zone feeling like the music had taking me into another world. I loved the feeling so much that I bought the album that week and to this day it's still one of my all time favorite records.

I survived all of seventh grade with the usual after-school fights and a few suspensions, but eventually my fighting ways caught up to me. In the second half of eighth grade I got thrown out of Methuen East Middle School because of this motherfucker named Steven that always gave me shit. Steven was this nerdy, goofy kid with short brown hair and glasses and he talked with a lisp like this: "Fuck you, Shully!" We'd always tease him about that and he'd go, "You shuck, Shully!" And I'd go, "Oh yeah, Shteven?"

Anyway, this kid was also a decent drummer and we played in the school band together. In some ways he was a lot like me, always wanting to be the leader, so he hated me because I was the first drummer in the drum corps and he basically had to take direction from me. One day we're arguing about this drum part and why he wasn't playing it right. He got so aggravated with me telling him what to play that he took the drum stick mallet that was in his hands and swung it at me. I raised my hands up to block my face and he ended up smashing my arm with it. I immediately grabbed him by his face, pushed him over the radiator and smashed his head so hard against the window that the glass cracked.

So once again I was suspended for fighting. I was so mad at him for getting me suspended, knowing that my mother was gonna flip out, I waited for him after school. As he exited the building, I stalked him like a wild animal waiting for the right moment to attack, hiding behind trees and staying out of his sight. As he got down the hill and far enough away from the school I jumped out of the shadows and ran up behind him, calling him from the distance. I expected him to drop his books and chest up to me like the tough guy he claimed to be in school, but instead he ran like a coward down the hill and right into someone's yard. Dead end! Right there we went at it and I ended up beating the living shit out of him. The first chance he got, he broke away and ran off down the street. By then I was way too tired to chase him, and felt that I had proven my point anyway. But little did I know, to get home, I had to walk right by where he lived.

As I was passing his street I could hear someone yelling, "Hey, Shully!" I looked up the hill and there he was, standing at the top of his street swinging a pipe so big that he could hardly even hold it up, let alone swing it at me. Of course, it was just another challenge for me.

I go running up the hill after him. He starts cussing and swinging this huge pipe at me, telling me he's going to kick my ass. It was actually really funny. The pipe was so heavy it took him three or four seconds after swinging it to get it around to its starting point again. I have no idea what he was thinking, but I just kept my distance and waited for the right moment, then I kicked him square in the chest and once again beat the snot out of him.

His father and his brother came out of the house. His father grabbed me and held my hands behind my back to break us up while his brother grabbed Steven and held him.

"Do you want to fight him?" his father said to Steven. Steven, already whipped twice, said, "Yeah!"

His father turned to me. "Do you want to fight my son?"

"Only if you let my hands go," I said.

Would you believe that son of a bitch wouldn't let my hands go? He sic'ed Steven on me while he was holding my hands behind my back. So here comes this raving maniac about to tear my head off and his father isn't letting me go. I lift up my leg as he's charging at me and he ends up running right into my boot, stomach first. He falls to the ground, his dad lets me go, thinking I'm going to take off, but instead I jump on Steven and…Bing, bang, boom! It didn't last as long as the first or second beating though because his dad yanked me up by my shirt, slapped me upside my head and sent me on my way. The next day his dad made one phone call to the school and I was out. Man, I held a serious grudge after that for a longtime.

It pissed me off so bad that one night, years later when I was drunk on tequila, me and a few friends happened to be driving around Steven's neighborhood, and all those memories resurfaced in my mind about his father cracking me one. So we all gathered up a bunch of rocks, stuffed them in our hooded sweatshirts, and at about 3am began smashing the windows out of his house. Once the lights came on, we all scrammed out of there and that was the end of that.

I finished the eighth grade at the Henry K. Oliver Middle School in Lawrence but I basically skipped school the rest of the year. I just had no interest—to me, school was like a mall to hang out and find new people in.

It was also right around this time that I lost my virginity to a Methuen girl named Kim. What a strange experience *that* was. I had always heard that getting laid for the first time was supposed to be this milestone achievement...well, at least for a guy. But I don't remember it that way.

We met each other sometime around the eighth grade at Methuen East Middle. If we skipped school, I would walk down to where she lived, which was about a mile or so from my house, and hang out with her while her parents were at work. We would hang in the living room and make out for hours. unless her little brother Keith was around. Then we'd go up into her room to get some privacy.

Isn't it funny to remember those big long make-out sessions you had when you were young? Whether you're a girl or a boy, we all go through that naïve stage where you think you know how to kiss, but you really don't know what you're doing. You haven't mastered the art yet. And it is an art.

You remember...you'd lock your lips together in that wide open position with your heads completely still. Then your tongues would start banging into each other and flopping around like they were having a sword fight or something. Or how about those times when you'd be locked together for so long that when you pulled your mouths apart, you'd get that long strand of spit that still connected the both of you. How embarrassing. Oh yeah, we were pros, all right. But that was typical eighth grade behavior, as far as I know.

A punk in the making at 14

Eventually all that kissing led to the big moment for us. Me and Kim found ourselves naked on her bed one hot, sweaty afternoon. Don't worry, I'm not going to give you the details about our amateur sex encounter. But I do remember thinking, "Am I doing this right? And how long do we go for?" I wonder what she was thinking.

I run into her from time to time, and to this day she still doesn't believe me when I tell her that not only did I take her virginity, but she also took mine that day. Maybe she'll believe me now.

From a very young age, my show-off tool was my drumming, so when I went to a new school, I never thought about getting good grades, I just thought about drumming and new ways of getting into trouble. And when I did show up, I was usually destined for detention. But that was ok with me because detention was where all the hoodlums hung out. It was better than class, that's for sure.

The first so-called band that I put together was with some musicians I met at the Oliver School. These kids were just total punks like me: pot smokers, drinkers and school skippers. We set up a jam room at my mother's house in the spare bedroom and learned songs by Judas Priest, Iron Maiden and Sabbath. I don't think we even came up with a name for the band and we sure as hell never gigged. But we practiced a lot and it planted the seed for wanting to be in a band even more. And after I actually graduated the eighth-grade, I was excited to get into high school and meet some new people to jam with.

One day there I was, stoned out of my mind and playing hooky from school with a couple of my friends—nothing out of the ordinary for me, that's for sure. We all went back to my house knowing that my mother was at work, my sister was at school, and no one would find us there. I had this room I'd made in the basement with black lights, cool black light posters and an old sofa for me and my friends to hang out on, get baked and jam to Zeppelin and Sabbath.

In my stoned blur, I happened to notice this awesome wax sculpture that my sister had carved from scratch. I have to hand it to my sister; she was always very creative, great with sculpting, drawing, anything that had to do with art. She would buy these wax blocks, melt them down and mold all kinds of cool objects. In this case it was a stone castle—the windows were etched out, the drawbridge door was carved perfectly, it really was beautiful. The problem was, we didn't get along to begin with and I was stoned and bored. And most importantly...it was in my space!

So I made a blowtorch out of my mom's can of Aqua Net hairspray and a Bic lighter, and I began to melt down the castle. It was so awesome. It melted so perfectly that even my friends were in a trance watching this thing go down.

Later that day I was in my bedroom, crashed out, taking my stoner's afternoon nap and got woken up by my sister screaming, "Sully, I'm gonna fucking kill you!"

I jumped out of my bed, realizing she'd found the castle. I opened my door and there she was, screaming at me, "How could you do that, you asshole?"

Being the cocky little bastard that I was, I told her, "Get the fuck out of my face, Maria, before you get a slap."

Before I could finish my sentence, she wound up and kicked me so hard in the balls I thought my eyes were gonna fall out of my head. I dropped to the ground face down, gasping for air, she jumped on me, put her knees on my back and pinned my arms down so I couldn't get up, then she started wailing on me, smashing my head off the floor over and over again.

I would look up at her between bashings and tell her,

"You're so fucking dead when I get up." In the meantime I was completely helpless until she got off of me.

She finally got brave enough to make a move. Pushing her body weight on me, she slowly got up, keeping one knee in my back. I could feel my blood boiling, knowing that in seconds when she made a break for it, I was gonna beat her ass. Finally she made a break for it and ran right into the bathroom. She slammed the door shut and I could hear her scrambling for the cheap little hook latch we had on our bathroom door.

Now I'm worked up into a frenzy, losing my mind. My face was all red and bleeding and all I could think of was beating this girl senseless. I began kicking and pushing on the door trying to get her off the other side of it. She's yelling at the top of her lungs for our Uncle Bill to come down from upstairs and save her, which only made me more desperate to get through the door to shut her up.

After a few minutes of this, I decided to go with another plan. I ran into her bedroom and grabbed some more hairspray and a lighter and began to blowtorch the doorknob. I figured if I heated up the doorknob long enough, it would get red hot, just like in the cartoons, and burn her hands so she'd let go of it. Then I could kick in the door and get the bitch. I was so crazed about getting in that bathroom that I didn't even notice that the door had caught fire.

Now I really started freaking out because I knew my mother was going to have a fit when she got home from work. So I started furiously kicking the door again yelling, "You fucking asshole! Ma is gonna kill me for this. You're fucking dead!" Then I suddenly realized two things: first, I'd cracked the door right up the middle and second, my sister wasn't yelling back at me anymore. I looked through the keyhole and saw Maria going out the bathroom window. So I spun around and ran out the front door to catch her, but she was gone like the wind!

When my mom got home from work that day and saw the door roasted and nearly cracked in two, she instantly knew I was responsible. She grabbed an extension cord and began chasing me around the house. Man, I was so scared because I knew if she caught me I was *fucked!* I had never seen my mom so pissed. She'd frequently go after me because of the stupid things I'd do, but the older I got, the less it bothered me. You know how it is—you grow up and the occasional slap or broomstick over the head isn't a big deal anymore. You just fake hurting to humor them, but this time was different—I knew this whip she had in her hands was going to really hurt if she caught me with it, so I ran for my life.

She finally backed me into the living room. I had nowhere else to run so I jumped up on the couch like a scared animal and curled up into a little ball, covering my face and praying this wouldn't hurt too badly. She whipped me like I was a stranger for what seemed like forever, but in reality was no more than a minute or two. It was the first time I'd ever felt any kind of distance from my mom. Out of all the times she had punished me or smacked me around for doing stupid shit, I still always felt the love she had for me, and I knew I was being punished for my own good, but this time was different: she had a blank look on her face as if she didn't even remember I was her son.

Then all at once, she realized what she was doing and stopped. My back was bleeding and glowing with big welts. When she saw this, she began to cry and apologized to me, putting Vaseline on my wounds. I think she scared herself. And

I began to feel guilty that I'd made her that upset. I knew that she'd fucked up really bad and she hadn't meant it to get that far. She'd probably had a horrible day at work and on top of that she comes home and her bathroom door is burned up and broken. She couldn't afford to go buy a new door. We just didn't have that kind of money. So it put her on tilt that day.

I didn't see her upset that often. She's the type of woman who won't tell you what's wrong if she's not feeling good— she'd rather deal with it on her own than ask for help from anyone; very stubborn in that sense. I never held that beating against her because I felt like I deserved it – I was being careless and irresponsible, not to mention dangerous. I mean, you can't just go around lighting doors on fire.

My mom never laid another hand on me after that. Well, actually, there was this one other time. I was fourteen or fifteen years old and had been out way past my curfew when I crawled in drunk as a skunk. Now, if you've ever been in a situation like this before, you'll understand what I'm talking about when I say that parents have this built-in radar system. They could be sound asleep and still know when you're sneaking in at the wrong hour. Everything seems to make noise when you're sneaking around, right? Even your own shoes seem to squeak when you're walking. And their eyes are already adjusted to the dark so they're watching you while you're creeping around the house trying to make your way to your bedroom, and you look like an idiot to them doing it.

So here's me crawling in the house completely wasted. I didn't turn the lights on because my mother's room was right off of the kitchen. Little did I know that my mom was sitting right at the table looking at me stumbling around in the dark. Besides, I wouldn't have gotten away with it for much longer anyway because I ended up tripping over the kitchen chair and making all kinds of noise. I go crashing to the ground thinking, "Oh my God! I just woke up everyone in the house." The lights immediately go on and my mom is standing there with that look on her face. I tried to make light of it by laughing at my stupidity, but the more I seemed to not care, the more she got pissed and told me to get my ass over to her so she could slap me and send me to my room. She got so frustrated going back and forth with me, running around the table trying to catch me, that she finally just picked up her keys off the table and cocked her arm back as if she was going to throw them at me. Her key ring was *huge*. My mom worked at a hospital, so she had about a hundred keys on this ring, literally.

In my drunken mind there was no way she was going to hit me with those things. She had always thrown stuff at me when she couldn't catch me, but she was never able to connect. She had the worst aim ever. So I just laughed out loud when she cocked her arm back and signaled with her eyes for me to come to her.

I stuck my face out at her and dared her to throw them. She fired those things at me like she was pitching for the Boston Red Sox and caught me square on the chin. I hit the floor like a ton of bricks. My jaw was cut open and I was seeing stars.

My mom stood over me, "That's what you get for being a smart-ass. Now get in your room and go to sleep." Which is what I was trying to do in the first place.

Whether it was starting trouble or simply just pulling pranks on people, it didn't need to be Halloween for me to try a new stunt. And me and my friends never got into stuff like egging houses, breaking windows, stealing little kids' candy, or lighting paper bags full of shit on fire on your neighbor's porch. No, we were more into permanently damaging things, like wrapping up our neighbor's rusty old car in toilet paper, wetting it down and letting it dry overnight, so when she peeled the paper off her car, the paint would peel off with it; that was payback for her always calling the police on us when we would play wiffleball in the middle of the street and have to jump her fence to retrieve the ball. She was a real bitch!

Or there was the time the mailman kicked my dog in my yard when he thought no one was looking. He didn't realize that my neighbor snitched on his ass when I got home. Boy, did he pay for that. At first I thought I'd just confront him and chew his ass out, but then I thought about it and decided that it would be so much better if my dog had the chance to get him back.

So the next day I planned my attack. I brought my dog outside so he could take a nice fresh crap, then I scooped up a spoonful of it and brought it up to the porch where he delivered our mail. I took a screwdriver, pulled out the doorbell button, stuck a razor-sharp tack in the hole of the doorbell backwards, then filled the hole in with dogshit. When the mailman came up to the porch to ring our doorbell, he not only stabbed his finger on the tack that awaited him, but he ended up sticking his finger right into his mouth to stop the bleeding. Mmmm! How did that dogshit taste, Mr. Mailman?

Not very mature on my end I have to admit, but it sure was funny! And mighty damn clever I'd have to say.

Besides, was I really concerned about maturing at that age? Well, I guess I needed to be...especially since, after all the schools I'd fought my way out of, I was about to step foot into my first high school classroom.

CHAPTER 3

ROCK 'N' ROLL HIGH SCHOOL

I always thought "The Regional Vocational Technical High School" was way too fucking long for the name of a school. Everyone else who went there thought so, too. So it was nicknamed the "Voke" for short. Much better, wouldn't you say? The Voke was a trade school. One week we would have classes, and then spend the next week in shop.

During my freshman year I decided to take up metal fabrication, which is learning how to install the duct work for heating and air conditioning systems. Or as we used to call it, "our little factory for making marijuana pipes and smoking them in the welding booths." On top of that, being in metal fabrication had its perks, because the part of the school that we were located in was right next door to the Culinary Arts Department. It was really convenient for us when we got the munchies to raid them and steal all the fresh-baked chocolate chip cookies.

I was fourteen years old and growing up fast. I started becoming even more independent now that I was entering high school. I even remember *feeling* older. I was meeting girls, going to house parties on weekends, ignoring my mom's request to be home by 11pm and staying out all night, and yes... smoking pot all the time! High school is where I also began meeting some very important people in my life—*my friends.*

I think that most people would agree if I said that throughout our first decade or so in life, we meet some of our so-called "friends" in passing. You know, the people that we play in sand boxes with and on little league teams. But our real, true friends start surfacing throughout our high school stages. These are the kinds of friends that you can end up staying close to well after your high school years are over. Or at least that was the case for me.

Remember Steven, the kid with the lisp? Well, his older brother Johnny went to the Voke. And I heard that this kid named Freddy Cristaldi had beat up Johnny and stuffed him in a locker. So when me and Freddy met, I told him how I beat up his younger brother Steven in the eighth grade. Naturally, we hit it off and became great friends.

A good six months or so passed and I hadn't even got into any trouble in this school. Everything was cool at the Voke. They even had a smoking area outside, which is where I hung out most of the time. And it was right next to the cosmetology shop, so the view was delicious, if you know what I mean.

The cool thing about this place was, when you were in class week, you were with your own grades, but when you were in shop week, you were with all the grades: freshmen, sophomores, juniors, and seniors. I always hung with the older kids. I just never felt like I jived with people my age. Plus the older dudes loved me because I was a fighter and didn't take any shit from anyone, and they loved to egg me on and see

the scraps go down. Yup, things were pretty cool for a while—
or at least until I met this kid named John.

Me and this kid hated each other. We were the same size
but he was even cockier than me. He was always being a
smart-ass and fucking with me, although it's funny how he
made sure there was always a teacher or some other kids
around that could help him out when he did.

One day I was in the shop by myself—it was lunchtime
and everyone had left to go eat. I'd decided to hang out that
day and just kill time. The big garage door in the shop opened
up and who walks in? That's right, my dear friend John. He
looked up in complete amazement that I'm standing there by
myself, no teachers or seniors around, no one for him to
show off in front of, just me and him. I'm thinking, "Oh
man, this is gonna be good."

He sees me smirk at him and looks away. Keeping his head
down to the ground, he walked past me. I started to follow
him, taunting him, "Hey John? You feel like going 'round and
'round right now, bro'? Seeing that you have such a big mouth
when everyone's around, I thought maybe you can say some of
that wise-ass shit now." He wouldn't say a word.

I got bored pretty quick trying to get him to fight me,
so I decided to make the first move. I grabbed him by the
back of his shirt assuming that I would get a reaction from
him and maybe he'd swing at me, but nope, he wouldn't do
anything but whimper and try to get himself out of it. Being
the nice guy that I was that day, I decided not to punch him.
But instead I dragged him over to the metal clamp (which is
about nine-feet wide with handles on each side to open and
close it) tied his hands behind his back using his own shirt,
then pulled the rest of his shirt out of his pants and stuck his
shirt in the clamp. Then I clasped it shut and left him there.

Even if he got his hands free, this machine was so wide he would've never been able to grab the handles and release himself. He stayed there for the whole lunch break while I took off and had a smoke.

Now, I thought I'd been pretty nice about the whole situation, and if he would've let that be the end of it, I probably would've never fucked with him again. But what did he do instead? He ratted me out the very second the class got back to the shop. I guess he had to say something considering the entire class walked in on him clamped to a machine. But the fact is, he still ratted me out and I got suspended for it.

I return to school one week later, just itching to find this rat bastard and beat his ass. Once again, I wait in the shop for John to show up during lunch. For some reason he always headed for the shop early, before lunch was done, so I knew he'd be coming soon. I hadn't spoken a word to him all day, didn't even look at him. I didn't want him to catch on at all that I was going to smack him one.

So here he comes, out of the snowy outdoors, heading for the shop garage doors. The doors open and he walks through them again, only to be surprised by little ole' me. I didn't even say a word to him; I just looked him dead in the face and drilled him right in the nose. He goes running off to the principal's office to rat me out again. And so I was expelled—again!

After I got expelled from the Voke, my mom felt like she had exhausted all her options with me. She saw where my life was going, all the trouble I was getting into, all the bad people I was attracting, the incidents I was getting involved in—and she was very worried. She tried the hardcore approach at first—

"Go live with your father!"—but that didn't work out. She tried grounding me, but it was too easy for me to climb out my first floor bedroom window when she would fall asleep and go party some more with the boys. So that didn't work for her either. Feeling like she had come to the end of her rope, and knowing that there weren't too many schools left for me to go to, she reached out for help.

My Aunt Rena (my father's sister) and my Uncle Ray had always been some of my closest relatives. Although they lived in Connecticut, whenever they did come around for the holidays I had always got a long with them great.

After my parents spoke with them on the phone one afternoon, my Aunt and Uncle offered to help out by letting me live with them. Big mistake.

Aunt Rena and Uncle Ray lived in Berlin, Connecticut. Berlin is a very clean, upper-class, low crime kind of town. And Uncle Ray was a very successful contractor in the state; he and Aunt Rena had also owned some nightclubs in the past so they had always done really well for themselves. It was a whole different league for me – they were rich. And they assumed that *maybe,* if I was taken out of the city life, away from all that crime and trouble and put in an environment like Berlin, that *maybe* I would start looking at life from a different angle. You know, appreciate the wholesome things that country living offers and become more responsible. Especially since my uncle was offering to put me to work in his construction business on the weekends. I could make some money and buy my own stuff. It was worth a shot and it was comfortable out there, very different from Lawrence. I was used to houses being right up against each other all the way down the block; in Berlin everyone had their own yard. Lawrence was very dark and claustrophobic; Berlin seemed

like the skies had cleared and it was blue out there. Lawrence
was full of dirt and graffiti but Berlin was clean, with no
trash on the sidewalks. The kids were well-mannered and well-
dressed. It truly was a breath of fresh air.

My uncle put me to work doing construction for him—
I was up at six o'clock in the morning working for him on
the weekends and then going to school weekdays. Their strat-
egy was to try to keep me focused on the right things. But
I was on a different page than they were. I was focused alright,
but it was more about finding new girls at a new high school
and seeing who the pot smokers were.

Of course, the first day there I find the worst kid in the
school to hang out with. His name was Sibby. (I assume it
was short for Sebastian or something.) His brother dealt hash,
so Sib always had a chunk with him the size of a tennis ball.
Getting baked before class every morning was never a problem. Needless to say, we became really close in a really short
time.

We spent most days in the boys room getting stoned or
just killing time until lunch. About two weeks into me starting at this school, we were hanging out in the bathroom
smoking a cigarette, stoned out of our minds. Sib had his
lighter out and as we're shooting the shit, he started lighting
the corner of this plastic paper towel dispenser that's hanging
on the wall next to the sink. There was only a little blue
flame lit on the corner of it, so we didn't think anything of
it. We were so amused by it that we just stared at it thinking,
"Wow, that looks really cool!"

Then the lunch bell rang and we ran to the cafeteria to
chow down. Pot munchies, I guess.

About halfway through lunch we're sitting in the cafeteria

and a shitload of policemen and firefighters come running into the building. I'm thinking, "What the fuck is this?" They start heading right for me and Sibby and I realized, "Oh no! We forgot to blow out that little blue flame!"

Well, that little blue flame had grown up to become a very big flame that caught the whole paper towel dispenser on fire, and then caught the entire drop ceiling on fire. The whole bathroom was ablaze.

As the cops get to us, they didn't even look at me, and I was sitting right next to Sibby. Instead they grabbed him from the table and dragged him out of the cafeteria, out of the building and into a police car, then hauled him away. They knew exactly who was responsible for this. Poor Sibby— he was known as the troublemaker in that school and I hadn't been there long enough yet to show them what a terror I was, so he got the rap. I don't really remember what happened to him for that, but I do remember that he was back in a couple of weeks to partner up again. I had some pretty good times in Connecticut and met some very cool people, but I fell right into the same bullshit I was pulling in Lawrence—drinking, getting stoned and being a punk.

Back at the Voke I had met this guy named Bill DeMonaco who I also became good friends with. He was a musician, a singer that I'd spent a lot of time jamming with. About six months into my stay, I decided I'd had enough of good old Connecticut. It was time to go home. So I called up Bill and told him to come get my ass out of there. I gave him directions and told him, "Be at my uncle's house tomorrow, right after school."

That morning I got up and went into Berlin High School for the last time. At the end of the day, I gathered up my

books, threw them all in my locker, took a bottle of lighter
fluid, soaked them all down, and set fire to my locker.

Then I ran my ass off out of there and right home to my
Uncle Ray's house. Just as planned, Bill was there waiting for
me in his Chevy Nova. My aunt and uncle had no clue what
had just happened at school so everything was cool. I told
them I was heading home, that I didn't want to stay in
Connecticut anymore. They didn't stand in my way because
they knew what I was like and how stubborn I could be. So
we said our goodbyes and I got the hell out of Dodge, *real*
fucking quick!

I never got caught for torching my locker but to this day,
people still walk up to me and tell me that that story still
floats around Berlin High.

When I got back to Lawrence, me and my mom had a
sit-down and came to an agreement that I would try to do
a little better. Freddy had told me over the phone that he had
also been kicked out of the Voke and was going to Lawrence
High School, and that I should go there. So I told my mom
that if she enrolled me at Lawrence High, I would most likely
do a lot better because I would be with friends, rather than
in Connecticut with people that I don't know. What a sales
pitch *that* was. But I got into Lawrence High, and once again
I had a fresh new slate to work with.

CHAPTER 4

JUST A BUNCH OF PUNKS IN THE STREETS

If someone asked me what was the most defining memory of my childhood, I'd have to tell them that it was when I met the guys in my life who have meant the most to me—my partners in crime. The guys I've grown to love, respect and admire through the years. We've laughed together, cried together, lived together, fought together. We've even fought each other. We've experimented with drugs, experienced women together, been in love, out of love, you name it; we've done it all! We've literally all molded our lives through sex, drugs and rock 'n' roll. So let me introduce them to you.

Freddy Cristaldi you've already met. Jim Mustapha, who we call "Muskrat," I met at Lawrence High through Freddy. The way Jimmy and Freddy knew each other was pretty amusing in itself. Jimmy and Freddy lived only a few houses away from each other but Jimmy had hated Freddy ever since they first met. So one day Jimmy told his friend Johnny (ironically the same Johnny that Freddy had stuffed in a locker at the Voke) to go and kick Freddy's ass. But when Johnny ran up to Freddy, Freddy gave Johnny the old one-two punch and laid him out cold. After that, Jim stopped hanging out with Johnny and Jim and Freddy became best friends.

They were both tough kids growing up. Street boys just like me. Jimmy was always the tallest one, standing about six feet tall, but weighing next to nothing. He's fairly mellow and not especially dynamic. Instead he just absorbs life around him and goes with whatever comes up. His father, Joe, was a Golden Gloves Boxer, and let me tell you, he was one tough son of a bitch! I would have to say that he was the guy responsible for making Jimmy as tough as he was. If Jimmy got out of line, Joe sure had a way of showing some tough love for it.

Freddy stands about 5'10" and is a little more high-strung than Jimmy—and very competitive. He was born with a cleft lip and had something of a speech impediment, so he had to stick up for himself as much as I did for being short, but became quite the fighter because of it.

Shortly after we all began to hang on a regular basis, we bonded by getting our first tattoo together. It wasn't at the local Tattoo Fever shop in New Hampshire, however, because we were still underage. So we learned the art of tattooing a different way.

We would hang out with dudes on the streets who were in and out of jail all the time and had all these jailhouse tats on them. They showed us how to use India ink and a sewing needle to tattoo ourselves. Jimmy would steal India ink from art class, heat up a needle so it was sterile, wrap thread around it, dunk it in ink and then we would stab ourselves for two hours until we got some kind of picture going. I wouldn't recommend it.

Our first tattoo was a cross (more like a plus sign) on the middle fingers of our right hands. And out of all the tattoo's that we have today, it is the only one that we said we would never cover up. It just became a very sentimental symbol for us, symbolizing our youth and the times of the streets.

Then Jimmy tattooed my name on my arm, his name on his arm and "Rush" on Freddy's arm because Rush was Freddy's favorite band. After that, it was a lightening bolt here and an iron-cross there, but all of those have been covered since. Only the crosses remain as the original.

I met Jeff "Fro" St. Hilaire a couple of years later through Bill DeMonaco. We call Jeff "Fro" because he has this nappy Afro-ish kind of hair that would always grow up and out, not down. And it pissed him off so bad because he is the biggest old school metal freak that there is and can't grow his hair long. He still loves and listens to Overkill, Metal Church, Metallica, Megadeth, Flotsam and Jetsam, and so on. He's just one of those guys who always wanted to have the killer long hair and be a guitar player in a heavy metal band.

I'll never forget the first time I met Fro. It was in the summer of 1984 and I was sixteen. Me, Jim, Freddy, Bill, and several other people were hanging out at the beach that afternoon waiting for the night to settle in so we could have a bonfire party on the beach. I was walking down the strip to get some fried dough and I happened to notice this dude with a set of headphones on and a Walkman clipped to his jam shorts, standing in front of a Coke machine. The tunes must have been wailing because he was playing the best air guitar I had ever seen. He would stand there, drop a quarter in the machine, then start jamming to the guitar solo that was playing, then he'd drop another quarter in and start tearing up the lead again with his head banging away and singing out loud. It must have taken him ten minutes just to get his money into the machine. I remember standing there thinking, "What the fuck is this guy doing? What a freak! I love it!"

Later on that night, we all got together to party on the beach and lo and behold, the crazy Walkman guy showed up with his girlfriend to hang with us. Bill introduced us and from that point on we have remained best friends.

As much of a brother as Fro is to me, the majority of the real crazy shit went down with Jimmy and Freddy, so let's keep going from there. Me, Muskrat and Freddy, the Terrible Trio—that's when life really began.

Jim, Freddy, and I all lived about two blocks from each other. We would start our day by meeting at Jimmy's house to get baked before walking to school, check in for an hour, and then skip the rest of the day. Jimmy's older sister always had the killer weed and would hook us up with a big fat bag of sticky buds to sell for her. Yeah, right...that plan never worked too well. We'd always smoke that shit up and then have to find a way to pay for it so she wouldn't kick our ass.

God forbid we didn't have any weed—that was like the end of the world for us. One time I snuck through Jimmy's bedroom window to get him up for school. We hadn't had any weed for days and I was dying. Jimmy had planted some seeds in a flowerpot weeks before and left it on his window-sill, hoping to grow a massive plant. I made all kinds of noise sneaking in, but he still didn't wake up. It didn't surprise me though—when Jimmy's crashes out, you can light off a stick of dynamite next to his head and he still won't wake up. Don't even make me tell you about all the times we've lived together and I'd literally stick socks in his mouth to keep him from snoring so loud.

I went over to the plant and began to pluck off every little leaf, leaving nothing but a crooked little stem sticking up out of the flowerpot. I zapped the leaves in his microwave to dry it out and then rolled it up. Jimmy gets out of bed and sees me sitting there on his floor rolling a joint. "Where the fuck did you get weed?" he says. Then when he noticed the disfigured nub on the windowsill, he starts going off on me. "What the fuck, Sully! It's not ready yet." I'm like, "Jim! C'mon man, it looks fine. Let's just smoke it." Bad idea! Have you ever heard the expression "headache weed"? Well, I think we invented it, because that's about all we got out of it.

Sometimes we'd gather in Jim's room, which was no more than 10' by 10', and get stoned after his family went to sleep. Then we'd find things to entertain ourselves with in the wee hours of the morning. Sometimes it was just a friendly game of Nerf basketball that would wake up the whole house as we'd body slam each other into the walls trying to block shots. Or we would take codeine out of his dad's medicine cabinet, crush it up and snort it to get a quick buzz, then see who could head-butt the refrigerator the hardest. Yup, we were a bright bunch, that's for sure.

One night we decided to take Jimmy's father's car for a ride. I was only fourteen years old, Freddy was about fifteen and Jim had just turned sixteen, so all he had was a learner's permit. We quietly pushed the car out of the driveway around two in the morning and just cruised around the city. We were behind Market Basket in Methuen when I noticed that the bread truck had just made a delivery. There were all these loaves of bread stacked up just sitting there, so I had Jim pull up and I grabbed a rack of bread that had about nine loaves on it.

As we were leaving, we noticed a police car behind us. At first we thought it was just a coincidence, but then we realized he was following us everywhere we turned. We tried to lose him by taking rights and lefts and rights and lefts, but we ended up turning onto a dead end street, so we panicked and started throwing all these loaves of bread out the window, thinking that getting rid of the evidence would help us lie our way out of it. All of a sudden, about seven police cars, some with K-9 units, came screaming around the corner with their lights on, screeching their brakes. Then all these cops piled out and start running towards us.

As the cops approached our car they're looking around, wondering where all this bread came from. There was bread all over the road and loaves of bread literally hanging in the trees. A cop asks Jimmy to step out of the vehicle, and when he did, would you believe it? A loaf of bread falls out of the car. The cop says, "What's up with all the bread, guys?"

Assuming that they'd seen us take it, we all started to confess that we'd stolen it from behind Market Basket. And you know what happens when you assume, right? The cop said, "Well, first of all, I was following you because your back taillight is out. Secondly, there's been a bunch of car stereo thieves in the area, and once you started running, I thought you might have been them. That's why we pulled you over."

They arrested us, brought us down to the station and called our parents. When our parents got there later that morning, they stuck us all in a conference room together and the district attorney starts telling our parents what we did. "Your boys are being charged with larceny of bread." Freddy lets out a little whisper of a laugh as if to say, "What a joke." His father looked over at him, wound up, and backhanded him right off his seat. I thought I was going to piss my pants laughing, but I knew I would've been next, so I just kept my mouth shut.

We went to court several days later and once again the D.A. says to the judge, "These boys are being charged with larceny of bread." The judge looked at the D.A., confused, and said, "Mr. District Attorney, can you please use the proper terminology in my courtroom?" He must have thought that he meant money.

The D.A. says, "No, your honor, you don't understand, they are being charged with stealing Wonder Bread—the kind you eat." The judge started laughing out loud, so we all look at each other and we start laughing, too. Then everyone in the courtroom starts giggling! Finally the judge yells out, "Hey! All three of you, get up here right now!" All three of us approach the bench and the judge says, "First of all, wipe those smirks off your faces." And we did, real quick! Then he says, "Can I ask you boys a question? What in the hell were you doing stealing bread? Were you hungry or something?" We tried the puppy dog-eye approach and said, "No, your honor, we just thought we could take some bread home to our families....blink, blink." After all, It was the early 80's and times were rough. Our families were still very poor and struggling, so it was kind of the truth.

Ok, so it was a bad lie. The judge didn't buy it anyway. He just looked at us with his one eyebrow raised as if to say, "Do you really think I'm going to buy that crock of shit story?" Then he gave us six months unsupervised probation and set us free. The only other time I remembered seeing a look like that was when my mom surprised me with a bag of weed she had found of mine.

Right: Fro looking buff! 1992
Below: The terrible trio, Freddy(l)
Sully and Jimmy

Jimmy "Muskrat" Mustapha, Freddy Cristaldi, and Jeff "Fro" St. Hilaire have stuck by me through thick and thin and have been in the front row to just about every show I have ever played with whatever band I was playing with since I was fifteen years old. More than twenty years later, they're

all still in my life. Fro works me as my drum tech and stage
assistant, Jimmy is now our lighting director, and Freddy has
run several tours with us driving the big rigs.

And yes, we're all still best friends.

It is so bizarre sometimes when I think that after all the
changes in our lives, the places we've moved, the people we've
met along the way, the girls we've fucked over, the girls that
have fucked us over, the jobs we've had, the twenty-plus years
of shit that we have survived and all the shuffling around this
country we have done, that not only are we still best friends,
but we actually still live within miles of each other—obviously not in Lawrence anymore—and we have remained as
tight as ever. I am more proud of that than any fame or
success I have achieved. I would never have been able to
become the person I am without them.

Don't get me wrong. There are several other friends that
have been a very important part of my life, and I will talk
about all of them in this book. I cherish my moments with
them just as much, but as my life continues and I face its daily
obstacles, joys, pains and whatnot, I have realized who has been
there for me the most, and who has never let me down. They're
my backbone, and my love for them is unconditional.

So to Muskrat, Fro, and Freddy, thank you for my fun
days, for my dark days and for every day that you have been
there for me. You're my blood, my memories and my life. I
honor and love all of you!

CHAPTER 5
TRIPPIN' INTO A WORLD

Steven Tyler once said, "From the time you start doing drugs until the time you stop doing drugs are all lost years." So let's see—based on Steven's calculation—I smoked pot for the first time when I was eleven years old and I stopped doing drugs when I was twenty-two, so that would make me twenty-seven years old right now. Not bad for a thirty-eight year old!

There was a time in my life when drugs took over a big part of me. It's funny because these days, I can't even stand the *sight* of drugs anymore. Don't get me wrong, I never preach or try to convert people, and I still have my moments when I get drunker than hell. I have nothing against people who enjoy smoking pot or having a few cocktails, but it's the hard stuff that I refuse to be around. Not that any of it is good for you—it just seems that pot and alcohol are the lesser evils.

I don't regret anything I've done and I'm really glad that I did all my experimenting at a very early age. I might be wrong, but I believe that if I were to have done the amount of drugs I did at a later stage in my life, when my body wasn't young and strong enough to fight it off, I probably would've died. I damn near did a couple of times.

I've tried just about every drug you could think of: heroin, crystal meth, uppers, downers, you name it. But I never stuck a needle in my arm and I'm very proud of that considering my surroundings. There were four things that became habits for us: pot, alcohol, coke, and acid. They were our nightly ritual. We did so much acid back in the 80's that we would have to wait a whole day to trip again. Not because we were scared something might happen, but because a normal dose wouldn't affect us if we took it every day.

Back in the early 80's you could get a half ounce of killer green weed for ten bucks, or you could buy joints, big *fat* joints, three for five bucks or five for ten bucks.

One afternoon after school, me, Jimmy, and Freddy all bought five joints apiece. We all matched each other a joint on the walk home from school and I wrapped the rest of my weed in a baggie and stuffed it in my sock.

After we blazed up our three joints, my plan was to go home, take a shower and head back to one of their houses and hang with them until we went out that evening. I was so stoned I could hardly keep my eyes open. I unexpectedly found my mom sitting in the kitchen, having coffee with her boss Nancy from the hospital. She'd gotten home early that day but seemed to be in a good mood. I walked in trying not to look at her or her boss and slid through the kitchen real quick. I didn't want any nurses analyzing my blood-shot eyes if you know what I mean.

"Hi, Mom! Hey, Nancy!" No eye contact, straight to my room.

I undressed, wrapped a towel around myself and began focusing on the mission at hand: getting to the bathroom without a confrontation. I'd have to walk past them, and my only thought was, "Let me get the fuck out of here before Mom finds out I'm baked!"

So there I went through the kitchen, eyes to the floor, past the warden and her boss and right into the bathroom. I shut the door behind me and thought, "Phew! Made it."

After I showered, I felt a little more normal—not quite as stoned. But I was brave enough to walk back by them knowing that if they noticed my red-eye now, I could just blame it on, ummm... the soap in my eye!

I got back to my room and quickly started to get dressed. Just as I was ready to roll, I realized that I couldn't remember where I had put my weed. I started tearing apart my entire room looking for it: under my dresser, under my mattress, in my socks, everywhere. I was so baked I figured I'd just misplaced it.

My mom hears me rustling around in the room and asks me what I'm doing. "Nothing! Just looking for my, ummmm... my wristbands! Yeah that's what I'm looking for, my wristbands!"

She says, "Are you sure you're not looking for this?" Then she held up my sack of joints. I thought I was going to faint. My heart dropped, not because now she knew I smoked pot, but because *she had my fucking weed!*

I shut my door and my mind went nuts. I'm thinking, "How the hell did she find my pot? And how the fuck am I ever going to get those joints back and get out of this house in time to meet the guys for this party?"

Then I heard them step outside, and I hear my mom say, "Bye, Nancy! See you tomorrow...enjoy them!" I was like, "*Enjoy them*? You gave my fucking weed to your boss?"

When my mom returned, she looked at me and said, "Where do you think you're going?"

I said hesitantly, "Out?"

"No you're not," she said. "You're grounded until I tell you otherwise."

Knowing that I was busted, I had nothing to say. So I gave in and asked, "Where did you find it?" As calm as the midnight sky, she replied, "The baggie was stuck to your leg. When you walked by, it fell off right in front of us." Fuck!

Then she asked me what else I was doing. Since she was in a calm mood, I figured, what the hell; I might as well tell her now. The time felt right. I was fifteen years old and I was sick of hiding from her every time I wanted a cigarette. You know how that goes; you're on the street corner with your friends smoking and chatting away, then your mom's car comes around the corner and you nearly burn your fingers off trying to hide it behind your back.

So I told her I smoked cigarettes. And to my surprise, she sat me down at the table, slid over a cigarette pack and said, "If you're going to smoke, then you're going to smoke in front of me. Just don't tell your father."

I was psyched! But it was still weird for a little while, being able to light up in front of my mother. Well, at least the sneaking around was over, and in some strange way it brought me and her a little bit closer to each other. It was a bonding thing.

At this same age is when I joined my first *real* band. We called ourselves Slaughter. (This was 1983, so we had that name way before the other Slaughter came out.) We rehearsed every day and played songs that I loved and listened to all the time: music by Aerosmith, Rush, Y&T, Deep Purple, Led

Zeppelin, Black Sabbath and so on. And we were actually pretty good, considering how young we were.

Bill DeMonaco was the lead singer, the guitarist was John Machera and Mike (I can't remember his last name) was our bass player. We practiced in the attic of Mike's house. We often skipped school to rehearse, knowing that nobody would be home. And being kids, we were relentless—we'd go at it for six, seven hours sometimes.

John Machera had long black hair that covered his face, a leather jacket, and ripped jeans. He was able to play guitar solos with his teeth or behind his head. Mike was very similar to John in his street presence—ripped jeans, scraggly dirty blonde hair and very laid back.

As far as Bill goes, well, he didn't have it together as much. He was extremely obsessed with Steven Tyler and would do a terrible job trying to act like him on stage, strutting around and wrapping his mic stand with scarves. He wore glasses that slid down his nose when he sang and had this goofy Aerosmith hat on all the time.

John and Mike were total Lawrence boys and had a much edgier street vibe going on. Bill wasn't raised on the streets. He was from a good family that did well for themselves, so he had no natural attitude in him. He was a bit nerdy and very uneducated in the women department. Even up until the age of eighteen he still didn't know how your dick got hard.

Me, Jimmy, Bill and someone else (I can't remember if it was John or Freddy) were on our way to an Aerosmith concert one night, and for some reason we got onto the subject of how easy it would be for a girl to bite your dick off if she wanted to. So Bill says, 'What do you mean? How could she bite through the bone?" We're like, "*What? The bone?* There's

no bone in your dick. It's all blood pressure that gets it hard."
But he insisted that there was a bone that pivoted out of your
stomach and into your dick to make it hard. What a laugh
we got out of that one. Regardless, he was our singer and for
the most part he did a decent job covering the melodies.

With a little help from my mother, we landed our first
gig after a couple of months. My mom worked at Ft. Devens
Army Base in Ayer, Massachusetts, not too far from Lawrence.
She was the Director of Reserve Components, overseeing the
budget for the ROTC. She told some people at the base about
our band and they agreed that we could play a show at one
of the function halls for the people on the base—no money
of course, but who cares? We were on our way to playing our
first real gig!

For a P.A., all we had were these two little speaker col-
umns that were meant for speeches in banquet halls or something, not for a rock band. We had one microphone on the
whole drum set and one microphone for the singer. I can't
even imagine how bad we must have sounded but the crowd
seemed to like us a lot, all seventeen of them. I'll never forget
how awesome it felt to play the first song and then have these
military guys stand up and clap. I felt great. We didn't stink—
people were clapping for us!

Our second show was the big one! Or at least it was
supposed to be. We played a club in Salisbury Beach, Massachusetts, called the Frolics. This is the club where I had
seen bands like *The Joe Perry Project*, so it was a big deal
for me.

That night we were the last band to go on. The "Head-
liner" I guess you could say. And from living in Massachusetts our whole lives, we had tons of people there waiting to
see us. There must have been over 200 people packed at the

front of the stage chanting "Slaughter! Slaughter!" after every act that went on. Our girlfriends, parents, friends, everybody was there to see this, so we were as pumped up as we could be.

We were backstage in the dressing room hanging out with Muskrat, Freddy, and a guy named Greg Goguen, who I'd met through Freddy. Greg had a few years on us so we always got him to buy the beers for us.

About fifteen minutes before we go on, Greg whips out this bag of coke and says, "Let's do this, guys! This show is gonna rock so let's get in the right frame of mind here!" He lays out two huge lines for each of us, pulls out a twenty-dollar bill, rolls it up and snorts up his two lines. I had never done coke before so I was a little intimidated. But I was also ready not to puss out in front of my friends.

After Jimmy and Freddy did there's, I grabbed the twenty-dollar bill, strolled over to the mirror and I cranked my two fat-ass lines up my nose. At the same time, the door flies open. I lift up my head to see who came in the room, the twenty-dollar bill still stuck in my nose, and lo and behold, two cops are standing there. Everyone's face dropped and turned as white as the pile of coke on the table. I ripped the bill out of my nose and tried to hide it along with the mirror, but the cops saw me. It turns out there was a screen above the door that none of us noticed, and they were up there snooping on us, so even when he asked us what was going on and we tried to lie about it, it got nowhere fast because they'd witnessed the whole thing.

One of the cops approached Greg and asked him if he was the oldest. Greg's reply was "Yes, sir!" Then he asked the rest of us our ages. When he heard that we were fifteen and sixteen years old, he immediately went back over to Greg and

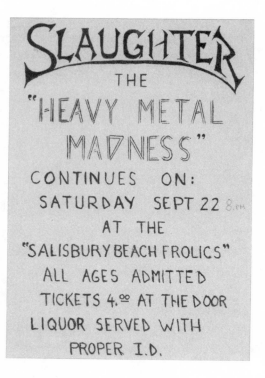

Flyer for Sully's second show ever in 1983

started drilling him about contributing to minors and blah, blah, blah. By this time we were all gacked out of our minds and trying as hard as we could not to sniffle and really piss the cop off, but coke was in our nostrils and it was beginning to drip, so it was real hard not to sniffle. Then the inevitable happened.

As the cop stood there reprimanding us, Greg's nose starts leaking and he sniffled really loud right in front of the cop. The cop looked back with a real nasty look on his face as if to say, "Do it again, smart-ass!"

Now it was my turn. The cop approaches me, grabs the mirror I'd slid under a bandana that I thought I hid so slickly, and blows the rest of the coke onto the floor. He turns to all of us and says, "Pack your shit up and hit the road—you're not playing tonight, fellas!" Greg responded right away with, "Yes, sir!" and began picking up his belongings, not questioning another word. This guy was giving us a break and everyone was relieved about it; everyone but me, that is.

I thought I was going to throw up right on his polished shoes. My heart dropped to the bottom of my stomach and I started to sweat. This gig was what I had dreamed about my whole life. This was what we had practiced so hard for, and now, in a blink of an eye, it was over. I lashed out at the cop, "What do you mean, pack our shit? We're on next!"

"I don't care," he says. "Pack your shit and get your asses out of here, or you can go to jail as an alternative."

I couldn't believe what he was saying to me. I was crushed. Plus, I was totally wired on this coke, so I put my hands behind my back, turned around and said, "Well, looks like you're gonna have to arrest me then, because I'm going up there and playing this show." Bill and Greg started freaking out on me, telling me to shut my mouth and get the hell out of there, but I wasn't hearing it.

Just then Bill's mom came flying into the dressing room, frantically asking what's going on. She saw me pacing around the room all pissed off as the cops started to explain what happened. They asked her if she's my mom and she answered, "Yes!" then turned to me, shooting me a look with her eyes that told me to keep my mouth shut. I looked at her in complete amazement that she had covered for me like that. So out of respect for her, I chilled right the fuck out.

She could have just come in, got her son and left us all hanging, but she didn't.

Meanwhile, I grabbed my bass drum and started heading out of the dressing room, but in order to get outside, I had to walk right through the club. There I was, carrying a huge bass drum, Bill right behind me with more of my drums, Greg, Jimmy and everybody else carrying other equipment in a single file walking through hundreds of people as they asked us what was happening. So lame!

To make matters worse, when I got outside these two huge beach-bum Italian drunken idiots came up to me and decided to start fucking with me because I was wearing a leopard-skin shirt and moccasin boots. (Okay, I admit it was tacky, but it was the early 80's and that's what was going on back then.) Nothing came out of that. I kept my mouth shut on that one because there were two of them, and they were way too big for me. Eventually they went away and that was it. I went home, wired, frustrated and depressed.

If anything, you'd think we would've at least learned our lesson about coke after that. But instead it worked more like an introduction to another level of partying.

Cocaine soon became a regular part of our routine. If you've never done this drug before, trust me, *don't!* Cocaine is the shittiest drug you can do. You get absolutely no satisfaction out of it, you talk for hours about everything in the world that you really couldn't care less about, and you look ridiculous while you talk because your jaw is moving from side to side. You'll sell or do anything to get more once you're wired out of your brains, your heart beats a million miles an hour, and to top it all off, it's way too expensive! Oh, and did I mention it can kill you? It's just an all-around stupid drug. Unfortunately I went through years of cocaine abuse before I realized all that stuff.

One weekend Jimmy and Freddy wanted to go partying. We all needed some money for beers, pot and whatever, so we decided to steal some of Freddy's mother's stash. His mom dealt coke and always had huge bags of it in her dresser, so we figured what the hell, we'll pinch a little and sell it to get some money. She'll never know, right? What we didn't know was, when you deal coke, dealers can tell when there's even the smallest amount missing because it's all weighed out right down to the last speck. We didn't realize that the "little" amount that we took was an eighth of an ounce, or an "Eight-ball" as they would say on the streets.

At the time, the street value of an eight-ball was about four hundred dollars. We'd sold it to a dude in a wheelchair for twenty-five bucks.

By the end of the day, Freddy's mom had found out and kicked the living shit out of Freddy. She threw him in the car and made him bring her to the guy we sold it to. Luckily he still had it and she got it back. And to her credit, she never ratted on me or Jimmy to our parents. What a lady!

I quit high school half-way through freshman year. I just got tired of teachers always yelling at me and telling me what to do. From a very young age I'd known that I was going to be a musician, so it never made any sense to me to learn about who discovered that the world was round. It's here, we live on it, and we know it's round! I actually enjoy history now, but then, who cared?

I would ask myself, "Why do I need to learn algebra or trigonometry to play the drums?" I have always believed that learning to read and write are the two most important things. Once you know that, you can educate yourself in anything you want, and I did, and I still do.

I went back to school the following year and gave it another try, but it didn't take much more to get me to quit at that point. One day this lunatic teacher screamed at me in front of the whole class. I was talking to some girl, trying to get my groove on, when Ms. Lunatic started freaking out, telling me to shut my mouth or get out of her classroom. So I yelled back at her, "*Why are you yelling at me? I can hear you just fine!*" Well, she didn't think that was so funny, so she told me to go to the principal's office. When I refused, she came over and tried to rip me out of my chair herself. I stood up, pulled her hand off of my shirt, sat her down in my seat and told her to take a fucking pill. Then I walked out the door and slammed it so hard that the glass broke. It was the last time I ever set foot in a classroom.

After that I knew in my heart that I was finished with school, and it was time to face the music and tell Mom. I knew she was going to be pissed at me when I dropped the news on her, but I also knew that I was not returning to school whether she approved of it or not. I was done. I was too involved with hanging out on the streets with my friends and trying to play music. Those were the only two things I cared about at that point. So we sat down at the kitchen table and had our little chat, and to my surprise she was a lot more receptive than I thought she would be. But she did make it very clear that I was to get a job and help out around the house. Of course I agreed without hesitation, even though I hadn't the slightest idea what I was going to do for work. I was just relieved that I was school-free!

Jimmy and Freddy had also dropped out around this time, which worked out great for me. I had friends to hang with, although I did think Jimmy dropping out was very strange. I was a freshman and still had four years to go, Freddy was a sophomore and had a few years left himself, but Jimmy was a senior and only had two weeks left before he graduated.

Even as hoodlums excited that our other brother was available to hang out, I remember me and Freddy telling Jim,
"What the fuck are you doing? You only have two weeks left.
Go graduate!" But Jim had his own reasons for needing out,
and who were we to say anything? Practice what you preach,
was his answer to us.

I never bothered getting my G.E.D. I'm not saying anyone
should do what I've done—it was just the path I chose. It
worked out for me, but let me tell you this, it was thirty
years of hell before anything paid off for me. So in case you're
getting any crazy ideas: stay in school.

After a few months I honored my mom's request by finding myself a job at the Golden Cue Pool Hall. Me, Jim and
Freddy had been hanging out at that place for quite a while.
It was the new place in the neighborhood where all the punks
and partiers were hanging out, and it was literally one block
away from my house. From being around there all the time
we had become very well-known and liked by all the bosses
and pool sharks. So, a gentleman named George Rippy gave
all three of us jobs. All we had to do was vacuum the carpets
and pool tables and clean all the glass on the windows and
video games. In return we made $40.00 each a night and got
all the free pool we wanted.

By the time I was sixteen years old, me and Jim had
gotten so good at pool that we were invited to play in the
Golden Cue Tournaments with people like "Shorty Johnson"
and all the other big dogs from the region.

Even though we never won any of them, we ended up
making the finals a couple of times, which made the old-
timers sweat some.

When we didn't make the finals, we'd amuse ourselves by

going down to the Cue to watch the rest of the tournaments while tripping on acid. We had to stay awake until 1am waiting for the place to close so we could work, so we figured, what the hell? Why not eat some acid and have a few laughs while we waited?

We would eat a couple hits of Purple Micro-dot mescaline and trip our brains out for nine hours, laughing our asses off and annoying all the players who were trying to focus on their game. Sometimes it got to the point that we were sent home for being too obnoxious.

One night when me and Jim were waiting to go into work, we decided to catch a buzz before heading in. We had a friend of ours pick us up a bottle of Mad Dog 20/20. For those of you who don't know what that is, it's probably the cheapest bottle of wine that you can get. They call it the poor man's wine. It's $4.00 for a fifth and it tastes like grape Kool-Aid. But it gets you fucked up! Me and Jim had never drank it before, but because it went down so smooth we chugged the whole bottle in seconds. As we walked over to the Cue, the buzz kicked in. It got to the point that when it was time to start vacuuming the tables down, I started spinning real bad. Next thing I know I'm in the bathroom puking purple all over the place and barely able to stand. Jim and two other guys walked me home. Till this day we have never touched the Mad Dog again.

Another time when me, Freddy and Muskrat did a bunch of mescaline and went wandering around, we ended up at a small party at the home of some girl Freddy knew. I had taken two hits of "orange sunshine mescaline" and I was fucked up!

I was sitting at this girl's table with Muskrat when we noticed a bottle of strawberry foot powder on the shelf. Now,

I don't know if any of you have ever done acid before, but that shit makes you do stupid things.

Jimmy brings the foot powder over to the table and starts cutting up lines, just playing around, staring at it. I remember saying, "Wow! That looks and smells so awesome." So Jimmy dares me to do a line of this strawberry foot powder. Of course I'm so fucked up that I accept the dare and snort up two lines. Real smart, Sully!

A little later we left and started walking home. All of a sudden my body started reacting to the chemicals I'd just shoved up my nose. I don't know if it was bad acid or a combination of the stupid ass foot powder I snorted, but I started shaking uncontrollably like I was going into a convulsion or something. I began hallucinating. I was seeing all kinds of fucked up shit: faces on leaves, the ground opening up beneath me, people laughing and yelling... aw man, I was feeling really funky.

I started freaking out, telling the guys to get me to a hospital because I thought I was going to die right there. They're telling me, "No way, bro'! We can't. We'll all get busted if we take you to a hospital." I'm thinking, "Are you kidding me? I'm going to die here and you're worried about getting in trouble?" But that's where it stood. No one was taking me anywhere where there was a chance of getting arrested. So instead they suggested we go to my house and lay low for a while to let the drugs wear off.

It seemed like a good idea at the time—or at least until I noticed all the people in my yard. "Great! My mom's having a cookout today." All my relatives were there—aunts, uncles, grandparents, everybody. I was fucked! I slid my way into the house, dodging everyone so I wouldn't have to look them in the face with my pale-ass skin and wide-eyed pupils. We got

ourselves into my bedroom and I laid on the bed. My body
was shaking like a fish out of water and Jimmy and Freddy
were holding me down trying to get me through it. I'm telling them over and over, "Please guys, get me to a fucking
hospital!" But it wasn't happening.

So Jimmy says to me, "Your mom's having a cookout right?
Go get yourself some food, maybe it will help absorb some
of the drugs and you'll feel better." Once again, it sounded
logical to me.

So I grabbed a piece of steak, ran back outside and sat on
the porch trying to eat. Within the first bite I found myself
chewing and chewing, but I couldn't swallow any of it. It felt
like my throat had closed.

After a few minutes of that, I bailed on the idea of food.
I spit it out and looked up at Jimmy and Freddy and I said,
"Bro', this is not working." So they say, "All right, forget that.
Go into the living room and try watching some TV, maybe
that will help take your mind off of this." Good idea? *Nope!*

I got up and headed for the living room, peeked around the
corner and noticed no one was in there. Perfect! I laid down on
the couch and looked at the TV set, and the first thing I saw
was a guy with a clown mask on from this movie called *Terror
Train*, chopping people up with an axe. Man, I freaked out! I
jumped up, thinking, "I gotta get the hell outta here!"

By this time Jimmy and Freddy had taken off. I ran out
of the house and hid in my backyard for at least six hours,
just lying on the ground and staring at the sky until the drugs
wore off. God, that sucked! But that was our life. We partied
all the time, and sometimes had to pay the price for it.

CHAPTER 6
ON THE RUN

By the time I was sixteen years old, me, Jimmy and Freddy had spun way out of control. It wasn't just the drugs and alcohol, either. We also started getting good at thieving, vandalizing and outrunning the cops. It was a new addiction for us.

We would go to the Showcase Cinemas in Lawrence every weekend and smash the side windows out of Audis and BMWs with these little metal ball bearings we called "blips." Then we'd tear the stereo systems out of the cars and sell them for drug money. A friend of Freddy's sister even hired us once to take her convertible Mustang, which she couldn't afford the payments on anymore, and total it for her so she could claim the insurance money and pay it off. We couldn't think of a better way to enjoy a beautiful Sunday afternoon!

She gave it to us in the morning and we drove it around all day, beating the shit out of it—burn outs, break lifts, donuts, you name it. After we had our fun with it, we drove it up to a place called "the crusher" in Haverhill, Mass. It's basically just a big cleared out spot in the woods that everyone went to on the weekends and partied at. Jimmy was driving, Freddy was in the passenger's seat and I was in the back cutting up the seats with a knife.

As we started coming down the dirt road of the crusher, Jimmy, without warning any of us, starts speeding up and sideswiping and smashing the car into all the trees, forwards and backwards. He continued to demolish the car until it wouldn't start anymore. Then we all got out and fucked the rest of it up with hammers and tire irons. At one point, I jumped on top of the convertible roof. Not realizing that Freddy was right below me on the inside of the car, I plunged the knife through it to tear it up. Then I hear him yell, "Dude! What the fuck? Watch what you're doing! You just missed my face." Whoopsie!

We got away with so much shit like that;, I'm surprised we never did any real jail time. We hardly even got caught for the most part. Even when we'd get chased by the cops, we were able to outrun them nearly every time.

One of the stories we enjoy talking about the most was about the time we were hanging around in Sean DesRoche's neighborhood. Sean is Freddy's cousin and lived in a wooded area directly behind the mall in Methuen, the next town over. We knew those woods like the back of our hands, and they saved our asses many times.

It became a regular routine for us to get baked, hang out at the arcade in the mall playing video games and then pull a quick chew and screw at the York Steak House for dinner. We never had that much cash on us but we were always starving from getting high so much. So we would go into the York Steak House, order all kinds of food and then make a run for it once we were finished eating. It was real easy to do considering their bathrooms were conveniently located right next to the exit doors.

We would finish our meals, go wash our hands in the bathroom while one person stood guard outside the door, then when the coast was clear, the guard would give the signal knock and we would quietly slide out of the bathroom and straight out to the parking lot. Most of the time we did it undetected, but there were a few occasions when we would get spotted and chased away by the mall's local rent-a-cops. But that's when the woods came in handy. It was the perfect escape, especially during a seven hour chase.

One day me, Freddy and Jimmy, along with Freddy's cousin Sean, a kid named Andy, and a couple other guys were up in Sean's neighborhood raiding this guy's tomato garden. After filling up a huge garbage bag full of tomatoes, we ran down to the street corner, hid behind some bushes and threw them at passing cars. Smart, huh? I told you we were a bright bunch.

When the supply went dry, we went back for a refill. This time the owner of the garden was waiting for us with a shotgun. He started yelling at us and chasing us off his property. As we're trying to get away, we hear the gun go off, then we hear Andy scream at the top of his lungs.

As we turned around to see what had happened, we saw that Andy had got shot right in the butt by the owner. Even then, he was still running his ass off right behind us (or at least what was left of it). The gun had been loaded with rock salt instead of real bullets. And as you may or may not know, rock salt won't kill you, but it will sure as hell give you a sore ass for a few days.

Freddy was right in front of me running like the wind,

but he was looking back in the other direction to see if anyone was getting close to catching us. As he turned to look one last time, he ended up running right into one of those wooden stakes in the tomato garden. He flipped into the air, landed on his back, and all in one motion I ran up to him, picked him up by his shirt and kept on trucking right back into the woods. Thank God that stake was cut flat on the top and not pointed or he would've been shish kebob.

When we came out the other side of the woods, we were in this area that was just being developed with new condos and townhouses, so a lot of the woods that we had known so well had been cleared away. There were still plenty of woods to hide in. but the cool thing was that now there were these huge dirt mounds that were twenty-five or thirty feet high from the holes they had dugout for the foundations. Once we climbed the dirt hills we were able see the whole street. It was a good hiding spot to chill while the owner of the property calmed down. Once enough time passed, we figured we would sneak back into the garden and pick more of his tomatoes.

Six o'clock rolled around and we started heading back into this guy's area, but to our surprise he had called the cops, and as we turned the corner, we just about walked right into them. The guy spun the cops around and pointed us out. The police began telling us to come over to them, but instead we hauled ass back into the woods. Now the cops were chasing us, and even though we were sprinting like rabbits, they were so close to us at times that we could hear them breathing down our necks. After we gained some distance on them they gave up and stopped. This kind of thing happened several times. We would poke our heads out of the woods to see if the coast was clear, then a police car would come down the road and spot us as they circled the neighborhood. They would chase us, we would lose them, and so on it went.

Eventually we got split up. Me, Jimmy, and Sean were able to stick together, but Andy, Freddy and whoever else were with them ended up in a different part of the woods. We tried to find each other, but every time we would peek out of the woods, a police car would come racing down the road, so we would have to duck back into the woods and hide for awhile.

One of the times the cops were chasing us, Jimmy was in front of me, Sean was behind me, and we were running like crazy trying to gain some distance on them. Nightfall had come so it was getting pretty hard to see. I was doing my best to stay right on Jimmy's tail so I could see where I was running, when all of a sudden he dropped straight out of sight, like the earth had swallowed him. He was running so fast that he didn't see this huge dirt hole in the ground and fell right into it. I remember looking down to help him out, and his face was smashed flat up against the wall of this pit. It looked like something from a Bugs Bunny episode.

By this time hours had gone by and we hadn't seen Andy, Freddy or the other two. Sean's house was close by, so we ran back to it, grabbed some flares and smoke bombs and anything we thought we could signal the other's with, and back into the woods we went.

We climbed back up to the tops of the dirt mounds and started lighting up the flares and smoke bombs, throwing them into the air trying to find the other guys, but nothing worked. We could see cops all over the place, patrolling up and down the street, waiting for us to pop our heads out again.

After we got sick of sitting in the dark, waiting for our friends to find us, we went back down to the street level and began scurrying through the woods again to find them.

As we got to the edge of the road, we heard a sound from across the way. Something was rustling around in the bushes but we couldn't see who or what it was. The coast seemed to be clear, so we walked out onto the street and began to carefully whisper into the trees, *"Freddy? Andy? Is that you?"*

Then we saw them stick their heads out and say, *"Yeah! It's us!"* So we all gathered in the street and started talking about what a crazy night it had been. Then, out of nowhere, the cops came flying around the corner, and again we had to dive back into the woods and lose 'em.

1:00AM rolled around and we're all exhausted from running all night. We hadn't seen the police for awhile at that point so we carefully walked back up to Sean's house and snuck in his basement. We grabbed some vodka and whiskey from his parents' liquor cabinet and headed back outside so they wouldn't hear us partying.

Around the corner from Sean's house, we noticed more newly built condos; they seemed to be finished but no one had moved in them yet. While everyone looked through the windows trying to figure out how to get in, I walked around back with Jimmy and Freddy and kicked in the basement window. Then we went through the house and opened the back door for everyone else. For a good half hour or so we had a blast in there, like it was our own apartment. We were drinking vodka and whiskey, laughing and wrestling each other, just having a good time. Then Sean yells "COPS!" Everyone immediately scattered throughout the house trying to get out. Me and Freddy went flying out of this bedroom, Freddy was running with a cup of vodka in his hands and he was right on my tail.

I cut through the bathroom that was connected to the bedroom, not realizing that Freddy was so close up my ass, and I slammed the door shut behind me. All I heard was "BAM!" I stopped, turned around and opened the bathroom door, and there was Freddy, lying in the bathtub with vodka all over him. You could almost see the stars spinning around his head. I helped him up and ran for the door.

As we got to the backdoor we noticed that everyone was on the ground picking themselves up. They had fallen right out of the house because the door that they were running out of had no stairs built for it yet.

There was Sean, laughing his ass off watching everyone fall one by one. "Hey guys, I was just fucking around. There's no cops!" Man, I thought we were all gonna kill that boy right there.

CHAPTER 7
SAINTS AND SINNERS

As far back as I can remember, my family took me and my sister down to the Italian Feast in Lawrence every Labor Day weekend. At that time of the year, the air starts to get crisp and cool from the summer ending. The streets are decorated with flashing lights and tinsel that hangs from the lamp posts, little kids run through the streets waving Italian flags and pinwheels that their parents just bought for them, and the smell of sausage and onions from street carts is enough to make your mouth water.

During this celebration, one of the favorite traditions is what the Italians call "Bringing in the Saints." They honor Saint Cirino, Saint Filadelfio and Saint Alfio by putting statues of them on a float and carrying them through the streets. As they pass the crowds of bystanders, people pin money on them and chant "Con vera fede," which means, "With true faith." Viva Saint Alfio!

For years and years, and still to this day, my father's marching band has been in charge of leading the saints through the streets of Lawrence and into the heart of the feast. You can hear them coming from blocks away playing the Italian "Marcia Reale" ("The Royal March").

It was really exciting to me as a child, but as I got older, things gradually changed. The feast was becoming more and more corrupted by the same kinds of people who were making Lawrence a much harder place to live in. Gangs, drug addicts, hookers and ethnic tension amongst the Portuguese, Italians, French, Hispanics and a lot of other groups were too much for the local police to monitor all the time. At the same time, I pretty much had lost interest in the whole deal. And no matter how hard we tried to avoid trouble, it always seemed to find us one way or the other.

One time when I was about seventeen, me and Freddy were enjoying ourselves walking through the streets of the feast looking around for cute girls or something. As we passed this small group of Hispanic kids, I heard one of them start talking shit to us behind our backs. So being the little hot head that I was, I spun around and got in this kids face; confronting him and asking him if he wanted a piece of me. Just as we began to argue, his buddy whistled, and within what seemed like seconds me and Freddy were completely surrounded by a group of at least twenty-five Hispanic guys. There were big ones, small ones, fat ones, tall ones, bald ones, muscled ones—every kind of bully you could imagine. I just looked at Freddy and thought, "Holy shit, we're in for it now."

As we're standing there back to back, the little twerp who started this whole mess stood in front of me and kept mouthing off. My blood was boiling from head to toe because I knew I could easily knock out this little shit, but with every one of his friends and relatives standing around us it was looking a lot more grim. Then, in the middle of his blabbing, he wound up and punched me dead in the face. Luckily he was too small to do any damage; instead he just got me madder than hell, but still I was in a hopeless position to fight back. I just stared him right in the face and gave him a smirk as if to say, "Nice try, you little shit!" They all started speaking in Spanish to each other and I could just hear them getting restless, wanting to kick our asses.

Finally, this huge bald guy stepped in the middle of the circle and said to me, "You two should get the hell out of here fast, they're talking about stabbing you."

Well, that was enough for me. I looked over at Freddy and without saying a word to each other, we just knew that our only way out of this mess was for me to go one way and him to go the other. Splitting up was the best thing we could do. It would lessen our chances of being caught by all of them at once.

I turned to the little twerp, looked him right in his eyes, clenched my fist and punched him square in the face. And in the same breath I busted right through that circle and ran my ass off. Freddy looked for his out by picking out the biggest dude in front of him, smashing him down to the ground and breaking through the opposite side of the circle. As I was running, I could hear the sounds of chaos behind me. I knew Freddy was back there scrapping but I couldn't turn around to do anything about it. We were on our own.

I ducked into one of the buildings off the street where the old-timers sat around playing cards. I knew that none of the punks would go into a public place and fuck with me, so I was safe in there. As I busted through the door like a scared little mouse, the old-timers could see I was in some kind of trouble, but of course they weren't about to get involved in that crap. They just ignored me and kept on dealing the cards.

I rushed over to the pay phone and called my father's house. His band would break for lunch, and whenever they did, my dad always went home to eat because he lived only a few blocks away from the feast, and I knew he had guns, which seemed like the only way I was getting out of this mess alive.

When he answered the phone I was ecstatic. I began spitting out words a mile a minute, ranting and raving about what kind of shit I was in, then he told me his two step-brothers were with him and that they would all come together to get me. Yee-fucking-haw! My dad's brothers were both black belts at the time, so I was feeling safer by the second. He told me that they will be driving down General Street in five minutes in their van, and that I should meet them there. Knowing that General Street was right around the corner I agreed, hung up the phone and sat there for a second contemplating how I was going to get from here to there.

When I peeked out the door, I was surprised to see there were no hoodlums lurking around waiting for me. They must've gone after Freddy, thinking I wasn't coming out. So I took a deep breath and made a break for it, hauling my little ass down the street toward the road my dad said he'd be on, praying the whole time, "Please be there, please be there, please be there."

I only had to run two blocks to General Street: one left turn, then a quick right and I was home free. It should've only taken a minute, but goddamn if it didn't seem like an hour.

As I made that first left, sure as shit, a group of about five of those kids came around the corner and spotted me. I could see the road my dad was going to be coming down right behind them, so I wasn't stopping now. The worst that could happen was, they would get a hold of me, and hopefully within seconds my dad and his entourage would come to my rescue. I sure as shit wasn't turning around and going backwards.

In a full-on sprint, I headed right towards the small pack of punks that stood there wondering what the fuck I was doing. I could tell they were planning their attack as they hovered in a line waiting to take me down.

I eyeballed the smallest one on my approach, and when I got within a few feet of him, I jumped up, kicked him in the chest, knocking him to the ground and kept on trucking full steam ahead. On the way through I felt the hands of the other guys trying to grab a hold of anything that they could. Luckily I was a squirmy little bastard, flailing my hands and swatting at them like I was some mental patient deprived of his medication.

I got around the corner, and just as I did, I saw my dad's van come rolling down General Street. There's no way he would have missed me either, because when I saw that van, I ran straight at it. He would have had to run me over to miss me. I'm sure he saw the pack of wild animals chasing me, because he had the side of his van door wide open for me as I got to him. I jumped in the side door like a stunt man from a Jackie Chan movie and we got out of there real fast.

Later on I checked in with Freddy, who also got away fairly clean. He told me he got a shot or two in, but he made a run for it as well. All in all, it was just another day on the streets!

Back then, all we knew was drinking, drugs and getting into trouble. Music was never on my mind when we hung out. I hadn't done anything important enough with music for it to occupy my thoughts, and the streets made me think differently, especially when I was with my friends. If shit like that went down, it was about winning and not looking like a pussy in front of my buddies.

We never thought at any time that we were looking for trouble when we got into shit, or that we could've gotten killed. But looking back at the situations, we could have avoided almost all of them. Things just got weirder and weirder the older we got. What were once friendly little jokes or simple street fights later became violent drunken mistakes.

Some of those mistakes almost cost us our lives, or someone else's—like the story I told you back at the beginning. There I was, standing in front of this drunken maniac who was about to stab me with this knife that looked like something out of *Rambo*. And I'm there stuffing a sawed-off twelve-gauge in his face. Before you could blink an eye, I pulled the gun up, pumped it once and pulled the trigger.

"Click!" That's all I heard. The gun wasn't loaded.

Looking back on it now, it seems comical to me, because when I heard this big-ass gun go "click" I almost shit my pants. I looked down at the gun and I thought, "Aw man, I'm fucked now!" So I turned the gun around like a baseball bat, but before I could hit him with it, he lunged at me with that fucking sword.

I dropped the gun, and grabbed his wrist so he couldn't stab me. We hit the ground again, and for the second time, the fight was on. This time I'm freaked out because I knew if I made one wrong move, I was dead. I held on to his wrist with a grip I never knew I had. People began pulling us apart to stop the fight. Jimmy and Freddy pulled me up and Freddy was screaming at me to get in the car so we could get the fuck out of there before the cops came. He was so pissed at me for taking the gun out of the trunk that I thought he was

going to smack me around next. Then I looked over and saw
the dude that owned the house wrestling with the kid with
the knife, smashing his arm into the curb to get the knife out
of his hand. The whole scene got way out of control and I
didn't bother sticking around to see the end result. Instead we
all got in the car and screwed out of there.

That's when I noticed a stinging feeling in my side and
realized my shirt was ripped in the same spot. I hadn't even
realized he had got the knife into me. He'd stuck me just
enough to open the skin, but not far enough for it to be
threatening. Thank God for that, and thank God Freddy didn't
load that gun. To this day I love him for that.

It really freaks me out when I think about those times,
mainly because it was so long ago and I've grown so much
since then. I don't even feel like it was me that it happened
to. It's like I've lived two separate lives. Sometimes these
memories just seem like scenes from a movie that I know
really well and have watched a thousand times. I could have
spent the rest of my life in prison if that gun had been loaded,
and it scares the shit out of me to know that I was ready to
throw my life away over a bad temper and a lot of pride I
wasn't willing to suck up.

There were plenty of kids in Lawrence who were a lot
worse than us, though. The difference was, we realized there
were different levels of danger. We were a little bit smarter
than the people who got into the real dark stuff, like murder
and shooting junk into their arms—we knew that was out of
our league, and that there's no happy ending to that story.
We were just tough kids who were always up for a good
fight, but shooting people just wasn't our style. Weapons in
general really weren't our thing, unless of course it was a

situation like the one I just told you. Then it became simply about survival.

It makes me think of that scene in the movie *Friday*, when the character that Ice Cube's father played came into Ice's bedroom and found him holding a gun. He said to his son, "What do you need that for?" Then he held up his fists and said, "This is what makes you a man. You win some and you lose some, but you live to fight another day." Powerful statement.

That was us. If you had a problem with us, well... put up your dukes and let's work it out. But don't be a pussy and pull out a weapon. Unfortunately not everyone we knew thought that way.

There was this group of kids we knew that lived around the corner from Freddy and Jimmy. Two or three of them were brothers, but there were probably five or six of them who hung out together. Everyone called them the Quaito's, which was the brothers' last name, and they were trouble!

The other guys in the neighborhood that we would hang with from time to time got into their own share of trouble, but very sporadically. They weren't real bad guys, they just got into small bits of trouble every now and again—you know, caught smoking weed by the cops, or stealing something from a store, nothing major. They all hung out at the Cumberland Farms convenient store on the corner of Lawrence street and Fern. The only real bad one was this one guy Paul. He was a junkie and very unpredictable. He was usually harmless, but you never knew what he would try, so you kept your distance from him.

One of the mistakes Paul made was when he sold a bag of weed to the Quaitos so he could buy some dope for

himself. The problem was, it wasn't weed—it was oregano
or something.

That Saturday afternoon, as usual, the Terrible Trio were
hanging out on our stoop right next to Freddy's house when
the Quaitos and some of the other guys that they hung with
came marching down the road carrying machine guns and
handguns. They weren't even trying to hide them. You could
just tell they were on a mission. As they walked right by us,
we said, "What's up guys? Whoa! Where the hell are you goin'
with all that shit?" and they responded, "Fucking Paul! We've
had it with him ripping people off. Now he's gone and fucked
us and he's gonna pay for it!" All this was said as they rolled
on by us. They never turned to even look at us. They didn't
seem to be worried about the cops driving by or anything.
They were just determined to find this dude and kill him. We
just sat there and watched them walk on by. We definitely
weren't going to follow them with all that hardware around.

Within seconds after that, all you could hear was "bang-
bang-bang-bang, BOOM, BOOM, BOOM!" By the time we'd
jumped up and ran down to the corner, all we saw were
innocent bystanders scattered, running for their lives as the
Quaitos just unloaded bullets everywhere. They didn't even
look to see if there were women or children around, they just
held these guns down at their hips and blasted away when
they saw Paul standing there. There were bullet holes everywhere, through the glass of the store, through the gas station
across the street, houses nearby, *everywhere.*

They hit Paul in the back with a shotgun that was loaded
with pheasant-load. For those of you who don't know what
that is, it's a shotgun shell that is loaded with hundreds of
tiny bb's, unlike a deer slug, which is one big piece of lead
that will blow a hole in you the size of a grapefruit.

Luckily for Paul that was the case. When they shot him in the back, he was at a good enough distance that the bb's just sprayed him. Not that that doesn't suck anyway, but it saved his life. If it had been a deer slug, he would've been dead.

Paul stumbled down the road and hid in some lady's hallway until an ambulance arrived. The Quaitos were soon arrested and sent to prison for a long time. Some of them might even still be there. I know that the youngest brother got out a while ago. I was told that soon after his release he went down to one of the worst areas of Lawrence to cop some dope. He met up with some dealer who told him to go inside the house to do the deal. When he entered the building and went upstairs, they were waiting for him with base-ball bats and two-by-fours. They caved his head in and now I hear he's got a metal plate in his head and is slightly para-lyzed. Word has it, it was all for $8.00 worth of acid.

The other groups of real bad boys that floated around the neighborhoods we hung out in were called the Fogertys, which again was the last name of two of the brothers.

Freddy's mother was dating this guy named Carlos, who we all kind of looked up to. He was a good guy—a big muscular hispanic dude with lots of ink and a nose ring. He was well over six feet tall and drove this kick-ass custom Harley.

One day Carlos had a run-in with the Fogertys. I'm not sure exactly what went down, but I know that the Fogertys were pulling some shit in Carlos's neighborhood, so Carlos ended up going to where they hung out one night, told them not to come around the neighborhood anymore and slapped some of them around.

Shortly after, Freddy had heard through the grapevine that the younger brother of the Fogertys was talking shit about getting even with Carlos, and how they were going to get that bitch he was with too. Well, that bitch they were referring to was Freddy's mom, and Freddy wasn't too happy about hearing that. So he got word back to the young Fogerty that if anything happened to his mother, he was going to kick his ass himself.

The young Fogerty took Freddy up on his challenge one afternoon when Freddy was pulling up to his girlfriend's house. The Fogertys lived in her area and happened to be driving by when Fred was getting out of his car. So they approached Fred and the young one offered to take him up on his challenge. But Freddy wasn't going to fight all four of them, so he told him that if the rest of them didn't butt in, he had no problem with a one on one. The young Fogerty told his boys to stay out of it, and just like that it was on.

They went punch for punch for several minutes and Fred says he got the best of him, up until he put the dude in a headlock and the kid started biting Freddy's finger. At that point Freddy dug his finger into the kid's eye until he let go. Then the young Fogerty took his beating and split the scene. After that day, Freddy claims that none of those dudes ever fucked with him or his mother again. I can't say the same for Carlos though.

One night they took their revenge by waiting for Carlos to come out of this club he hung out at, and when he did, they attacked him with a sledgehammer. They smashed him over the head with it and down he went. That's how big this guy was—it took a sledgehammer to put him on the ground. Then the real horror started. They laid his head on the edge of the sidewalk and began to stomp on the back of his skull. They left the poor guy lying there paralyzed and bleeding to death. Fortunately he didn't die, but he suffered severe brain damage. He had to have a metal plate in his head, too. Today, he walks with a cane and his face is slightly slouched from being partially paralyzed. The Fogertys went to prison for that, just like the Quaitos.

Like I said, there's no happy ending to that kind of lifestyle. Nor did I ever want that kind of life. I'm an Aquarius re-member? We're dreamers, not killers. And as for me, I still dreamed about being a rock star one day.

CHAPTER 8
HEEEEEERE'S JOHNNY!

A band called Meanstreak was the next step towards my musical dream. After we did a couple of small gigs with Slaughter, our guitarist John Machera had found a guitar player named John Hartado, this rich kid from Andover. This dude was no Machera, but he could definitely play his ass off. Hartado was a bit more schooled and polished while Machera's playing was more attitude than anything, but they worked great together. As a bonus, Hartado's parents let us rehearse in the basement of their big, fancy house.

The singer was Derek Jean, who I found through a mutual friend. Derek was fucking great! He could hit all those crazy-ass high notes like Rob Halford from Judas Priest and Bruce Dickinson from Iron Maiden. And that's exactly what we jammed on: Priest, Maiden, Y&T, etc. It was unbelievable. Playing songs like Priest's "Victim of Changes" and Maiden's "Where Eagles Dare" was so much fun, especially with a bunch of guys who could pull it off so well.

Unfortunately Meanstreak didn't last all that long—we spent more time practicing and inviting girls over to Hartado's base-

Meanstreak: Derek Jean, Sully, John Machera, Dave Galley and John Hartado in 1983

ment to watch us jam than we did playing out. I think we only played one show. My sister set us up at a V.F.W. hall for fifty bucks or something. We made a bunch of fliers and hung them up around town and maybe a couple hundred people showed up at best, but it was fun while it lasted. I was really starting to come out of my shell and show my talent. It was clearly a graduation in my playing and performance. And it gave me even more confidence to go and hunt for my dream.

Right around the time that Meanstreak began rehearsing regularly, my mom bought another car for herself. Her old car was getting ragged, and she had finally saved up enough money to get herself some transportation that was a bit more reliable.

It was a 1982 light blue Buick Regal. I'll never forget that car, for two reasons. For one, I was able to benefit from her new purchase by inheriting her old car. Now, don't laugh too hard. I was sixteen years old with a fresh new license in my pocket, and we were poor, so I wasn't going to be picky about what I got to drive. But my first car became my mom's 1977, rusted, *pink* Cadillac Fleetwood. Driving that car felt like jumping into bed with a woman who was way too big for me. This thing was a fucking tank! And yes, it was *pink!*

It had a 500 cubic inch motor in it, and you could hear every inch of that engine from miles away. Not because the motor was so big, though. One afternoon when me and a couple of friends went up to Hampton Beach for the day, I tried to sneak into the parking lot through the rear entrance so I wouldn't have to pay, and when I and drove the car up onto the curb it knocked the muffler clean off.

Heading home after that, doing seventy miles an hour on the highway, the noise level was so obnoxious that we couldn't even hear ourselves talk. Halfway home, the police stopped me and handed me my first ticket for being mufflerless and making too much damn noise.

But the real reason I remember my mom's Buick Regal the most was because one night after I blew out my muffler on the Cadi, I asked... no, begged my mom to let me borrow her wheels so I could go to rehearsal. After a lot of relentless persuasion, she finally caved in, but told me that if I didn't get my ass straight home after practice I would be grounded and never allowed to use her car again. So I gave her my most sacred promise to be home by 10:00PM sharp.

Around 9:30 or so, we wrapped up rehearsal. I remember that it had been a great night. We had had a killer jam and gotten really stoned. But since I'd promised not to piss off my mom, I got in the car, dropped it in gear, cranked up the stereo and headed down the highway back to Lawrence. A 10:00 ETA was right on schedule.

About 15 minutes or so into the ride, something just didn't feel right. I looked down at the speedometer to check my speed and saw that I was doing a cool seventy miles an hour. No problem there. Yet the car just didn't seem to be running right, so I let off the gas then hammered it again. Every time it got up around seventy, it felt like it just couldn't go any faster. Finally, I decided to turn the stereo down and try to figure out what was going on.

As the music came down to a normal level, all I could hear was the sound of the engine racing and wheezing so much that I thought the car was going to blow up. So I let off the gas and watched the speedometer drop. Just then, I realized that the car was in the wrong gear. I was so high when I left practice that I hadn't realized I put the car in first gear. I'd been doing seventy miles an hour for 20 minutes on the highway.

I immediately pulled off at the next exit to let the car cool off, but when I threw the shifter back up into drive, the piston rod went right through the oil pan and blew up the motor. Goodbye, Buick Regal. Hello, ass-whooping!

Once Meanstreak split up, me and Machera became very close and hung out together all the time. Even though we had no band, we knew that *we* were a match and wanted to keep the chemistry alive that we had with each other. So we would randomly jam with different musicians when we could find them and see if they had the attitude and the talent that we were looking for.

When we weren't jamming, we were finding some kind of trouble to get into. Whether it was stealing, getting into fights or simply getting wasted together, it all became a part of our bonding. And we became as close as any two brothers could become, which made it so much more painful when things went wrong for us.

It hurts to see somebody you once loved as a brother,

someone you would have done anything for, go down in flames and destroy his life through drug abuse or crime. You eventually get to the point where you feel he can't be helped, or at least you've exhausted all your options, and now it's a matter of escaping for yourself or getting caught in the downward spiral with him.

For me, that person was John Machera. He was a legend in his own time to me and to everyone who knew him. John dressed in ripped jeans and a black leather jacket and grew his long jet-black hair to cover his face; this was way back in the early 80's when everyone else was still wearing Spandex and teasing their hair with hairspray, way before grunge or even before Metallica was popular. He was truly a man ahead of his time—for some reason he just knew what the new cool thing coming up was. He was listening to punk rock like Black Flag and G.B.H. way before anyone in our little group was. And man, could he play the guitar.

John was well respected for certain things, but he was also very feared for other things, and sometimes being feared and respected is a bad combination. It reminds me of what Chazz Palminteri once said in his movie *A Bronx Tale*. It's a movie about this young kid who lives in the Bronx and is strongly influenced by the local mafia, growing up under their wing even though his parents don't approve. The boy asks the mafia boss one day whether it's better to be loved or to be feared. The boss replies that it's nice to be loved, but he'd rather be feared—it keeps his men loyal to him. As for me, I'd rather be loved. Being feared takes too much work.

John was stuck between worlds. He had, and still has, a heart of gold, so I know he enjoys being loved, but as a teenager he made bad decisions, as we all have; unfortunately some of those decisions were so bad that it became dangerous to be around him. I found that out like I found out a lot of things in life—the hard way.

When I was around sixteen, I met this girl named Lisa T. Lisa had light brown hair, shoulder-length. She looked kind of like Pat Benatar and had a perfect ass, which she'd show off in these really tight Jordache jeans. She was a little older than I was and she was tough—she was raised by two brothers. She worked as a waitress and she had her own car. She actually came on to me at a bowling alley in south Lawrence.

It was empowering to be with an older woman, and she was cool, like she was one of the guys—you could talk about anything with her. I really fell in love with her, or at least what I knew love to be at the time. Unfortunately, she was hard to trust. She worked the night shift at Howard Johnson's and met a lot of people that way. Some of them, I'm sure, were drunken guys going in for late-night food and putting their moves on. Fair enough, we all have our skeletons—I'm no angel myself—but it sucked for me because at the time I was feeling that she was it for me. I was experiencing love for the first time and I really thought she felt the same way.

Although I never caught her in the act, there were plenty of signs that I was probably being played for a fool. You kind of get the hint when you're out with your girl and some dude rolls up in his car asking her when he could get together again and get some. Then their face drops when she says, "Oh hey, Steve, this is my boyfriend Sully."

Eventually she confirmed my worst suspicions, and in the worst way possible.

I found her over at John's house a couple of times. Long story short, they eventually hooked up and started seeing each

other. Surprisingly, they became inseparable and their relationship lasted for years. I'm still not sure why I forgave John
so quickly. I wonder if it was because I really loved him like
a brother and a bandmate, or because I feared him snapping
on me. I guess it was a little of both, but for what it's worth,
I was at least glad to know that he loved her and hadn't
broken us up just to fuck her and dump her.

And it's not like I was going to duke it out with John
anyway. As I explained earlier, for the most part, I could carry
my own when it came to fighting and I never really feared
anyone, but John was in a whole other league. John was simply the toughest dude I had ever known. He was also the
craziest dude I'd ever known. He feared absolutely no one. He
was one of those guys who you were real happy was on your
side. He wasn't always the biggest guy, although he went in
and out of weight-lifting phases that would leave him at times
weighing about 200 pounds and ripped, but most of the time
I was hanging with him, he was about 5' 10", 140 or 150
pounds—skinny guy. He was one of those guys that you would
never guess to be tough, but trust me when I say that if you
got on his bad side, you'd better watch the fuck out!

One time John, Jimmy Mustapha and myself all walked
down to the Store 24 to steal some food because we were
broke and hungry. As we got out of the car, these two muscle-
headed guys started fucking with John, teasing him about
being a scrawny little fuck, having long hair and calling him
a faggot and whatnot.

John's deadliest weapon was that he would never let you
know he was coming at you. He would simply let you get in
his face, yell and scream and let you feel like you were in-
timidating him. Then out of nowhere, he would lash out at
you like a cobra and relentlessly beat you with anything he

could get his hands on, to the point that we always found ourselves pulling him off of whoever he was annihilating to make a break for it before the cops got there. It's like he would black out and not even realize how far he was taking it. He would literally leave people lying in a puddle of blood.

That's what our friends at the Store 24 got that night. John stood there as quiet as a mouse while they went off on him, yelling all this shit and sticking their noses right up against his. Next thing you know, John pulls out this lead pipe from his trench coat and begins to smash one of the guys right over the head. The other guy, who happened to be on crutches, goes into complete shock when he sees his friend go down; he takes one of his crutches and smashes John across the back with it. Not even flinching, John turns around and starts beating the other guy until he had them both on the ground begging for their lives. As usual, we ripped him off those poor guys and got the hell out of Dodge.

Another time, while sitting at a bar having a few cocktails, some drunken lug was staring John down and making sarcastic remarks to him, really testing his patience. Once again out of nowhere John picked up his shot glass, tossed back his drink and fired this glass at the guy, shattering his entire face. There was no question in any of our minds that John's temper was way out of control, and eventually Lisa and even his own father became victims of it.

When Lisa and John started dating, everything was real cool for a while. Yeah, they would get into their fights, but those didn't seem too different from anyone else's—until one day when I bumped into one of Lisa's friends. I asked her how Lisa was and she told me John had beaten her pretty bad during their last fight. They had argued about something and it got so bad that Lisa tried to make a break for it and leave John's house. He chased her down the stairs and caught up with her outside the house, dragged her back inside by her feet and made sure that her head hit every step on the way back up to his third-floor apartment.

At some point his father approached John to try and reason with him, but I guess John felt like his dad was taking Lisa's side, so he and his dad started fighting. John's dad was one big son of a bitch, too. He went to the gym religiously and had to have been at least 240 pounds jacked, so for John to even think of going at his dad was insane in itself. But he felt betrayed, so he decided to take matters into his own hands.

After escaping the argument with his father, he went out that night and partied with his friends. I'm not sure exactly what they did as far as alcohol or drugs, but something must have fired him up. He must have been stewing all night, because he eventually decided to go back and take it up with his father again.

When he got back to his house, he went down to the basement and grabbed a rusty old axe. Then he climbed up the stairs to the second floor where his dad's girlfriend lived and started to pound on the door, yelling for his father. John's dad opened the door, leaving the chain on, only to see his crazed son standing there with an axe. He immediately slammed the door and locked it. John started chopping away at the door, trying to get through, yelling and blasting his axe into the wood.

He finally got a huge piece of the door busted in, stuck his head and arm through the hole to undo the chain and began quoting lines from the horror movie *The Shining*. "Heeeeeere's Johnny!" Then he got the rest of the door open and stood in the middle of the kitchen looking his father dead in the face and said, "Dad? I'm home!"

He began swinging the axe around, trying to hit his father, bashing and cutting into the floor of the kitchen. John's dad eventually got hold of him and they began to wrestle on the floor. At one point, when John swung the axe at his dad, his dad was able to get the axe under his arm and actually snap the handle in half. Holy shit! Now can you imagine how big this dude was? John made a break for it after that (can't say I blame him), leaving his father's girlfriend's apartment in shambles.

Now here's how I know all of this: I fell asleep on the couch that night, like I often did, and when I woke up the next morning the first thing I did was go to my room to get some clothes and have a smoke. When I opened the door, I heard someone rustling around in my bed. It was like Goldilocks and the Three fucking Bears. I jumped back in shock and turned around to see John awakening in my bed.

He opened his eyes and said very quietly in his morning voice, "Hey dude! What's up?"

"John? What the fuck are you doing in my bed?"

"Your bedroom window was unlocked, so I crawled in late last night. I didn't want to wake you up so I just crashed in your bed," he said.

This wasn't anything new to me—everyone climbed through each other's windows. My room happened to be located right off the driveway, so it was easy access for late-night visitors.

Then he sat up and started spitting it. "Sully, I'm in some deep shit..." And on and on the story went.

I asked him, "What are you gonna do? You can't stay here. My mother will freak out if she finds out."

"That's cool, I'm gonna make a break for it and jump town."

All I could think was, "Is he telling me everything? Is

that the extent of it, or is his dad a lot more injured than he's saying? Or dead?"

Either way, I still gave a shit about John—he was my bro' and no matter how bad this was, I wasn't a snitch. I would do anything for my friends. I told him to call me if he got stuck, but I was at a loss for words beyond that. Then he left. I remember thinking, "I'm never gonna see this guy again."

It's easy for some people to sit there and wonder how I could give a shit about someone who seemed so dangerous and unpredictable, but if they knew John's story, they might think differently. He had it rough as a kid. His dad, being as big and masculine as he was, put pressure on John to grow up a lot faster than he probably should have. I could sit here and write a whole chapter on the stories John has told me about the abuse he went through with his father—like how his dad tied him to a pole in the basement and beat him with baseball bats over a bad report card. But it's not in my place to do that. Maybe John will write his own book one day and shock the world. What I *can* tell you is that this went way beyond the argument over Lisa. This was just the straw that broke the camel's back.

Surprisingly, he turned himself in two days later. He was arrested, convicted and sentenced to six months in jail. I'm sure it could've been worse for him, but his dad, loving his son unconditionally (as every parent should), decided not to turn his back on him and instead got him help. He knew that the first thing he needed to do was let John do some time for what he did, but he forgave him eventually and they worked it all out.

Once he got out of jail, John started hanging with the

wrong crowds and eventually it led him into experimenting
with heroin. John was the first person I ever witnessed shooting up, and it was a very disturbing sight. Once that started,
I pretty much bailed on the whole idea of hanging out. Sticking a needle in my arm just didn't seem like fun to me.

At one point I hadn't seen John for several months. Then
I heard that he'd overdosed. Me and Jimmy rushed to the
hospital to see him. He was lying there in bed, tubes attached
to him everywhere because he'd slipped into a coma. When
he finally snapped out of it, he was still a mess. He would
sit there and tell us how scared he was and that he would
never do that shit again, then a second later he would start
hallucinating and yelling at us, telling us to watch out for the
rats that were crawling all over his bed. I was heartbroken.
Here was the strongest guy in mind and body that I had ever
known, and now he was helpless. I was devastated.

John went clean for a while. He started to get back into
weight lifting, but because of the coma he was in, his right
arm had become paralyzed and had shrunk down to almost
nothing, so he could only do limited exercises.

I really believed at that point that he had learned his
lesson, but as the months passed, I would hear about him
getting into the dope again, which was shocking—he was
partially crippled because of this shitty drug, and now he's on
it again? It just didn't make any sense to me. All I knew was,
I had to stay away. There was no helping him.

I don't see John around anymore—he has his life and I
have mine. I hear about him from time to time and I find
myself still feeling concerned about how he's doing. Sometimes I hear he's back on the dope and it makes me sad,
hoping he'll rid that shit from his life before it kills him.

Other times I hear he's doing great, lifting weights again, and staying in shape.

Whatever it is you're doing John, I just hope you've been able to find a happy life for yourself. I know you had it real tough growing up, but you're an amazing individual. Jimmy and I talk about you from time to time. We both miss you. Just know that we had to move on and get our lives together, but you will always be, in our eyes, the wildest fucking guy we've ever known.

CHAPTER 9
LOVE HURTS

When I was seventeen years old I met this girl named Michelle. She lived about ten houses away from me. Michelle was kind of poor and lived with her mom and her two sisters, and they were all beautiful, especially Michelle. This girl was absolutely gorgeous—perfectly defined body, a beautiful face framed by long, wavy brown hair, the whole package. She was a ten, like a Playboy centerfold, or Kate Smith from "Charlie's Angels." She carried herself well, and she was very quiet, shy and reserved, but very sexy. I immediately fell for her.

Little did I know she was just getting out of a relationship when we started dating.

One day, about two months after we hooked up, I was walking home from a store that was at the corner of my block, and I heard a car screech on its breaks and pull up behind me. I looked back to see what the noise was, when four guys jumped out of the car and started approaching me. Before I could even think about running, they backed me up against a wall and got all up in my face.

One of the guys came forward and asked me if I was dating Michelle. I answered yes, then he began threatening me and telling me they're all going to kick my ass, and that if I'm seen with her again I'll be in the hospital and blah, blah, blah.

So needless to say, I was pretty scared at that point because it was four against one. I was just standing there waiting for one of them to lose it and start smashing me around. Just then, out of the corner of my eye I happened to catch Freddy's car driving by with a couple of my friends in it. That changed my whole attitude. I started thinking, that these motherfuckers were going to get a run for their money now.

Of course it was just my luck that Freddy and the boys didn't even see me. They were ready to keep driving right on by. I remember thinking, "Fuck! Those bastards are probably getting stoned right now and cranking the tunes so loud that they're not gonna hear me if I yell for them." But then I decided that it would still be my best opportunity, so I pushed one of the guys to the side and I whistled as loud as I could. Freddy was driving so I had the best view of him. He looked over and locked eyes with me, seeing that I was surrounded by idiots, and spun his car around to check out what this was. I started feeling a lot more relaxed knowing that they were seconds away from helping me. Even if they decided to jump me right then, I wasn't getting my ass kicked for long.

The dude who was up in my face looks back at me and says, "Oh...you wanna get your friends involved?" and I'm thinking, "It's four on one, what do you think?" Then he says, "No problem dude, we'll be back with our buddies!" They jumped in their car and split before Freddy or anyone else could get there. I'm thinking, "We just evened out the odds and you run away?"

Freddy and the boys pull up, they have no clue what was

going on, but they see me all freaked out and ready to fight. As I'm explaining to them what went down, they start getting all worked up themselves and suggest that we go look for them. We spent a good hour or so driving around the neighborhood looking for these guys but we couldn't seem to find anyone that resembled them, so we figured we'd drop it. They brought me back home and we just assumed that it was over and we wouldn't hear from them again.

Later on that evening I hooked up with Michelle and told her what had happened. I asked her who those guys were and she told me it was her ex-boyfriend and that he was a nutcase, but reassured me that she wasn't going to get back together with him. So I forgot the whole thing.

The next day Michelle and I were hanging out here and there, and we decided to go back to my house and chill for a while. We were both pretty burnt out from smoking pot all day, so we went into my room and crashed. We were both sound asleep when I was woken up by cars screeching outside of my house. This wasn't anything new because we always had accidents on my block, but I jumped up and ran to the living room window to see what was up anyway. As I lifted up the shades and tried to focus my eyes in the bright sun, I noticed there were fifteen or twenty guys outside arguing with this guy named Rick Jarvis, a good friend of mine who was staying with me and my mom for a while. His father had been physically and mentally abusing him for some time and my mother and I decided to let him stay with us until he found his own place. He was a fairly big guy and definitely capable of taking care of himself.

I could hear them saying to Rick, "Get Sully out here, we're gonna kick his ass!"

I hear Rick respond, "Oh really, you mean all twenty of

you? Well, why don't you start with me first?" That was that, punches started flying and in a flash it was twenty on one. I started shitting myself watching this, knowing that when I got out there I was going to get my ass beat, but I couldn't let Rick be out there on his own, so I ran into my room and grabbed a baseball bat and started heading for the front door. Just as I got my hand on the door knob, I felt my mother grab me by the back of the shirt and pull me backwards; she was screaming and begging me to stay inside, grabbing at my hair and whatever else she could grab on to. We struggled for a few seconds but I broke away pretty fast and got onto the porch.

The first thing I saw was Rick on the ground punching the shit out of this one guy as another guy was running up behind him holding a lawn mower over his head. We had this old-style manual lawn mower that had a round swirling blade connected to a T-handle, so when you pushed it, the blade would turn and cut the grass. And it was made out of real heavy iron. Well, this Neanderthal picked it up over his head and started charging behind Rick to bust him over the back with it, so I yelled, "Rick! Behind you!" Rick spun around just as the kid launched the lawn mower at him and was able to get out of the way before it hit him.

My mother came flying onto the porch and locked her death grip on me again. And once again I had to wrestle her off of me so I could get out there and help Rick.

Just then my Uncle Bill came flying out of the house with a shotgun in his hand. My Uncle Bill is a redneck from Arkansas and is also a pretty big guy. He's about six foot one and probably weighed about 220 lbs. at the time, and he had a nasty temper. So I was thinking, "Somebody is definitely about to die!" He ran past all of us and right into the brawl. All the guys started scattering one by one, backing way up into the road. Some of them just plain ran for their lives. My uncle ran over to Rick and the guy he was fighting and smashed the butt of his shotgun right into the guy's ribs. Man, let me tell you, I could literally hear his bones crack from the porch.

Then this one idiot stood in front of my uncle and started waving his hands around like he was some martial arts nut. My uncle looked over at the Bruce Lee wannabe and stuck the barrel of his cocked shotgun right into his face, with his finger on the trigger. My aunt Barbara was yelling at the top of her lungs for him not to do it. I was standing there with my hands over my ears waiting for the gun to go off. Then this dude does the funniest thing I ever saw. He started slapping the barrel of the shotgun and toying with it like a cat would with a piece of yarn. Here and there he would try to grab the gun out of my uncle's hands. I was thinking, "This guy is really asking for it."

My uncle pulled the gun away from this kid's reach, turned it around and jacked this guy right in the face with the butt of the shotgun. He hit him so hard, it sounded like a window had shattered.

Then I realized that a window *had* shattered. The guy who was trying to hit Rick over the head with the lawn mower had gone up to our house and smashed both his fists through one of the windows. He punched through so hard that he sliced his arms up. He turned around, hopped over the fence and ran away. There was a puddle of blood below the window and a trail of blood all the way up the road. At that point, all the other guys got freaked out and split.

The cops showed up and we explained what had happened. The cops told us that they were well aware of who these guys were and would go look for them. It turned out that they were a part of a gang that lived seven or eight blocks away from us. Michelle had just kind of forgotten to tell me that part.

When I got back into the house, my mom was a mess. She was sitting at the kitchen table with my aunt Barbara just shaking and crying. I went up to her to comfort her, but she wouldn't have it. She just kept saying, "I can't do this anymore. We're leaving this state. It's just too much for me. You're going to end up dead or in jail for the rest of your life!"

What I hadn't known was that my mom was already thinking about relocating us because of all the wear and tear of the city life. Not to mention that she hated the winter!

I was more upset seeing my mom in that condition than I was about what had just happened. What she said really had an impact on me. I started thinking, "She's right! I *am* going to end up dead or in jail." And I had way too much talent to waste it on a senseless situations like that, or on a piece of shit city like Lawrence. Plus I had never been anywhere but New England my whole life, so I said fuck it, it might suck leaving my friends, but I need to go check out the rest of the world. Me, my mom, Rick and his girlfriend all began planning our way out of Lawrence.

I had no idea what was in store for me, or what I would do when I got to this new place, but I knew in my heart that it was the right thing to do. It was just time. I was tired of life on the streets—all the violence, all the crime, never being able to walk to the store at night without having to watch my back or carry a weapon, and always worrying about being in the wrong place at the wrong time. It was a life I was no longer interested in.

It was December of 1985, I was seventeen years old and I was leaving the only life I had ever known: life in the ghettos. I would never live in Lawrence again.

PART TWO

CHAPTER 10
SOUTH BOUND

Fayetteville, North Carolina was our destination. My mom had been working at Fort Devens near Lawrence for some time and she had met this lady there named Susan, who was now a realtor in Fayetteville. Susan's husband was a colonel at Fort Bragg and because of my mom's experience working on an army base, he said he could get her a job. Susan also promised that she would help my mom find a great deal on a house. It was exciting for me to think about— we had lived in that old run-down house in Lawrence for so long, and now we were going to have a single family home in a fresh new town.

But when we actually got down there, we got no help from anyone. We moved into a house in a development called Devonwood Estates, and although my mother bought our house there, I don't think Susan even helped. Mom never got that job at Bragg, either.

Fayetteville was a small town loaded with military people. So many servicemen had passed through Fort Bragg on the way to Vietnam and packed into the nearby bars, strip joints and whorehouses that the locals still called it "Fayettenam." Fort Bragg, one of the biggest army bases in the country, is about ten miles away from the house my mother bought, so it was a real treat for us the first time we felt the house shaking and heard all the pictures rattling off the walls at 6:00AM because the Navy decided to show up and test all their bombs on base. I had no idea what the rumbling was the first few times I heard it. I remember thinking, "North Carolina has earthquakes?" I didn't care though, it was a new place and I was ready for some new scenery.

My main focus was to find some guys to start a band with. Being new in town, it was going to take a while because I had to go out and find people that were like me, but I've always been a sociable kind of guy so I wasn't all that concerned. Plus, I was just about to turn eighteen years old and that was the drinking age in NC at that time. So I was psyched to go and party in the clubs.

Before I could do any of that, of course, I had to get some drums and some wheels. My mom, being the saint that she is, had a few extra bucks from selling the house back in Massachussetts, and hooked me up with a 1976 Trans Am. Coolest fucking gift I ever got! Then she took me to a pawn shop, and I found a killer eleven-piece candy apple red Ludwig Rockers drum set. Let me tell you, I was in heaven after that.

My mother always made it work for us no matter how bad we struggled, but this was over the top for me. I was a ghetto boy feeling like a rich kid. With everything looking so perfect for the first time in my life, I decided to go out into this strange town and find me a band.

* * * *

Shortly after my eighteenth birthday, one of the first things I did was go down to Bill Clayton's Tattoo Shop to get myself my first real piece of ink. Animal from the Muppets was and still is my hero as a drummer, so he became my first tat on my right shoulder.

Then it was off to the Cross Creek Mall. It was your typical small shopping mall equipped with a food court, fine young women and of course an arcade. Any stoner, punk, or musician I would be looking for was probably going to be found there.

The first time I visited the Cross Creek Mall, I couldn't have been in Fayetteville more than a month. I was excited— I was 900 miles away from trouble and it was time to start a new life.

I was probably not even twenty steps through the entrance of the mall when I heard someone say, "Hey, freak! Yeah, you! Ace Frehley!" OK, I admit I had long hair and I was a freak, but I sure as hell didn't look like Ace Frehley. I turned around to see who had said that, and there before my eyes were two GI's, fresh out of boot camp, neatly shaved heads and being complete assholes. I remember thinking for a second, "No, Sully! Don't do this. You're here to get a new start. Leave it alone!" But of course I never listened to anyone else, so why would I listen to myself? Besides, they were both my size and they weren't seasoned soldiers yet—you could tell by their scrawny little arms and the "not so sure if I want to do this" look on their faces that they were definitely not trained killers.

I walked over to both of them, the adrenaline already screaming through my veins, and I said, "What's up, bro'? Is there a problem here?" They stood there for a second before

answering, completely in shock that I had the balls to call
their bluff when it was two against one. The first kid said
under his breath, "No dude, we weren't talking to you," and
tried to play it off like they were just having a loud conversation and I was hearing things. Then his friend cut him off
and said, "Yeah, we were talking to you, you wanna do something about it, you little faggot?" Before this kid even finished his sentence, the blood had run to my face so fast that
there was no turning back. If I got my ass kicked, well then,
so be it, but I was hitting this motherfucker first.

I bowed my head down and put my hands up in the air,
as if I was suggesting to them that I wasn't going to fight.
Then, within a second of him ending his sentence, I hauled
off and smashed this fucker so hard in the nose that he
dropped instantly. Blood started pouring out of his face as he
lay there whimpering like a little girl.

I immediately turned to the other dude, ready to rock 'n'
roll, when I noticed that the look on his face said that he
didn't want to have anything to do with this—he was just
interested in helping his buddy up. As I walked by the kid
that I just leveled, I said to him in passing, "Next time keep
your fucking mouth shut!"

Feeling all proud and pumped that I just defended myself
against two guys, I decided to get the hell out of there before
I got in trouble, but of course my life can never be that
simple. I was greeted by two sheriffs that just happened to be
walking in the door that I was leaving by. I had just got past
them when that little weasel that I didn't smack yelled to the
cops, "Hey, officers! Help us! That dude right there just hit
my friend!"

I heard it, but I couldn't believe it. Here we go again! I
just got to this town and already the kettle was boiling. You

know how that ol' saying goes: you can take the boy out of the city, but you can't take the city out of the boy.

I was hoping to make the escape and kept walking without turning around, pretending like I hadn't heard anything, but they knew who to grab. I heard the cop say in his southern accent, "Hey, you! Stop right there." All I could think was, "*Fuck!* I can't believe this shit! My mom is gonna kill me!" The first officer came to deal with me while his partner checked on the other dude. He told me to have a seat while his partner brought the other boys out. As the other officer made his way out with the two boys, I noticed the one I hit was really hamming it up for the cops, making it look way worse than it was. They asked the two guys what had happened, and of course they told them everything, except for the part about them antagonizing me first. So I stepped into the conversation and told the two cops that they started the whole thing, and that it was two on one. I had to defend myself.

Now if I had a southern accent, maybe I would've gotten away with it, but not this time, not with my long hair, tattoos and my Boston accent. These two guys were clean cut and served in the army, so of course the police weren't going to believe me. I was cuffed, stuffed and brought down to the station where they gave me a big lecture and let me go. I don't think I have to tell you how relieved I was that they didn't call my mom. That could've been ugly.

For quite a while after that I spent my time struggling to find something to do or someone to hang out with. Most of the time I would go out to the bars and watch the cover bands jam on weekends. But mostly, I would hang out at my house, strap on my headphones and jam out to all my records.

Either that, or I would just sit on my steps outside the house and stare off into nothing, thinking about how to get something going in that town.

On one of those afternoons, I began realizing that a group of about four kids were frequently cruising my neighborhood on foot. They looked to be a few years younger than me, and I noticed that they carried themselves like little punks. Hey, I'm not trying to be the pot calling the kettle black here, I'm just saying that a punk can smell another punk a mile away, and I got very suspicious of them. They would walk by smoking butts and glancing over at me, whispering shit and flicking their cigarettes on the ground. But they never said hi or anything like that, so I'd just stare back at them and they'd keep on walking. Sometimes I'd be inside the house and I'd see them walking by, scoping out my Trans Am and peeking inside the windows of my car. I never said anything to them; I just kept a close watch, making sure they weren't going to pull any funny business with my new wheels.

A few days later when I got into my car to leave, I noticed that my lock on the driver's side door was broken. When I got in, I saw that my radio had been torn out of my dashboard.

I had this amazing Alpine digital car stereo rigged in there that I loved, and the fucking thing was gone. I got really pissed off because I knew who did it, but didn't know where to find them.

The next Saturday morning when I was outside in my yard, I saw two of the four kids walk by. I immediately stopped what I was doing and ran after them. One got away, but I was able to catch the second one. I quickly gave the little shit his only option. "Tell me where the stereo is or I'm gonna knock your fucking teeth down your throat!" I lashed out.

He didn't hesitate for a second. He rolled over on his

friend faster than a rabbit gets fucked! "Dave took it!" He shouted. "Not me. I can show you where he lives."

So I threw the dude in my car and had him bring me to Dave's house. As we screeched into Dave's driveway, I cut the rat loose. I walked up to the front door and rang the doorbell. "Ding-dong!" His mother answered with the perfect southern charm. "Hello young man. Can I help you?"

"Is Dave home?" I replied ever so sweetly.

"Sure." She said, "He's home. Would you like to come in?"

"No thanks." I said. "I'll just wait here." Oh man, was I steaming! A few seconds later Dave came to the door with his mom standing directly behind him. He must have caught a glimpse of my car in the driveway when she told him he had a visitor, because he looked nervous as hell. Busted!

When he came into my sight, I called him outside. "Hey Dave!" I said, like a true pal. "Can I talk to you outside, buddy?"

His mom was standing behind her boy, smiling gently. She had no clue what was going on. But he wouldn't have anything to do with that. He just shook his head, "No" and stayed frozen. He knew something was up.

Then my attitude started to shift. Right in front of his mother, I said to him firmly, "Where's my stereo dude?"

"What are you talking about? I don't have your stereo."

Without hesitation, I punched him square in the face, dragged him by his shirt onto the porch and repeated myself, "Tell me where it is or I'm gonna knock you out right in front of your mother."

His mom started going nuts trying to calm down the situation. As I held him by the collar of his shirt, I turned to her and told her the story. Surprisingly she didn't argue back with me, but instead looked at her son and asked him if he had stolen my stereo.

Finally he confessed, "I don't have it, but I can get it back." So I told him he had 24 hours to have it sitting on my porch or I was coming back to beat his ass. Judging by the way his mother dragged him back in the house by his ear, it looked like he was going to get his ass beat regardless.

Sure as shit, 24 hours later that stereo was on my front steps. And I never saw those kids again.

Months and months passed and I had no luck finding any musicians to start a band with. I went to every rock club in town, from Doc's to the Flaming Mug to Bahama Joe's, searching for some kind of action, but couldn't find anything. I began meeting people and hanging out at house parties more frequently, and some of those kids were actually in bands, but none of them were looking to switch out their drummers.

There was a band called Rough Justice, who was one of the better local bands in the area. Then there was The Mighty Overlord, who were these guys who wore spiked wrist bands, leather clothes and big hair; they were total Judas Priest rip-offs but they played all originals and signed some indie deal with Metal Blade records or something. How appropriate. They weren't all that good either, and everyone in town called the lead guitarist "OverGeorge," which I thought was hilarious. It was pretty slim pickings in the whole area.

When I finally got to the point where I felt the search was going nowhere, I decided to call Bill DeMonaco up in Boston and sell him on moving down to Fayettenam. Of course I lied and bragged about how cool Fayetteville was so he would go for it, and it worked. He got on a plane and moved in with us.

Not that Rick wasn't cool to hang with, but he was always tied up with his girlfriend and wasn't a musician, so it was great to have one of my friends to go out and work the town with. Not to mention that Bill was a singer, so that was one less dude I had to worry about finding.

Once Bill moved in, we both became club rats. All we did was hang out at the rock bars, drink lots of alcohol and look for new people or musicians to hook up with.

3:00AM rolled around one morning and we had just gotten back from the Flaming Mug. My mom was sound asleep so we tried to keep it down (even though we were drunk as hell) by hanging in the living room and watching TV. This movie called *Spring Break* was on HBO and me and Bill just happened to notice how beautiful and sunny it looked down there in Florida, not to mention all the hot chicks partying in bikinis. And it just so happened that it was spring break that week.

Without saying a word, Bill and I looked over at each other and nodded, reading each other's minds like we'd always done. We grabbed some clothes and a twelve pack of beer, jumped in my Trans Am and headed south on I-95 – 480 miles to Daytona Beach, baby! My mother had no clue that we were gone. We only had $150 on us but we figured we wouldn't even need that. Once we got there, we'd just find some people to party with and mooch off of them.

Halfway through South Carolina we got stopped for speeding. After the State Trooper pulled us over and ran my license, he came back to us and says, "It's a fifty dollar fine for speeding around here."

"I understand officer," I replied, thinking that was it. Then he says, "You have to pay now! Fifty bucks or you boys go to jail." He hadn't sensed that we were drinking yet, and I

wasn't about to argue, so we just forked over the fifty bucks
and got back in the car.

A hundred miles later, we cross the line into Georgia and
another cop pulls us over for speeding. "Fifty bucks on the
spot or you're going to jail!" I started thinking, "Is this legal?"
I'd never heard of such a thing, and I was getting a bit aggravated feeling like they were playing us for the fool. Plus,
my buzz was peaking so I had what they call liquid balls! I
tried calling his bluff by telling him that we didn't have the
$50.00, which got me absolutely nowhere except into an
argument with the Trooper. Bill, knowing, that I was shit-
faced, began to see where this was heading and decided to
butt in. He jumped out of the car and told the trooper that
he had the money. I looked over at Bill as if to say, "Don't
pay this dickhead anything!" Bill looked back at me with eyes
that said, "Shut the fuck up!" and paid the crook off. I'm
surprised he didn't ask us to bend over and grab our own
ankles before he fucked us.

Now we're down to fifty dollars and we weren't even over
the Florida line yet! We stopped at a convenience store, spent
forty dollars on gas and about another ten bucks on a pack
of cigarettes, a loaf of bread and a jar of peanut butter.

Eight hours and a brutal hangover later, we arrived at Daytona
Beach. We had no money, nowhere to go and we didn't know
a damn soul in town. Our breath smelled like cigarettes and
peanut butter and we were parked on the side of the road, out
of gas and wondering what we were going to do.

I called my mom at about noon, hoping to get her to
wire me some money so we could at least get home. She
thought we were still in Fayetteville sleeping late.

"What the hell do you mean you're in Daytona? I thought
you were in your bedroom."

I tell her, "Mom, please! We need some money down here or we're fucked! $50.00 and we can at least get home." Not knowing if she had the money or if she could find a Western Union that was open, she told me to call her back in a couple of hours.

In the meantime, we met this guy on the beach who told us that we could leave the car in his driveway for the night and sleep there if we needed to. Having driven all night we decided to take him up on the offer and get some rest before we had to drive all the way back. Once we woke up, I tried my mom's again, but kept getting no answer, and for a whole day we were wandering around, starving. Finally I got through to her and she told me that she had wired some money to me. We were so excited that me and Bill ran down to the local Western Union, and with a quick flick of my license, we were in the money!

To our surprise, my mom had wired us $175.00. Woo hoo! Our way of thinking changed *real* fast. We weren't about to head home yet. This was enough money for food, gas *and* a hotel room. We were staying for Spring Break!

The first thing we did was walk over to the Burger King and ordered about $15.00 worth of food. And in 1986, knowing how cheap Burger King is to begin with, you can just imagine how much food that got us. We were stuffed and happy. The next step was a hotel room. Once we got in, we showered and hit the beach to look for some fun. When we returned later that evening, this big southern redneck guy who was running the little shit-breather hotel had gone through our room and confiscated our belongings. Just what we needed to ruin our big plans. When we confronted him he started yelling at us, "You hippies are a bunch of no good pill-poppin' Yankees," stereotyping us because of our tattoos and long hair. He definitely didn't want us there. So he kept Bill's bag and told us to beat it, physically threatening us and whatnot. Bill was really upset because he had just bought a new hair dryer that he wanted back, and as you know, in the 80s, you needed a good hair dryer. We got into a big argument with the fat fuck, and when he began threatening to call the police, we decided to leave and go back to Fayetteville. We didn't have enough money to get another hotel room and pay for gas, so we left Daytona and never got to enjoy spring break.

Bill and I eventually found a few guys to start a band with. Doug Robinson on guitar, Derek Thomas on bass and Kip Griner on guitar completed our first out-of-state band, Meliah Kraze. It was a name that we ripped off from a high school band back in Methuen that wasn't doing a whole lot. We didn't feel that bad about it since we were 900 miles away from them, and besides, they'd ripped the name off themselves from a Boston band called Meliah Rage. We'll talk about that later.

We were quite the sight. We were dead smack into the middle of the 80's, so Spandex, big hair and makeup was the thing to do. Bill fucking hated it. He was a jeans and t-shirt guy (which I was as well) but I always liked to entertain and look like I was in a band, so I was more adventurous then he was. Now, our bass player Derek was a whole different story. He was way more overboard with this kind of style than all four of us put together. He loved wearing lipstick and hairspray way too much. I remember it was so extreme with him that it would actually worry us. He dressed like that all the time, at malls, movie theatres, house parties, you name it. Hey, to each his own.

The rest of the guys lived in Georgia, but moved to Fayetteville to join the band. They didn't have a place to live so they crashed at my house, sleeping on the couches and rugs.

Now, my mom has always been the greatest "rock mom" ever, but this was a little bit too much even for her. There was an extra four guys added to our living arrangements and it was no longer cool to stay and torture her. Kip had inherited a house in Georgia so we decided to move the band down to Georgia and work out the details there.

Now, I thought Fayetteville was country, but Fayetteville was New York City compared to this town. Douglas, Georgia, had nothing but trees, corn fields and peanut farms. We were destined to be a great rock band simply because of the fact that there was nothing to do there but practice. And since we all lived together at Kip's house, it was pretty convenient for rehearsing all the time.

Every day for months we practiced in Kip's living room, working out songs by Motley Crue, Alice Cooper, Aerosmith, Led Zeppelin, and so on. Yeah, we thought we were cool all right, but the only problem was, we weren't! We played songs from cool bands and we played them great, but we looked like idiots. We were trying to compete with the looks of Whitesnake and all those other huge, chick-friendly 80's bands, and it just didn't work.

Back then you had to know at least forty songs because when you played the clubs, you had to do four, sometimes five sets a night, and each set was forty-five minutes long. It was hell! After about four months of hard work we finally worked up enough material to go find an agent and hit the local circuit.

I was feeling great—I was finally going to play drums in a heavy metal band for a living! The suck part was, we didn't have a following yet, so we could only get the lowest piece of shit booking agency out there.

Our booking agent looked just like Andre the Giant. He was a big, cigar-smoking thug. He got us on what they called the "C" circuit: they put you in the shittiest hotels (if you even *get* a hotel), they stick you in the shittiest clubs on the shittiest nights, and they pay you shit. We felt like a bunch of cheap hookers getting pimped out. It's one of those situations where once you're in it, it's real hard to get out.

The places we played were smoky biker bars—dusty, dark holes filled with low-class people. We ran this circuit for months and months. We were dying out there. It was so bad we would offer to do gigs for a case of beer and some fast food just to keep going. We would literally sleep under people's porches and eat cheap ramen noodles five days a week. We would pick up fat girls at the gig (not that there were any cute girls anyway) and sweet-talk them into taking us to their place, hoping to bribe them into cooking us up a steak or something. Plus we'd have a couch to crash on. We called it the Torture Tour.

After about half a year of that, the band decided to split up and try something else individually. Bill went on to jam with Rough Justice after they lost their singer and did really well with them for some time. But that didn't last either— they fired Bill and eventually the whole band broke up. Once again it was back to Bill and myself, and we were bandless.

We went on to find some other opportunities, but nothing worth mentioning. This one cover band that I joined down on Atlantic Beach in North Carolina was actually responsible for getting me on the path I needed to be on. I was with them for such a short time that I can't even remember the band's name, but I do remember we played a lot of

Dokken. A guy named Gary was the singer-guitar player and a guy named Roy was the bass player, and they were a lot older than me. We did a few lame gigs and made no money (what else was new), but I have to admit it was pretty cool living right on the ocean for a while—or at least until I found out what it was these dudes did to get cash. They would dig clams out of the ocean just to make a buck or two.

Really, it sucked! We would stand out in the middle of the ocean where there were low spots, with our pants rolled up to our ankles, looking like Jesus Christ walking on water, digging in the mud with this claw-like contraption to find clams and try to sell them for ten cents a pound or whatever they went for that week.

It was definitely not my idea of how to become a rock star, but before I quit, we played the right show one night and I met this dude named Todd Jackson. Todd owned his own P.A. system and he was running sound for us that night; he was also in a band called Lexx Luthor. I know the name sounds silly, but they were really good, and they were playing all the shit I wanted to play: Metallica, Queensryche, Slayer, Anthrax, Sex Pistols, G.B.H., Murphy's Law, you name it. Todd and I hit it off right away, swapped numbers and he said he would call me if they were going to replace their drummer.

CHAPTER 11
WHORES AND SCORES

In the middle of all of my band searching, I had fallen in love with my first southern belle—or should I say, southern hell!

It all started when I was riding with a friend in this big-ass Ryder truck down Raeford Road in Fayetteville one day and spotted these two beauties driving towards us. I hung myself out the window to get their attention, and then gave them the old Gene Simmons tongue action as they drove past us. It's such a typical Italian male thing to do, but for some reason it worked. I looked back, saw their brake lights go on and watched their car head into a gas station for a U-turn. I told my friend to whip the big rig around and go catch these sassy little things.

I got out and I went up to the blonde on the driver's side and asked her what her name was. "Arlene," she says in her little southern accent. I asked her if she was interested in hooking up later for a drink or two, and she said yes, so we exchanged numbers and I called her later. It didn't take us long to start spending every waking moment together either.

It was instant magic for us, and within a blink of an eye, we were the ultimate couple.

Arlene was a hottie. I mean, she was Heather Locklear hot: a tiny little girl with bleached blonde hair and blue, blue eyes. She was the stereotypical ditzy blonde—you know, the kind you can trick into giving you a blowjob! You could tell she wasn't very bright, just silly, giddy and giggly (not that that's a bad thing), and I fell in love with her right away. What can I say—I've always had a weakness for blondes. My mom used to tell me that when I was a baby in the car seat and a blonde would walk by, she thought I was going to break my neck trying to turn around and look at her.

Unfortunately, Arlene's parents hated me. They were a very wholesome, Christian family. They owned a school bus company and had plenty of money. Then there was me—long, scraggly hair, tattoos, earrings and a rock musician—oh yeah, I had Satan written all over me.

I didn't like them either. They were that rich, stuck-up type that reminded me of the snobby people back in Andover, Massachusetts. But I did my best to impress them because I loved Arlene and I wanted them to like me. It's just really hard to impress people like that when you look like you're on skid row and talk like you're from Brooklyn. They weren't buying it and I didn't waste much of my time selling it. If Arlene and I were going to have any kind of a relationship, it would have to be without their blessing. So, since they were so nice and understanding to us, we decided to move in together anyway. Fuck 'em!

We rented a one-bedroom with a kitchen and a living room. It was small but it was ours—no parents, no roommates, just us. I worked a construction job and she was a waitress at the Rockola Café. Everything seemed great for the longest time.

Arlene's ex-boyfriend was a coke dealer and she was still friends with him, so she was able to get tons of this shit for nothing. He'd give her a certain amount to sell, but she would never get around to selling it. She'd bust it out when friends came over and after we'd start pinching a little here and there, the next thing you know we're eight-balls into the bag. That's cocaine for you.

One night at the apartment, I invited my friend Jon Robbins over and Arlene invited her friend Carla. The four of us sat at that table forever just doing lines and chat, chat, chatting away; religion, space, music, aliens, you name it. It's so ridiculous what you talk about when you're jacked on blow. It's always about crap that you normally would never discuss.

It felt like we were there for days. I don't remember exactly how much coke we did that night, but it was a fuckload.

The next morning we were still slugging away at it, to the point where nobody was even talking to each other anymore, we were all just looking at each other waiting for the mirror to come in our direction. Finally the coke was gone. We snorted up everything we had, and me and Jon probably smoked a carton of cigarettes between the both of us. We knew at some point we were going to start coming down off the drugs and feeling like shit, so we decided to go get some food, slow down the buzz and sleep off the inevitable hangover. After we realized that eating wasn't an option, Arlene and I decided to just deal with being wired until we were able to crash.

Next thing I knew, I woke up to Arlene shaking me. Apparently I'd been choking in my sleep. My uvula (that little thing that hangs in the back of your throat) had swollen up to the size of a walnut and was blocking my air passage and I just about swallowed it. Thank God she heard me gasping for air, or I might have died in my sleep.

And that was it for me. No more coke since that day. I couldn't help but think about my friend John and the coma he'd slipped into from a drug overdose. I was twenty years old, and it felt like God had tapped me on the shoulder and said, "Smarten up, boy, or next time you won't be so lucky." So I did, and my hard drug days were over just like that.

But Arlene had a worse problem with cocaine than I realized. She was still sneaking around with her ex-boyfriend, the coke dealer. She had no signs of slowing down and it was getting to be too much for me. It might seem weird that I didn't realize how hooked she was even though I lived with the girl. But addicts can be really good at hiding it – sometimes even the people closest to them don't know. When you're drunk with your friends, you don't notice them being drunk. But try and be around drunken people when you're straight and see how noticeable it is.

That's what happened with me. Once I went clean, it was plain as day that she was a cokehead. And she was so ditzy that it was just hard to tell if she was high on coke, or if she was just being a goof. She started not showing up to work and lying to me about hanging around with her ex-boyfriend. She hadn't gotten the scare that I'd had yet, so she had no intentions of stopping.

It was time to try something new. I decided that changing our location and heading north was the answer. So we loaded up her white Chevy Impala and moved up to New England. We bounced around a little and lived in a few different cities before landing in Haverhill, Mass., a ten-minute drive from Lawrence. I found us a one-bedroom apartment in a brick multiple-tenant building downtown. She started working as a waitress again and I found a job installing carpets.

Not long after that we got engaged. My mom was so excited when I told her that she gave me a diamond ring to put on Arlene's finger, which I did. It was a very special time for me because I had never, ever thought of getting married. It had never seemed right for me, but I loved Arlene to death and I felt like I could spend the rest of my life with her.

As time went on though, we got real good at fighting, and in the middle of one big argument I flushed the ring down the toilet. Part of the reason we were fighting so much was because she was still playing around with the coke, which made her really moody, and I was drinking all the time. And drinking and drugs only create pain, guilt and insecurities. We got to the point where neither of us trusted the other and we constantly fought about the stupidest things.

She felt that being in a relationship had made her tame and boring so she started hanging out with these girls from work, going out with them all the time and whooping it up all night. One night we got into such a bad fight, she decided she should go stay with a friend from work and cool off. So I said, "Fine!"

After three or four days she still hadn't called or come by, and my suspicions got to me. I began going to her work to see her, but when I'd get there, they'd tell me she hadn't come to work in days. This got me really freaked. I had no idea where she was and I felt responsible—I was the one who'd brought her to this town where she knew no one. I couldn't help but start to think that either she'd gone back to North Carolina or that something bad had happened to her. I decided to go over my friend John Machera's house and talk to him to get my mind off of Arlene.

John and his girlfriend Rachel lived in Lawrence on the second floor of a three-story apartment building in a pretty rough area. He and Rachel had met Arlene a few times and hit it off pretty well, so I knew he would lend me his ear for awhile.

As I pulled down his road, I couldn't believe what I saw: there's Arlene's car parked in front of his house! Man, the blood shot right through my face like a steam train. I screeched on my brakes, slammed my car into park and jumped out, cursing up a storm.

"Arlene! Get the fuck down here!" I yelled. Then I saw the curtains move as someone looked to see what all the yelling was about, so I yelled again, "Arlene, if you don't get your ass down here I'm gonna smash the fucking windows right out of your car!" Still no show, so I pulled a hammer out of my trunk, went over to her car and smashed her driver's side window to pieces.

"You comin' down now?" I yelled. Nothing. Smash, bang, boom, I ended up losing my mind and smashing every window out of her car, then I dug the claw of the hammer into the metal of the hood eight or ten times. I opened the door, got inside and smashed up the stereo system I'd bought and installed for her. Finally I got the response I was looking for. People started coming out of the apartment, but it wasn't Arlene, it was John and one of his friends, and they didn't look too happy.

John wasn't someone I wanted to fuck with, but goddamn it, he was supposed to be my friend and I was mortified! I asked him flat out, "What the fuck is she doing here?"

I knew in my heart that whatever he was about to tell me was going to be bad, but I didn't realize that it was going to be *this* bad. He said, "Arlene told us that you guys were

through and she was free to do whatever, so she's been staying here with me and Rachel doing blow and fucking the
both of us!" Whoa! Way too much information for me. John
looked wasted. You could tell that they had been doing blow
up there for days. I looked at John in disgust, turned my
back on him, got in my car and drove home.

When I arrived, I started tossing her stuff out the third
floor window and onto the street. About thirty minutes later
I heard brakes screeching in front of my apartment. I looked
out the window and saw Arlene's car pull up with plastic
sheeting on all the windows and hammer gouges all over her
hood. Looking back now, it was pretty fucking funny to see
her pulling up in this hunk of shit that I created, but it
wasn't funny then. I knew her temper and how pissed she
was going to be once she discovered how bad her car was.

She came flying into the house losing her mind, yelling
at me to stop throwing her shit out the window. "I'll get it
out myself, you fucking asshole!" she yells. So, I'm thinking,
"Cool! She'll be out of here in a second." She walked right
by me and into the bedroom to grab whatever she had left
there, and as she did, she noticed my drum set stacked up
against the wall.

She grabbed a pair of scissors and went dashing for them,
trying to stab holes in the heads and then, I assume toss
them out the window. I thought, "Oh shit, *not the drums!*"
I ran over and grabbed the drum out of her hands and pushed
her down on to the waterbed to get her away from them.
Then, just like that, it was over. I thought I was in the twilight
zone. Within a blink of an eye she chilled right out, stopped
fighting with me, began talking really calm and cool, and
with a subtle smile on her face she said she was going to get
her things and just go. I said, "Fine, just leave," and she did.

I closed the kitchen door behind her and made sure to lock it. I remember scratching my head thinking, "Hmmm, that was way too easy...something's not right here." And of course the instincts were right, because when I went into the bedroom and laid down on the bed to get a grip on everything that just happened, I fell into a pool of warm water and sank to the bottom of the frame. The bitch had stabbed my waterbed with the scissors!

Water was going everywhere on the floor; there was so much water that it ruined the ceiling of my landlord's apartment below. The worst part was our landlord had told us when we moved in, "No waterbeds up here. It's not safe on the third floor in case of a leak." Well, leak was an understatement and I was tossed right out of there. "Buh-bye! Don't let the door hit your ass on the way out!"

Believe it or not, the next day I was just as stupid as ever. We talked on the phone, met up with each other and ended up working things out. Ha! Love really is blind. I should have just said, "You're a fucking douchebag, I can't trust you, you're a lying whore and fuck off!" But instead of just spitting all that out, we both apologized and decided to live with it. But the fact is, you can't live with that. It just brews inside of you and ticks away like a time bomb.

Relationships are tough enough as it is. Once you throw something like that into the mix, fahgettaboutit! You're done.

After several months in New England we decided to move back to North Carolina and get away from the whole scene. She called her parents and told them some lie about her crashing her car or something and she needed some help getting a new one, so they helped her finance a brand new shiny red Pontiac Sunbird.

We started on I-95 heading south back to NC. She drove first on our fifteen-hour journey, and within the first hour of the ride we stopped at a Wendy's and grabbed ourselves some burgers and a couple of chocolate Frosties, then put the pedal to the metal.

No sooner did we finish eating than we started fighting about all the bullshit that had gone on with John and Rachel. In the heat of the argument, she got me so mad that I head-butted her windshield and shattered it. Right away she lost her temper and tried to start slapping me while she was driving. But when she did, she ended up knocking my Frosty out of my hands and it went flying in the air and splashed all over her new car. What a sight that was. Her car smelled like a combination of new interior and chocolate milk. I thought, "Oh man, this is gonna be a long fucking ride!"

When we arrived in NC, we stayed with my mom for the time being. Arlene went back to the Rockola Café and I was looking for something to do.

Things weren't good for us anymore. Not that they were ever great, but after going through that kind of trauma, you can never trust that person again. I became paranoid whenever Arlene was a second late getting home from work. I would use my mom's car and go check to see if her car was in the parking lot. I would sneak around the places she said she was going to be, just to be sure she wasn't lying. All bad! When you start acting that way, it's hopeless. The relationship is over. The funny thing is, for the most part she was always where she said she was going to be—until one evening. Arlene helped me experience the most embarrassing moment of my life.

It was 3:00AM and Arlene still wasn't home. Sick to my stomach, I woke up my mom, concerned that maybe she had been in an accident or something. I had no wheels so I couldn't look for her and I didn't want to steal my mom's car to drive around and piss her off if she woke up. So my mom agreed to take me around and look for her.

As we were making our way all around Fayetteville, we ended up on Raeford Road (ironically the same road I met Arlene on) and I spotted her car in the parking lot of a motel. My heart instantly dropped to the floor—again! I knew something was wrong with this picture. I looked to my mom calmly and said, "I know where she is, Mom."

"Where?" she said.

"We just passed her car in that motel parking lot." So my mom spun around and pulled in to see if it was her car, and sure as shit, it was.

I got out of the car and my mom said, "Sully, please don't do anything stupid."

"I won't, Ma, I just have to let her know that she's busted. She has to see my face or she'll lie her way out of this." Very calmly I approached the door that her car was parked in front of, I gently lifted my hand up to knock on the door and then I decided right there, fuck it! BANG-BANG-BANG! I started pounding on the window instead. I saw the drapes move to the side, and there she was with her friend and two army dudes in the room doing God knows what. I looked at her right in the face, laid a gentle little smile on her, and walked away.

The important thing was just making sure that she saw me. As I turned around to leave quietly like my mom suggested, the manager of the hotel came outside with a baseball bat to see what all the banging was about, then said to me in his truest southern accent, "Who are you, boy? And what the hell are you doing?" I was so mad and numb from seeing the woman I loved with another guy for the second time that

I walked up to him and said, "Don't even think about swinging that bat on me or you're gonna find it stuck up your fat
ass. Go mind your own fucking business. I'm on my way out
anyway!" My mom flew out of her car, knowing that I was
feeling pretty much bulletproof at that point and hysterically
started yelling for me to get in the car and go. Once the man
saw my mother deal with me he pretty much backed off and
let us roll. I was so mad, I wanted to take that bat out of that
guy's hands and start thrashing everyone, but I could see the
fear in my mom's eyes, so I chilled out right away, not to
make her any more upset.

I hated that my mom was there, only because I felt so
embarrassed that she had to witness that whore being a whore.
But I was very appreciative that she was there knowing that
I could've got into a real bad situation between those dudes
and that manager guy. As much of a cloud that I was in at
that time, I could still recognize the disappointment in her
face as well that Arlene had let me down. Parents really do
feel their children's pain. She knew I was hurting.

I'd had enough of this. My heart (or what was left of it)
was completely shattered. I went back to the house, threw
out any remnants of hers and told her to stay out of my life
for good. After that, we were never together again.

I was sick for days. I would cry then I would sleep. Then
I would just lie on my bed and stare at the ceiling until I
would either cry or sleep again. I had no energy to go anywhere or talk to anyone. It took months before I was able to
get myself to feel normal again.

Finally the sun shone through one day when I received
a phone call from Todd Jackson, the guy I had met on
Atlantic Beach.

He told me that Lexx Luthor had gotten rid of their drummer and asked me to come to Kinston, NC and jam with them. I hung up the phone and sat there thinking, "What the fuck am I doing sitting here feeling pathetic for myself?" That was what I'm missing in my life. Not that bitch. Music! Music is what kept me alive. It was time to go and do what I did best…rock and fucking roll!

CHAPTER 12
LEXX LUTHOR

We looked cool, we sounded cool, and we had a great live show. There was Todd on guitar; a guy named Micky on vocals who was soon replaced by Dennis Bauer; John Bateman from Bogotá, Columbia on lead guitar, who talked just like Al Pacino in *Scarface* (my favorite movie ever); bassist Robert Sledge, who went on to play for a band you might know of called the Ben Folds Five; and myself on drums.

We did so many cool songs: "Creeping Death" by Metallica, "Post Mortem" by Slayer, "Take Hold the Flame" by Queensryche, "Bodies" by the Sex Pistols, "Slut" by GBH and on and on. We played a lot of great gigs and we had a lot of fun hanging together.

We rehearsed in Todd's garage in Kingston, NC, about ninety miles from Fayetteville. Todd was an auto mechanic and he set up a spot in his garage for us to practice.

Todd had a dog called Hercules that was the biggest German Shepherd I'd ever seen—he looked like a bear! He must have weighed at least 175 pounds, and he was so mean he could have been Jim Croce's junkyard dog. We had to walk by this incredible beast every day because Todd chained him to the garage so no one stole our equipment. The problem was, we couldn't get in when we got there early because this dog wouldn't let us approach the door. The chain that restrained this animal from mauling everything on the planet was thicker than a lead pipe. UPS showed up one day to

Lexx Luthor:
Sully, John Bateman, Robert Sledge, Dennis Bauer and Todd Jackson

deliver something, and as the truck tried to leave, Hercules started biting the tires relentlessly until he punctured one of them. At first I couldn't believe it, but I swear to you, *the dog bit right through a steel-belted truck tire.*

I rode to Todd's place every single day with our singer, Dennis, who was also from Fayetteville. It was nice to have someone to chat with, considering it took us an hour and a half to get there. We played in clubs all through the South. One club we played in was The Switch in Raleigh, NC, a club I'll always remember as the place where Lexx Luthor left me stranded one day. After a gig we had played, I decided to stay with my friend Diane who lived in Raleigh, sixty some-odd miles from Fayetteville. My band said they were hanging in town for the night, so they would give me a ride home in the morning. Well, they wound up taking off that night and weren't able to find me to let me know.

When I woke up the next morning, Diane had already gone to work. I had no car, no money, no ride and nobody was home to accept my collect calls. So next thing I know, I'm walking my ass home to Fayetteville. I figured it wouldn't be so bad—I'd hitch a ride and be home in an hour. NOPE! I was a longhaired, tattooed, scraggly-looking freak and not a single soul would even look at my sorry ass thumbing down Route 401. If you've ever seen the movie *European Vacation* with Chevy Chase, you know what I looked like that day.

I started walking at ten in the morning. It had to have been at least 100 degrees that day. When I was at the halfway point, the sun was so brutal that I literally took my pants off, wearing only my boxers, strapped them on my head like a jester's hat, and pathetically groveled up and down abandoned corn field roads looking for someone to help me before I died. I couldn't even get a bottle of water from the gas stations I passed on my journey because I had no cash on me, not a single penny. And no one was at my house when I would randomly try to call home to ask someone for a ride. After walking a good forty-five miles, I finally got through to my aunt Barbara who said she would come and get me. I was fifteen miles outside of Fayetteville. I didn't get home until seven o'clock that evening. God, that sucked!

Anyway, as time went on the whole band got real tight and opened for lots of acts like Kixx, C.O.C., Gang Green, and so on. During this period is when I met Shannon Larkin for the first time. Todd had been telling me about this dude Shannon since the day I met him. He kept saying, "Sully, you have to see this guy Shannon play the drums, he's insane! He stands up when he plays and slams his head off of the cymbals—its *killer!* Real showman." Eventually Todd dragged me down to a show at the Attic in Greenville, NC.

Shannon's band was called Wrathchild at the time, but they soon had to change it because of a European band that used the same name and claimed it first. So Wrathchild became Wrathchild America. They were playing a gig with Corrosion of Conformity that night. Till this day, it is still one of my most vivid memories.

I stood next to the drummer of C.O.C. As we watched Shannon—or should I say, got schooled by him—our jaws dragged on the floor like we had just seen our first pair of tits. Shannon was a monster! He was everything Todd said and more. Actually, the entire band was awesome. Their set was all originals with the exception of a few covers, including an amazing version of Sid Vicious of the Sex Pistols' cover of

Frank Sinatra's "My Way" and a version of "Time" by Pink Floyd with a flawless guitar solo.

Seeing Shannon play really made me re-think the whole way I thought about playing drums. I don't feel like I was ever a slack, but Shannon introduced me to a different style of playing. He had a way of bringing dynamics to the kit that I didn't realize was possible. He was hard-hitting and had great technique, just like my idols Bonham and Peart, but he also brought in a third element: the visual. Shannon was very animated, very passionate and extremely intriguing to watch. It was almost like he was making love to his drums, only in an "angry hate-fuck" kind of way. I hit it off with Shannon immediately, as drummers usually do. We kept in touch through the years and played together at some clubs in the South.

After I'd been bitten by the man, I became so influenced by his style that I began ripping off his moves. I couldn't help it—it was that cool to watch. And the more I went out to see other bands, the more I saw other drummers stealing Shannon's style. There was that godawful band called Jackyl who later came out with that stupid-ass "chainsaw song." Their drummer was a total Tommy Lee rip-off when I first saw them, then several months later he transformed into a lame version of Shannon. I noticed a band called Still Rain—their drummer Bevan was Shannon Junior, and Morgan Rose from Sevendust is *still* doing it. Don't get me wrong, I love Sevendust and Morgan is a dear friend of mine and Shannon's, but even Morgan will tell you where he got his style and how many drummers have ripped off the man's moves.

I saw Shannon whenever his band came through town on tour with Pantera or whoever they were with at the time. We'd hang out together when we could, but it was very random. The interesting thing about our relationship was that even though we rarely saw each other in person, we always kept in touch by phone and updated each other every so often on what was going on in our lives. Eventually my relationship with Shannon turned out to be more about destiny. He became one of the key people in my life and helped me connect the dots by joining several different bands, all of which led me to the birth of Godsmack.

But before that would happen, my life took a turn for the worse.

CHAPTER 13
SCARRED FOR LIFE

It started in the beginning of 1989 when I was rehearsing with Lexx Luthor in Kinston. Like I mentioned earlier, Kinston was about ninety miles from Fayetteville, and one evening after wrapping up, Dennis's wife came to pick us up. On the drive back I smoked a cigarette while we joked around and chatted about the band.

As I finished my smoke, I rolled the window down and tossed it out—and just then I felt this tightness in my chest. The pain got worse and worse, passing through my left arm and making it feel all numb, just like they say happens when you're having a heart attack.

I looked around in a panic, realizing we were in the middle of nowhere—corn fields, back country roads and no lights or civilization for miles. I got nervous thinking, "Shit! If I'm having a heart attack, I'm gonna die out here! There's no one around who can help me!" Man, I was getting real freaked out. I kept thinking, "I can't believe this! I'm gonna die at twenty-one?"

Dennis must have noticed something was wrong by the look on my face because he said, "Hey, bro'...you okay?"

I told him I wasn't sure, I was feeling unbelievably disoriented and I was having chest pains. He told me to lay the seat back and relax, because maybe I was just tired from jamming too long. All I could think was, "Breathe, Sully, just relax and breathe." It was, hands down, the scariest feeling I'd ever had in my entire life. I'd never felt so helpless. I eventually managed to get myself into a zone, calming myself with every breath I took, until finally I was home.

It must have been about 2:00AM when I got to my house. My mom was fast asleep and I hated to wake her up, but I had to. She was a nurse and I needed to find out what had just happened to me. She immediately saw the scared look in my eyes as I explained what happened. She agreed to take me to the hospital and get me checked out right away.

When we arrived at the hospital, the doctor hooked me up to every electrode, every EKG, every X-ray smorgasbord gadget they had. Then he finally broke the news: "You're as healthy as an ox!" I couldn't believe it. "What? Are you kidding me? I almost died a few minutes ago and you're telling me that there's nothing wrong with me?" He simply replied, "Yup—that's exactly what I'm saying!"

He gave me a prescription for a mild sedative called Ativan and told me that I had had an anxiety attack. I had no idea what an anxiety attack was—as far as I knew, people who had anxiety shook a lot and were nervous all the time. But that wasn't me—I was always the life of the party and extremely energetic. There's no way people could call me anxious. I told him, "That's not possible. I'm not stressed out or nervous about anything."

At that point I didn't know what to feel. I was relieved to know that it wasn't a heart attack, but I wanted to know what it really was. It wasn't my imagination. I *felt* this—it was *real*. So I left there confused and bummed out that something so scary just happened to me and no one could seem to explain to me what it was.

As time went on, it would happen so frequently that I became a regular at the local emergency room. I became afraid to go into public places because I thought it might happen again and I'd be embarrassed in front of whoever I was talking with. It really fucked with me, even when I went to bed. If I laid on my back I'd feel a pain in my back; if I laid on my chest, I'd feel a pain in my chest. I had to sleep in a face-down fetal position, resting on my elbows and knees because that was the only way I felt comfortable. Day after day I sat around my bedroom, constantly checking my pulse and listening to my heart rate. Sometimes I would get a hot flash and become really disoriented, which in turn would make me have another anxiety attack because I was obsessing about it so much.

I guess if you haven't gone through this, it may not seem so serious—it may even sound silly, which, for someone who hasn't experienced it, it probably appears. But people who have struggled with anxiety or still do will tell you it is no joke. Anxiety consumes you and alienates you from everything. Your ability to concentrate disappears and your body feels like shit every day. It makes you constantly feel weak and tired and you become extremely unmotivated and depressed. It's just not a good way to live. And it's not a figment of your imagination— it's *real!* And unless you identify the problem and figure out what's stressing you out mentally, it can eventually lead to physical health conditions and possibly even kill you. Or at least that's what the doctors told me. Granted, it could take decades of wear and tear to get you to that point, but who wants to waste their life living like that?

It was a very lonely and fearful way to live. I should have

been out there having fun with my friends and enjoying being young and healthy, but instead, life became a series of fears and struggles, trying to understand what this was and how I could get rid of it. It was very frustrating—I'd always been a very upbeat person, and from being a drummer my whole life, I was in excellent physical condition. So what was the problem? Was I chosen to be one of the unfortunate people in this world who happen to be cursed with an illness at a young age? Was this going to be for me like other people having heart conditions or getting cancer or AIDS? I wasn't sure, but I do know that I became quite the hypochondriac after that. Whatever was plaguing me was eating away at my life.

I tried to take the doctor's advice and think of things that I thought were bothering me, things that maybe I was stuffing down inside and wasn't dealing with. Was it my surroundings? Well, let's see. . . For one, I was in a place that was dragging me down. Fayetteville was very slow compared to Boston—everyone drove three miles an hour and it was very country compared to the city life I had known. Plus, I was missing the friends I'd grown up with my whole life—Jimmy and Freddy and Fro and all the rest. But people miss people every day. Was that enough to give me these anxiety attacks?

And I was drinking way too much. There were times when I would sit around with my friend Jon Robbins and drink a bottle of Captain Morgan's in one night. That couldn't have been too healthy for me, but I doubted that was it.

So what else could it have been? A girlfriend? Nope! I didn't have one. But after I thought about it long and hard, I realized that I had gone through a brutal break-up. My relationship with Arlene had ended in a very shitty way. The only girl I had ever loved enough to consider

marrying was fucking everybody in Fayetteville—and I had
only moved us back there because she was fucking one of
my friends in Massachusetts! Now that I thought about it,
it was no wonder I was having anxiety attacks! I needed a
change badly.

Even my band was slipping away. Lexx Luthor was doing
nothing—our bass player and our singer had quit, so Todd
took over bass and vocals and I had called my friend Doug
Robinson (from my last band, Meliah Kraze) and invited him
to fill the guitarist slot. With all the lineup changes it felt like
a new band, so we changed our name to Attic Bratt and
continued to play gigs. But it seemed like we were going
backwards—the crowds got real thin, the band got real lame,
and we got real discouraged.

Around that time there was a small wave of signings in
the south for hard rock bands – the major labels had stepped
in and signed bands like Jackyl and whoever else – but once
the labels scanned the area and pulled what they liked, they
moved on to other parts of the country. We were never a full-
on original band, so we missed that gravy train. By December
of '89, I'd had enough of North Carolina. I'd been there almost
four years and the last year had been eaten away by anxiety.
It was time I got my ass back home to Boston.

I told the guys, "That's it! I need to go back to where I
belong." They understood, we shook hands, told each other
it was fun while it lasted, swapped numbers, played our last
show at the Attic in Greenville, NC and said our goodbyes.

Jon Robbins had been telling me over some time that he
wanted to get out of NC as well, so I called him and invited
him to come with me back to Boston. He accepted my in-
vitation and in a flash we were off to the train station to
book ourselves a lift home.

My days of living in Fayetteville, North Carolina ended at that moment. And it didn't bother me one bit to make that decision. In my mind, it was the only decision to make. I was actually excited about it. It was the first time in a long time that I remembered feeling energized. If I was going to start rehabilitating my health and my state of mind, I needed to get back to a place where I was comfortable. I was searching for life, so I had to go to where life was: with my friends, my heritage, my home. That's where I belonged.

PART THREE

CHAPTER 14
BACK TO BOSTON

After a miserable eighteen-and-a-half-hour train ride, Jon and I arrived back in Boston. My sister Maria picked us up at the station and let us stay with her at her house in Derry, New Hampshire, about fifteen minutes north of Lawrence.

God, did it feel good to be back home! I immediately felt relief. I couldn't wait to go hang out with Jimmy, Freddy, Bill, and Fro—all the people I loved so much and hadn't seen in years. But there was also my continuing fear of anxiety attacks. I didn't want my friends to see me like that, and I was worried it would happen when I was around them and they wouldn't understand. Or worse, they might think that I'd gone off the deep end down in the South or something. So I stayed home a lot.

And because I was constantly isolating and examining myself, sure as shit, it struck again, often right in front of my sister. I would start feeling all disoriented, my arms would start tingling and pretty soon I would be on the floor, scared out of my mind, praying for it to stop. At first Maria would freak, not knowing what was happening because I'd never told her about any of this.

It got real bad again for a while. I remember my sister slinging my arm around her to carry me into the hospital because I was so dizzy I wasn't able to walk. But again, all the doctors said the same thing: "You're having panic attacks, not heart attacks. There's nothing physically wrong with you. Whatever it is that's on your mind, you'd better get it off because this could kill you!" Well, that was the clincher for me. After hearing those words, "It could kill you" it was finally enough to motivate me to figure this thing out once and for all.

We had also just lost my grandmother to a heart attack, so at first that didn't help the situation any. I was very close to my grandparents, and yet when my grandmother passed away it didn't seem to affect me like I thought it would. I never even cried. Something was wrong with me. All the distance from my friends and all the heartache I had endured through my relationship with Arlene was stuffed inside of me, and I wasn't releasing any of it. But finally, I saw that's what the real problem was. I never showed my emotions. I had conditioned myself to be a certain way—from living on the streets for so many years and being tough, never showing fear, or remorse, or weakness. I didn't know how to cry when I needed to, or how to talk things through when something was bothering me.

I realized that the anxiety attacks were created by my mind from feelings and emotions that I was keeping in and never letting out. All the little things that you should stomp your feet and yell about, but instead just hold back and hope go away in time, are the things that were causing this misery.

Avoiding problems doesn't make them go away—you think it does, but it really doesn't. They're just postponed. Those problems just stay inside your subconscious and brew until your body gets to a point where it's had enough and decides to release some of the stress itself. That's what an anxiety attack is! It happens when you don't know how to vent your frustrations, fears, stress, sadness, madness, whatever it is that bothers you, the things you should be confronting and getting closure with. If you don't confront these things and deal with them, your body does it for you. Think of it like a pressure cooker: when you stuff a million things inside it, and keep turning up the heat, eventually it's going to come to a boil, start whistling and release the pressure that has built up inside. And if you don't do something about it quick, the lid will blow clear off the pot. Same thing with your body—it will eventually release all the things that you have stuffed down inside.

I'm not trying to sound like a doctor or psychiatrist or anything, but I've had a lot of experience with this and I made it a point to research it, probably more than some doctors might have.

I recently acquired even more information about anxiety through a doctor friend of mine named Susan Randlet. She explained to me, "Anxiety is an illness that sometimes you have no control over because of what your body is made up of. The chemicals and the amount of adrenaline that runs through people's bodies are all different. We don't control that. It's what we're born with. Your engine may rev a lot higher than other people's because of the amount of adrenaline that runs through it.

"Think of someone who has diabetes," she explained. "It's what that person's body was born with. They have no control over whether their body produces enough blood sugar, or produces too much. They have to just surrender to it by taking their insulin and eating when their bodies tell them to."

So the fact that my body might have more adrenaline running through it at times was part of the reason why sometimes I could just be sitting there chillin' out, when all of a sudden my heart would start racing and make me feel weird, which made all these thoughts of heart attacks and whatnot snowball in my mind.

That brings me to the point of a panic attack. Once you understand all this, (which I know isn't all that simple, but then again neither is the human body), you're be able to rid yourself of the problem. Like Susan said, sometimes you just have to surrender to it. You tell yourself that you've seen this movie before, and the ending is always the same. You didn't have a heart attack. Nothing even happened to you. It was simply adrenaline running through your body, which will pass in a moment.

But you should never underestimate the mind and how powerful it can be. It can work with you or against you. It's all a matter of how you handle your thoughts. Eventually I was able to realize what was bothering me, and I spent a lot of time going through a healing process that helped me take back control of my life.

Anxiety is a surprisingly common problem. Once I started openly talking about it, I couldn't believe the number of people I met who had the same problem. I hid my anxiety attacks for the longest time because I was embarrassed to talk about them, thinking that people my age wouldn't understand or that they would think I was a nutcase or a weak person. That wasn't the case at all; the more I told people about it, the more I realized that there were tons of people feeling the same thing, and they were just as young and scared of dealing with the unknown as I was.

One thing I'd do: instead of getting nervous when I felt an

anxiety attack coming on, I would get pissed off and purpose-
fully do shit to prove to myself that it wasn't my heart. I'd do
sit-ups or go running, anything to make my heart race. Over
time I began feeling more comfortable again and the anxiety
attacks became a lot milder until they rarely happened at all.

The summer of '90 was a big turning point for me. Me,
Jimmy, Fro and Bill had reunited and were frequently hanging out at the beach in Hampton Beach, New Hampshire. I
started feeling a lot better about myself—partying with my
friends, meeting girls, meeting new people...just feeling human again. That summer also introduced me to some new
friends who I have maintained great relationships with over
time. One was a guy named Tony Cirella.

He was a good looking guy: dark hair, light eyes, Italian,
worked out a lot. But he also was a sarcastic, hot-tempered
pot smoker who wore Gold's Gym tank tops and showed off
a lot in front of the girls!

I walked into this cottage one afternoon where everyone
was hanging out, and there was Tony on the floor doing push
ups in front of these girls. He and I had met once or twice,
but nothing substantial. I had a good buzz from drinking,
and I decided to sneak up behind him and yank his balloon
pants down around his ankles. It turned out he was flying
commando, and he got pretty embarrassed when his freshly-
shaved ass was exposed to his audience. I thought for sure I
was gonna catch a beating for that, but we just laughed it off
and soon after became good friends.

We partied that whole summer. It was a filth festival—
drunkenness, nakedness and fights—you know, typical beach
behavior. Nowadays, we call Tony "T.C." He's still like a brother
to me, and has been Godsmack's tour security director.

That same summer I also met Dave Mesiti, another dear friend of mine who introduced me to Paul Geary, the drummer for Extreme. Extreme's big album *Pornograffitti* had just come out, so Paul was coming into the prime of his career and it was exciting to meet him. He was doing what I could only dream of doing: playing music for a living and being famous.

That summer changed a lot of our lives. Two separate groups of friends becoming one. Paul invited me and Dave to hang out with Extreme and tag along to their shows. Seeing Extreme gave me a lot of information about how to conduct a band. They were so professional and were at such a high level of success in my eyes—it taught me how to put a show together. For one thing, Extreme's guitarist Nuno Bettencourt used to get on the congas and a timbale and jam with Paul in the middle of their set, which planted the seed in my brain for the idea of the double drum solo that Godsmack does today. Of course it's evolved quite a bit since then, but it started out as something very similar.

Over the years I called Paul every so often and kept him posted about what I was up to. I'd give him some music and he'd come out and see the bands I was in. Even though he was famous and I was just some local schlub, he always helped me any way he could, whether it was getting me a gig, looking at some legal documents for me, or even lending me a few bucks to pay my bills. We became great friends and I felt very loyal to him.

Soon I started a new band with Bill DeMonaco, Jeff Abraham (my sister's boyfriend at the time) on guitar, and this dude named John on bass. Since the band I had left in NC hadn't done a whole lot with the name Attic Bratt, I suggested it to the guys and they liked it. We just changed a couple of letters and called it Addict Bratt. This band was a real joke, though—we didn't do shit! We didn't play a single gig. And Bill was still way into the Steven Tyler thing, which was kind of annoying. We recorded some demos and tried to shoot our own video, but it was obvious that the whole thing was going nowhere.

Jeff finally got an offer to join a band called the Fighting Cocks, so he left and Addict Bratt ended.

Soon afterwards, Jeff called saying the Fighting Cocks were looking for a drummer. The band was doing pretty well in the Boston area but they were more like old-school rock, Black Crowes meets Alice Cooper kind of stuff. As a matter of fact, the singer Jaime Sever had co-written "Trash," a song that Alice Cooper used and named his album after. So it was kind

The Fighting Cocks:
John Patingalo, Jamie Sever, Jeff Abraham and Sully

of cool to start getting involved with musicians who were at my level again.

Okay, our hair was big and we wore leather pants, but at least we were playing out everywhere and making a name for ourselves, and that's when it all started turning around for me. The Fighting Cocks might not have been the perfect band for me, but like I said earlier, it's all part of the path. Never regret where your life takes you—there's a reason for it and eventually you will find out why.

I told you that Shannon played a big role in my path to Godsmack, and this is how that happened.

I had started to become well known in the Boston area. Thanks to Shannon's influence, I was a very animated drummer and really into showmanship, which made me stick out a lot in my bands and got people talking.

A nationally-known Boston band called Meliah Rage happened to be looking for a drummer. They had two previous albums—*Kill to Survive* and *Solitary Solitude*, plus a live album called *Live Kill*. And they were heavy fuckin' metal, right up my alley. Their manager knew Shannon, and when he told Shannon they were looking for a new drummer, Shannon put in the good word for me. Pretty soon I got the call. I researched the band and decided that it was probably a good move. I told the guys in the Fighting Cocks that I was moving on, and so it was done.

Meliah Rage was a cool band and I had a great time working with them. They rocked harder than any band I'd ever been in, and they were all original. I was really able to open up and start playing my ass off with these dudes. Jim Koury and Tony Nichols were the guitarists, Keith Vogele played bass, and Mike

Meliah Rage:
Mike Munroe, Tony Nicoles, Jim Khoury, Keith Vogele and Sully

Munro was our fearless front man. Mike stood about 6' 2",
weighed about 210 pounds and looked like Conan the Barbar-
ian. He was a big guy with a big voice.

At the time, I was living with Tony Cirella and his girlfriend, Cheryl. T.C., had an extra bedroom in his place, so
that worked out great.

We'd rehearse in Jim's mother's basement in sleepy
Windham, New Hampshire, after everyone would get home
from their shitty nine-to-five jobs: I was still installing carpets, Mike did construction, Jim was in the screen-printing
business and Keith, well... I'm not sure what he did. I think
he just loafed around and scraped up money where he could.

Right before I joined they'd been dropped from Epic
Records, so they were in search of a new deal. Considering

that we were all still young and hungry and had a good name for ourselves, I was convinced that landing a new record deal wouldn't be a problem—all we needed was to write some kick-ass new material.

We wrote ten or twelve songs and saved up enough money to record at this small studio in Providence, Rhode Island. We figured if we shopped the demo around to all our contacts and kept doing gigs in the meantime, we'd land a new deal. (Today you can actually buy that demo under the title *Unfinished Business*. It's about as old-school metal as you can get, but a fun listen if you like that kind of music.)

We played all around New England, and the band still had a decent following, so kids would show up to sing along and jump around in the pit. I hadn't experienced that yet — usually the bands I was with were still new and were never together long enough for people to know our music. It was awesome! And I was having a blast with it. Tony Nichols was our business guy in the band so he kept us booked as often as possible, also trying to shop our demo to whoever he could. Mustapha, T.C. and some of my other buddies like Bob Erban, Tommy Mathews and Mike's friend Dennis Brennan all helped out on the crew.

Most of all, it was good to feel alive again!

CHAPTER 15

THE DEVIL IN DISGUISE

When I was in Meliah Rage, me and TC used to just about live in a strip club in Saugus, Massachusetts called the Golden Banana. The Golden Banana, along with another club called the Cabaret, were our homes away from home for years. We were at one of those places so much that the owner of the Cabaret used to tell us he had cots in the back in case we needed to take a nap in between our vicious drinking binges. We'd head over for the afternoon matinee, drink pitchers of beer, then we'd eat, go home and take a nap—maybe—and then come back and catch the night shift rolling in and stay there all night.

I wasn't doing much of anything for work in those days— I was more like a gypsy. I'd pop in at a job until I had enough money to blow on hanging with my friends and drinking, and then I'd quit. I worked in warehouses, loading docks, packing trucks, packing boxes, at Gillette on the assembly line putting caps on underarm deodorant, and even cleaning planes. Check this out: you roll under the plane on a dolly with a scrub brush that you dip in some kind of

From left: Sully, Muskrat, Dave Mestiti, Lee Gagnon, Fro amd Steve Mazzalia in 1991

nasty chemicals and scrub the black shit off the bottom of the planes. Yeah right! I started at eight that morning and by lunch I was history.

I think my record stint at one job was four, maybe five months. I just couldn't stand having a boss. And as you know from my school days, I didn't take orders very well. Plus, I've always had a problem with setting an alarm clock and getting up for work—I don't want the responsibility of having to be somewhere from 9 to 5. I'd rather come and go as I please.

Me and TC were making our rounds one evening and drifted into the Golden Banana to see Tony's girlfriend Cheryl. As I walked through the tinted glass doors and headed for the bar, my eyes became glued to this beauty I'd never seen before, dancing to "Sad But True" by Metallica. She had on a leather outfit with a leather biker's hat, chains on her skirt and high-heeled black boots. She looked like something out of the Motley Crue "Girls, Girls, Girls" video. And she was clocking me with every step I took.

I locked onto her like I had been struck by Cupid's arrow. She had a petite little body, long blonde hair, a beautiful face and tits like pow! I was all done. When she finished her set she walked over to where me, Tony and Cheryl were sitting. Cheryl introduced us: "Lisa, this is Sully; Sully, this is Lisa." I remember feeling numb, like all the blood had drained from my body and left me paralyzed. I was actually nervous talking to her. She was perfect!

There's two types of girls. There's the kind you meet and you go, "How's it going?" and they talk to you a little, then you try and nudge your way into putting your hand on their knee or something. And then there's the girls that are like, "Heyyyyyy!" and grab you and hug you, and you're like, "Fuckin' A, I'm *in!*" Lisa was the second type. She was as drawn to me as I was to her. It was instant chemistry.

As time went on, we became inseparable. We went out a lot, we laughed, we drank together and had the best of times. We were together every day for at least a year. Everything just seems so perfect when you're in love, doesn't it? Or is it lust? Either way, you feel like you could conquer the world. All your problems seem to go away and all you can think about is the next time you'll see each other.

But all that goes away in time, or at least this time it did. Lisa started to show me sides of herself that I couldn't understand: she had very drastic mood swings, stayed out all night and didn't call to check in, and started to make me feel insecure and unbalanced. I would stay up at night wondering why she was acting this way and trying to figure out what I'd done wrong. It was shitty!

This one time everything was going really good with us, no fights, no arguing—it was a very normal day. Me and Lisa were in her Jeep driving around and I was staring out the window of the passenger's seat watching the cars on the highway pass by. Then, as I turned back to face her, she punched me dead in the face for no reason. I said, "What the fuck was that for?"

She replied, "What the fuck are you looking at those girls for?"

"What fucking girls, you psychopath? I was spacing out watching the cars going by! We're on a highway doing seventy, for Christ's sake!"

That's the kind of episode we began to have on a regular basis. I'd had no idea how unstable and fucked up she was. She hadn't shown me that side of her until then.

It started to become a reality for me on the day that we went into a drugstore together. She was browsing through the birthday card section when I came up behind her and said, "Hey, babe! What are you looking for?"

So she tells me she's trying to pick out a birthday card for her grandmother. I said, "Umm…sweetie? Didn't you tell me that your grandmother passed away a few years ago?"

All of a sudden she started bawling her eyes out and ran out of the store. That's when it hit me, "Whoa! This girl is a nutcase!" But I loved her and felt obligated to stand by her, even though she was starting to act like a total bitch to me.

One of the funniest memories I have with Lisa was the time when she and I and Tony and Cheryl all went out to the Axis nightclub in Boston. We all knew everyone who worked there so we could drink for free most of the time and hang out after hours.

As the night went on, we all got pretty fucked up. I started getting the spins so I drifted into the bathroom to splash some water on my face. The bathroom was co-ed, so feeling as fucked up as I was I went into the stall and sat on the toilet to recompose myself, knowing that no one would bother me in there. Next thing I know, I woke up to a couple of girls kicking the door, asking me if I was OK. I stood up and stumbled out of the stall grunting and growling at the chicks and worked my way back into the club. Tony spotted me and said, "Where the fuck have you been?" I said, "Nowhere. I just went to the bathroom." He said, "For Two hours?" I was like, "Two hours? Have I been gone that long? Damn, I must have passed out on the can."

So we headed back to the bar and continued to drink. Tony and Cheryl were gacked to the nines on blow and had no problem staying awake. I'd been clean from coke for years at that point but I could stay up for days at a time with them, never touching a line, just drinking. Tony and Cheryl would always ask me, "How the fuck can you stay up for days with us and never touch a line?"

My answer to that: "Women!" They'll keep you awake better than any drug out there.

I figured out many months later that Lisa was just as jacked on blow that night, but like I said, love is blind, so I didn't know at the time.

3:30AM rolled around and we decided enough was enough. We headed into the East End of Boston and met a friend of ours named Jeff Freedman at a little mafia coffee shop/after hours bar to sober up. As we sat in the back, I was approached by this girl who recognized me and came up to say hi.

"Hey, Sully! How are you?" she said. She looked familiar to me, but I couldn't quite put the name to the face. I didn't want to feel embarrassed asking her what her name was since she obviously knew me so well, so I purposely didn't introduce her to Lisa or the others.

"I haven't seen you since you were this big!" she said.

Then it hit me! I remembered that I knew her from the eighth grade, but I still couldn't remember her name. She was real brief and innocent with her approach, she just wanted to shake hands and say a quick hello, that's all. It was harmless. She couldn't have been there more than two minutes.

As she said goodbye I purposely shook her hand so Ol' Psychopath sitting behind me wouldn't get all jealous if I hugged her or something. I could feel Lisa's tension when this girl rolled up to me so I kept it neutral. Just then... *smack!* I looked down and there's Lisa slapping our hands apart. Now this girl got all freaked out—she put her hands up, looked at me and said, "Hey man, I'm not here to start anything, I just wanted to say hi."

She walked away and I looked at Lisa and said, "What the fuck was that for?"

She said, "What, are you gonna hug and kiss her, too?"

I said, "You know what, Lisa? You're a fucking psycho! I'm outta here!"

So I started walking out of this bar in disgust. The girl that had come up to me happened to be leaning on the bar right near the exit doors, talking to the bartender and having a drink with her friend. I'm just about out the door when I hear running footsteps from afar, getting closer and closer. I turned around and sure as shit, here comes Lisa in a full on sprint, running towards me with hate in her eyes. Then, all in one swift smooth motion, she passed by this girl, grabbed her by her hair, smashed her face down onto the bar top, and without even batting an eyelash, continued to charge after me. She did all of this without ever stopping or taking her eyes off of me. I ran out the door, banged a left, then banged another left and somehow ended up in a dead-end alley. She came flying around the corner like a goddamn superhero or something, cussing up a storm and swinging at me like Mike Tyson.

Now, I have control to a certain degree, but when you have a wild animal slashing at you and backing you into a corner, your defenses kick in and survival mode takes over.

After her numerous attempts to scratch my eyes out and kick my balls in, I decided to grab her by the throat and put her up against the wall. Tony and Cheryl came whipping around the corner to catch up with us and saw me holding Lisa up against the wall. Cheryl got all wigged out thinking that I was kicking her ass, when in reality, she was kicking mine, and Tony was just standing there waiting for everything to settle down. Lisa turned around, walked away and left in her car, stranding me in Boston. Fine with me. That bitch was crazy that night.

Of course the next day everything was back to normal again, but as time went on, more of the same shit would go on and I eventually started to hear the wrong things from people, things you don't want to hear when you're in love. Things like being at a bar and overhearing someone saying that Lisa's sucking the owner of Axis's dick for coke. I got the double whammy on that one—not only didn't I know that she was a cokehead, but now I'm hearing that she's giving blow jobs for it. Great!

I was really hurting at that point, but for some stupid-ass reason, I wasn't letting go of her. We continued to see each other, yet we were never together. She would always go out with her friends and I would go out with mine, and we would bump into each other at the clubs constantly because we hung out at the same places. I couldn't help keeping a close watch on her when I did see her. I was feeling all insecure and messed up, and I couldn't take my eyes off her every time she walked away to talk to someone else. It was hopeless at that point. Our relationship had gone to shit and I was an emotional mess.

It's probably pretty hard to understand why I stayed with this person. But it was just one of those things where you're attached and you don't want to detach. And you think you can take the situation and make it back into the way it used to be. The problem is, you just can't admit to yourself that it's over.

One night at Axis I saw her talking to some dude. She hadn't seen me walk in yet, so I made my way up behind her to listen in to their conversation. Just as I got within range, I heard the guy say as he held her hand, "Since you're not with your boyfriend anymore, why don't we hook up and get out of here?" That was enough for me. I pulled around to the front of her so she could see me, and she jerked her hand back as if I hadn't seen them holding hands. The look on her face was priceless. The guy had no fucking clue who I was— I could just tell by the confused look on his face. But someone needed to be hit and I couldn't hit Lisa. So I grabbed this dude by his throat, smashed him square in the face and began to beat the living shit out of him. I wished it could've lasted all night, but unfortunately the bouncers came over and pulled me off him and threw me out of the club.

A week or so later, it somehow seemed like we had worked things out again, but something felt wrong one day when she wasn't returning my calls. I knew she had a day off and she was in the area, but she never came over or called. I was living with Fro at the time and I had no wheels, and I was going crazy in Fro's apartment thinking of the worst possible situations I could drum up in my mind.

Finally, I couldn't take it anymore. I stole Fro's car that night when he fell asleep and drove to her house to see if she was home. (Sorry Fro!) I felt like a loser doing it, but I couldn't control myself.

When I pulled up to her house, I noticed an unfamiliar car in her driveway, so I took it upon myself to just go in without knocking. Just as I entered her kitchen, I heard her come running halfway down the stairs from her bedroom. My heart dropped into my stomach knowing something was wrong. As I looked up the staircase, I saw the same look on her face that I had seen before: pure fear! I asked her who was there, but she just dodged the question, asking me what the fuck I'm doing there, and saying shit like, "We're through, get over it!" I'm thinking, "We're through? But we were fine yesterday."

We were right in the middle of it when Mr. Musclehead came down the steps behind her, asking her if she was OK. He was a police officer who was assigned to the Golden Banana on certain nights.

I was like, "Motherfucker! You are a fucking whore! Do you fuck everybody you meet?" I was in a complete rage, so I started calling this dude downstairs. Cop or not, I didn't give a flying fuck. He was off duty and I was ready to jam!

"Come on down those stairs, you motherfucker" I said to him. "Me and you can step outside and deal with this."

Lisa started pushing me out the door saying, "You don't wanna do this Sully, trust me!"

I said, "Fuck you Lisa, I know he's a fucking cop and I don't give a shit! You're a fucking slut!"

Blah, blah, blah, it went on and on. He never came outside, he just stood there like the big dope that he was. So eventually I just gave her Jeep a good swift kick and got in my car and left.

As upset as I was, and as disgusted as I felt, I still couldn't let her go. It was Arlene all over again. I tried so hard to put things back together by caring for her and loving her. I was in love and I didn't want it to end, so I did whatever I could to hang on to that. I was actually hoping that she was going to notice my pain and feel bad for me and turn things around. Maybe she would realize that she really did love me. Looking back on it now, that sounds absolutely ridiculous, but back then I was all messed up over this girl.

Early one morning while it was still dark out and I was fast asleep in Fro's apartment, someone gently shook me awake. It was Lisa. She had this nervous expression on her face, like maybe I would be in there with some chick. But I was alone and she got in bed with me. At that point, I just felt so good. I didn't question where she had been, or what she was doing. I was just really happy that she'd come back. We fell back asleep together after talking about making things right. But the next morning she was gone before I woke up and she never came back again. She had left me without any explanation. I guess she had become a full-blown junkie.

I was broken down to nothing. The girl I had tried so hard to love had suddenly vanished from my life, leaving me with no answers to any of my questions. I wanted to find her so bad, just so I could talk to her and get some answers—get some closure at least. But it wasn't happening. She stopped answering her phone. Her family and friends always told me that they hadn't seen her when I called them. She was gone!

* * * *

I tried to repeat what had made me happy in the past, by going back to the music and healing myself through friends, but nothing was working for me. There's nothing your friends can say to you that'll make you feel better when you're in that kind of a place. And as far as music went, Meliah Rage wasn't doing a whole lot either, so it all felt like time was standing still.

Me and Mike were the first ones to speak up. We were tired of feeling like we were getting nowhere with the band, and we were tired of getting lied to by this fucked up attorney named Frank who worked for us. He was always blowing smoke up our asses about how close he was to getting us a deal. He was full of shit! And Mike, even more than myself, was so over it. He had been with Meliah forever and just didn't have the energy or the passion to put back into the band. Plus, we were entering a whole new genre of music. The grunge thing had taken over and was wiping out all the glam and the metal bands. Nirvana, Sound Garden, Alice in Chains, Pearl Jam and many other greats were killing all the dinosaurs. And that's where Mike and I wanted to be. We wanted something fresh, something with a new sound, so we made the call and sprung it on the rest of the guys.

Tony and Jim took it the worst. They had also been in the band since day one and were really hoping for the dream to come back, but it just wasn't a reality. Me and Mike walked, and we did our best to part with the other guys on good terms. They hated that the band was breaking up, but they understood why we were doing it and didn't seem to hold a grudge.

After that, Mike and myself were really craving a new

project, so we started one: we called it Mangled Elf. How's
that for a name? Me and Mike joined up with this other guy
named Mike, and Bob Mayo from a band called Wargasm. (I
love that name.) Yeah, we rehearsed a lot like any other band
I'd been in, and we wrote music, but it was only two or three
months before it ended. It just wasn't going anywhere, either.
Things just started to suck again. Bored, depressed and anxious, I did the only thing I knew I had to fall back on—I
drank a lot and spent too much time by myself.

About the only positive thing that came out of my relationship with Lisa was being introduced to the Wiccan religion. I happened to be browsing through her bookshelf one
day and decided to flip through a book titled *Power of the
Witch* by Laurie Cabot. I had no knowledge of this religion
before I read this book, and I assumed, as most people do,
that it was all about demons and devils.

Witches *do not* believe in the devil—that's the biggest
misconception about witchcraft. No devils even exist in the
Wiccan religion, so how can you worship something that
doesn't exist? We believe in what the Hindus call karma, that
what you do will come back to you three-fold — and that
works for both good deeds and bad. I'll give you an example:
say you were at a house party and stole someone's CD because you were too cheap to buy it yourself. Two weeks later,
your whole collection of CD's gets ripped off from your car.
That's how karma works.

I'm not going to get too heavily into this subject, for no
other reason than that it's a very personal thing for me and
I don't want to come off as a preacher. What has worked for
me in my life may not apply to you in yours. When it comes
to spirituality, everyone has his or her own beliefs and opin-
ions on what is right, as they should. When I'm asked about

religion or faith, I simply tell people to do what they feel is right for them. I don't believe that anyone should be persuaded or pressured into any religion. It should be your choice, and that is exactly why Wicca has worked for me.

It's never told me that I can't explore the world and educate myself in other religions. It's never told me that if I fuck up, I will burn in hell or something. The first law of Wicca is, "Do what thou wilt and harm none." In other words, I can live my life the way I want to, I can do anything I wish, as long as it *harms no one*. With that as a template, how can I go wrong? So for the critics and religions out there that have tried to sabotage this religion and condemn it as Satanic, my advice to you is, educate yourself in all religions before you speak. We are all seeking the same thing.

If you really want to know what I believe, I believe that no mortal on this earth is qualified to dictate what the proper religion to follow is. *We are not gods* and no one but the one who created us really knows what happens to us, or where we go when our time is up. We can only hope that the after-life is as serene and glorifying as we envision it. I can't speak for anybody else, but Wicca supplied me with the tools I needed to regain my spirituality and find my balance in life. My advice to the people that are soul searching is: research as many different belief systems as possible. You'll find your bliss through one of them.

During the Meliah days, my friend Dave Mesiti was beginning to make a name for himself in real estate and had rented me an apartment that he owned in one of his buildings.

Over the years me, Dave, Jimmy, Freddy, Fro, T.C., Lee Gagnon, Bob Erban and Tommy Mathews had all become really good friends. We hung out every day for years at either

Dave's place or Fro's apartment, having the best times and laughs any good friends could have together. Then out of nowhere, Dave slipped away from the crowd. None of us really noticed for some time.

Sometimes I'd think about all the great laughs we had together and call Dave to see what was up with him not being around. I was lonely. I had no band and no girlfriend, and I needed friends. But he was always making excuses about why we couldn't hang out. At first it was no big deal, but after a while I got curious about why he was acting so weird with me. Then one day it all came together.

T.C. called me up and said that Dave had been seen hanging out with Lisa—a lot. "Oh my fucking God!" I thought to myself. I thought my heart was going to fall out of my chest. I asked T.C. if he was sure, and he said he knew for a fact. He also knew how much it would kill me to hear this, but he was loyal to me and he knew I would much rather know than not.

I called Dave the next day and asked him if he wanted to hook up and grab some lunch. I wasn't sure what state of mind I was in because this just didn't seem real to me. He just didn't seem like Lisa's type, although it makes perfect sense now. He was financially stable and she was a cokehead. Perfect!

He told me he couldn't hang because he'd already made plans to go to dinner with his sister and his father. I couldn't keep it in any longer. I had to say something.

I asked him if he was hanging with Lisa. He told me he wasn't and made it sound like he had no clue what I was talking about. I began to plead with him not to get involved with her.

"She's all fucked up," I told him. "Trust me, she's not stable, man, don't be blinded by this."

Sure, I was hurt and there was a part of me that didn't want to accept that my friend was hooking up with my ex, but the truth is, I really was trying to warn him about her and her evil ways. She has something about her that seems to blind most guys into giving her what she wants, but when she's done with you, she will walk without batting an eyelash. Fucking devil!

Again, he swore up and down that this wasn't the case. Well, sure enough, that night I found out that he hadn't gone anywhere with his family, but instead took Lisa out to a movie and dinner. After days of trying to reason with him I finally got to the point where I told him, "Look man, I don't give a shit about this fucking bitch anymore. She's fucking evil and you'll find out for yourself eventually, but quit fucking lying to me about hanging out with her. If you are, then you are, but you don't have to blow me off and lie about it."

Unfortunately, he couldn't hear or see me at that point. He was way too deep into her and fell out of touch with all of us after that. This bitch had not only fucked me up, but now she had fucked up a really good friendship, too. Everyone tried to warn him, Jimmy and Fro especially, but he couldn't hear them either. Deaf and blindly in love, he chose to separate from everything and start a new life with Lisa.

A year or so went by and the news came to me via phone call: Dave and Lisa were getting married. By this time I was so fucking numb to the whole situation that I didn't even give a shit. My heart was now broken twice, and as far as I was concerned, he was deleted from my life and they deserved each other.

Between Lisa and Arlene, it's no wonder I can't get my

shit together today with a girl. I still have a hard time with
trust. When you've been played for such a fool, you have
your guard up all the time. Like that saying goes, once bitten,
twice shy. It did some internal damage that I *still* struggle
with.

When things happening to you get really extreme, you
can't help but wonder how much worse it can get. It completely puts you into a frozen state of mind. When your life
is consumed by all the wrong things, you forget to put time
into the right things, the things that are important to you.
Sometimes I guess it's for your own good that something this
extreme has to happen in order for you to snap out of your
unmotivated life. It was inevitable that I was about to cross
the next road in my journey.

CHAPTER 16

STRIP MIND

B_y this time, everyone in New England who was any kind of a metal fan knew about Meliah Rage and had seen us many times. That was a good thing for me because it circulated my name through the Boston area, and because of that, I was eligible for the next thing that came my way.

One day in late '92 I got a call from David Robinson who was managing a Boston act called Seka (they'd gotten their name from an 80s porn star). They were a metal-punk band that landed a deal with Sire/Reprise Records, a subsidiary of Warner Brothers. They had been discovered in 1992 after they won this famous annual battle of the bands hosted by the Boston radio station WBCN.

Turns out my guitar player from Meliah, Tony Nichols, had bumped into David Robinson at a local bar. David mentioned to Tony that Seka was looking for a drummer, so Tony turned David on to me. I was a little surprised when I got the phone call, but excited at the same time. This was a huge deal for me. This is what I'd been looking for my whole life: a gig with a cool band on a major label. I knew I had to make this work. I wasn't familiar with Seka's music at all, but I knew they had a deal and it was aggressive music, just the way I like it, so I wasn't about to pass this one up.

I met with David, he gave me a tape of some music the band was working on and I got right to work on it. Since my apartment wasn't big enough to set up my drums, I asked Fro if I could set up at his place and jam to this stuff. Of course, being the sweetheart of a friend that he is, he agreed without hesitation.

I had at least a dozen songs to learn in a day or two, not because they were giving me that deadline, but because I knew if I didn't get right on this, someone else would land the job and I'd be back to the drawing board. I jammed these tunes all day and all night until I had every section down pat. Those songs weren't easy either—it was a real challenge. Their tempos were all over the place and the double bass drum work was insanely fast. I hadn't played that kind of double bass since before I was with Meliah Rage, but I wasn't letting anything get in my way. And thank God for my years of studying Neil Peart, because it really helped me get comfortable playing crazy time changes.

The day of my audition, I rolled into Boston in my piece-of-shit-brown carpet installation van. These guys rehearsed underneath a liquor store on Boylston Street in Boston, directly behind Fenway Park. As I pulled into the alley, the stench smelled like home to me. It was so dirty and sleazy— it reeked of rock 'n' roll. "Perfect!" I thought. "Let's do this!"

I opened the back doors of the brown bomber and began booting my drums out one by one. When the guys in the band came out to meet me and help me load my gear inside, they saw me literally kicking my drums out of the back. I was never the type of drummer who babied my drums. They're *drums,* they're *supposed* to be beat on, and the way I saw it, if they couldn't take getting thrown around a little then they definitely couldn't take what I was going to do to them on stage. But for some reason the guys found this strange. The guitarist said, "Dude, we'll help you carry these. You don't have to kick them down the hallway."

At first I hadn't paid much attention to the room where I was setting up my drums—I was really excited to get started, so after we all introduced ourselves, I got right down to business. As I got closer to finishing, I noticed that there wasn't a single inch of free space on the walls—it was totally covered in porno pictures. It couldn't get any better than this— I was back in the core of the city, in a room covered in porn, about to play with a cool-ass punk-metal band—*and* they were signed to a major label!

Billy O'Malley was one of the guitarists, and he turned out to be my favorite in the band. He had a great look: long, straight brown hair all one length covering his face and hanging down past the middle of his back, and he played the coolest guitar on the planet, the Gibson Les Paul. He hung his guitar down to his knees like Sid Vicious and could do a killer scream like James Hetfield. Then there was Tim Catz. Tim loved his pot as much as he loved playing the bass. Another very cool-looking dude, he played Gibson Thunderbirds and Les Paul basses. Stu Shoaps was the other guitarist and main singer for the band. Billy sang some songs, but most of the time it was Stu.

They told me what had happened to their last drummer. He'd been with them from day one and was really good friends with Stu, but he had a drinking problem and wasn't cutting it. The band had already been in the studio up in Ithaca,

New York, recording their debut record. About twelve days into it they realized they didn't even have one drum track down because of this guy's drinking problem, so they packed their shit up, drove back to Boston and broke the news to their buddy that things weren't working out and told him that he was out.

The rest of the guys in the band were no angels either—they did their share of drugs and alcohol—the only difference was, they were taking this deal very seriously and were incredibly focused on making a great record.

After the audition I felt like I hadn't played as well as I wanted to. I began to think I might have blown it. A lot of times when you audition for bands, they won't tell you right there that you didn't make it—they'll just say, "Cool man, nice job! We'll call you after we finish the rest of our auditions." Most of the time it's just bullshit to get you out of the room quicker. I don't think I played shitty, it's just that I really wanted to slam these tracks down their throats and I didn't feel like I'd blown them away. Apparently, they thought differently though, because they gave me the gig right then and there. Ya-fucking-hoo!

I was so excited to tell my friends and family that I was finally going to do a record and go on tour. It was my dream come true. I called everyone I knew, expecting them to share my enthusiasm, but instead I received a very monotone response. I ran over to Fro's house and began jumping up and down saying, "Hey, bro', I got the gig! I'm on Warner Brothers Records!" He laid there on the couch and said, "Oh really? That's cool. What's the name of the band again?" Definitely not what I was expecting. I don't think he even sat up.

I know they were happy for me, but people like Fro,

Jimmy and my mom had seen me go through so many bands and get so excited about every one of them that they were kind of immune to it by then.

I guess you have to be a musician to really understand the passion that flows through your veins and the hunger you have for music. It's a high like nothing else—better than sex, better than any drug, better than any meal. It's the purest form of adrenaline you can get. You can be stoned for days off of a great show you played or a new song you created. I understood that my friends and family didn't share that level of enthusiasm, but for God's sake, they could have livened up a little!

Of course once they saw it was for real, they supported me 150%, as always. I was in, and I was going for it. That was when shit got real serious for me.

We rehearsed from 7:00 PM every night until 1:00 or 2:00 AM, going over all the songs so many times that my fingers would wind up cracked and bleeding. We wrote some new songs and decided to demo some of them to hear what they sounded like. One thing this band had was funky song titles: "Pentapussy," "I Wanna Fuck Your Girlfriend," "Bastard," and of course the very popular "Lap Frappe" (a term for the surprise treat that follows a blow job), just to name a few.

Just before we entered the studio to start our pre-production, the band was informed that the porn star "Seka" was about to sue the band for using her name without permission. And since she was married to an attorney, things got a little hairy. Especially since the band didn't want to give up the name because of the following they had built over the years with it.

But no one wanted to be sued, either, so to make a long story short, after enough threats we decided to change the band's name to "Strip Mind," a name that was chosen randomly off of a list that everyone had contributed to.

We moved into New Alliance Studios, which was next door to where we rehearsed. It was a small recording studio and the guys had known the owners for some time, so we got a good deal. That's when I first met Andrew "Mudrock" Murdock. You may recognize Mudrock's name from the first two Godsmack albums, which he helped me produce. But when Mudrock and I first met, we didn't hit it off at all. He was a hothead and I was always full of piss and vinegar. We immediately got off on the wrong foot. The stupidest thing set off our first argument.

We had already recorded a few songs at New Alliance and we were coming back to do a few more. I was sitting behind the drums between takes and discussing the progress we were making, or *not* making, on the track. Mudrock was in the

control room setting up a new reel, but he had the microphones on in our room so he could hear us talking.

I mentioned to Billy that I wasn't as happy with the kick drum sound on this run as I'd been with the last session we did. That's all I said. Well, Mudrock came flying out of the control room, stomping his feet and yelling, "Why don't *you* mix the fucking thing yourself if you don't like my sounds!" I was pretty calm, just responding, "Wow! Who

Hangin' in Maria's kitchen, 1992

pissed in *your* Cheerios today?" Then he goes stomping out of the room, making me chase him down the hall like we were in high school or something. It was all I could do to patch the argument up so we could finish the demo.

Years later when we came across each other again, we worked it all out. We still get a good laugh every once in a while when the subject comes up. Mudrock has stepped up for me over the years and became one of the hidden heroes behind the success of Godsmack. I'll tell you all about that a bit later.

So we traveled to Ithaca, New York to record our major label debut album with producer Alex Perialas, who had produced so many of the great bands I grew up listening to: Metallica, Anthrax, Overkill, S.O.D., and so on. This was the big time for me—if I was any happier, I would've shit nickels!

We moved into this five-bedroom house one block from the recording studio. I don't remember there ever being any food in the house, but I do remember there was never a shortage of beer or whippets. For those of you who don't know what a whippet is, it's the N_2O (nitrous oxide) cartridge that you put in b-b guns. We would make these contraptions that screwed down on to the N_2O cartridge and punctured it, letting all the gas flow into this thick balloon. Then we took the balloon off and inhaled the gas. Man, does that shit fuck you up for about thirty seconds. It's just another one of those super-intelligent things that you do when you're young, drunk, and stupid.

Being the drummer, I was the first to do my tracks, laying down the foundation for everyone else. I banged out all eleven songs in two and a half days. Then the rest of the guys

went to town drilling riff after riff and completing all the
vocals. Five or six weeks later, the record was done, mixed,
mastered and ready for the stores. Our excitement kicked up
another notch. We knew that our first real tour was just a
little bit closer.

We came back to Boston and played some local gigs while
Sire/Reprise set up the album. We also got a few extra bucks
from the label to buy our first real touring machine, a brand
new shiny maroon Ford van. For those of you who have never
toured, trust me when I tell you, there is nothing cool about
touring in a van with seven or eight guys who do nothing
but reek of beer and fart a lot. And someone always has a
cold, which means everyone gets sick. So as far as getting any
kind of rest goes…fahgettaboutit!

Take my advice on this one: if you're in a band, tell your
record label to put you on a tour bus. Even the shittiest tour
buses are better than the best vans.

We toured everywhere in that van, from the east coast to
the west coast and everywhere in between. We shot our first
video—for "Bastard"—on tour in Virginia in the peak of the
summer of 1993. They put us in this abandoned warehouse
that felt like it was a hundred and fifty degrees with no food
except for crackers and sodas, threw us our instruments and
said, "Go ahead guys, jam for twelve hours!"

Later, we shot our second video, for the title track "What's
in Your Mouth," in New York City. It was the exact opposite
of the first video. It was midnight, in the middle of March,
and we were outside for hours and hours underneath this
walkway/tunnel that ran along the Hudson River. The con-
cept of the video was fairly simple. It starts off with a shot
of this redheaded punk rock girl who opens up her mouth
and the camera goes down her throat, seeing what looks like

sewer tunnels with rats and cockroaches crawling around.
Then, when it gets to the pit of her stomach, you see the
band performing in a wet, concrete underground. The only
problem was that when we filmed this it was so fucking cold,
we nearly froze our asses off!

We made our way out west and continued touring through
various states. That's when I met Tommy Stewart. He was
touring with a band called Lillian Axe that had the same
manager we did. They were more of a hair band, all good-
looking guys with that Guns 'n Roses kind of vibe, and we
were very drunk and punk. Most Lillian Axe fans didn't quite
get our music, but our management stuck us on tour together anyway.

We arrived in Hollywood to visit the Sire/Reprise offices
and hang out in town for a couple of days. We were all pretty
excited to check it out since none of us had been to that side

Strip Mind:
Stu Shoaps, Bill O'Malley, Sully and Tim Catz in 1993

of the world before. On our first day there we decided to go
see the famous Hollywood Boulevard, so we got in the van
and made our way into town.

In fifteen minutes of driving around we witnessed some
pretty intense shit. I noticed this black kid and his girlfriend
sitting on a bench at a bus stop. These four black guys walked
past them and said something to this dude's girl. The kid
stood up and said something back to them. Well, that was
that! They grabbed this kid off of the bench and beat his ass
so bad that I could hardly stand to watch. They punched him
down to the ground then beat him relentlessly. Even after he
was knocked out cold, one guy held up his limp body, standing him upright, while another dude ran and jumped off the
bench and kicked him square in the face. The kid crashed to
the ground, and then they would stand him back up, rip off
his shoes or some clothes and do it again. They were enjoying
it way too much.

In the meantime, his girlfriend was running up and down
the road screaming for help from anyone, but not a single
soul would help this boy. They simply turned their heads like
nothing was happening and walked away, which gave me the
impression that we were in some kind of gangland or something where people just knew to stay out of it. And we sure
as hell weren't getting out of that van to help. We were scared
shitless ourselves, just like anyone else.

It was a lame way to be greeted to Hollywood, but it put
things into perspective for us real fast. With most of us feeling pretty freaked out, we drove back to our hotel and stayed
in after that.

The next day we learned a bit more about this place. We
were at the Roxy on Sunset doing soundcheck when someone
from the club approached our sound engineer, J.J., who was

wearing a red bandana on his head. He told him it wasn't such a good idea to wear the bandana. J.J. asked why, and the guy replied, "There are gangs that float around here and they wear certain colors on certain days. If red happens to be their color today, they'll shoot you right in broad daylight over that bandana." Such was my first trip to Los Angeles.

We did run into a few pretty big problems along the way. For one, we never paid much attention to the business part of the band. It was just all about partying, hooking up with chicks and playing rock music. That was our biggest downfall—there was no one in the band who truly knew how to deal with the business. Then again, can you blame us? Why would we know about that? We were just musicians trying to play music.

As time went on, we all got worn out by touring and partying, and things got worse and worse within the band. Stu and I grew farther and farther apart. He had been raised rich and snooty, and I'd always hated that stuck-up, spoiled kind of attitude. He even got a Gold MasterCard for an Easter present once, which we all found pretty amusing. When he didn't get his way, to put it bluntly, he was a fucking baby. That side of him surfaced more and more, which really made things tense for everyone.

I was a street boy, as were Billy and Tim, and we were all trudging through it together, so the "I'm better than you attitude" just didn't cut it with me. Even though Stu was the founder and frontman of the band, I still had no problem telling him to shut the fuck up when he started that bullshit. It's too bad no one else in the band did the same. We should've just tossed his ass out and kept going. Me, Billy and Tim were the stronger part of the band anyway. But nothing ever changed.

As I said earlier, we were too young, drunk and stupid to think about anything other than music and partying.

Things really started to fall apart when we got back to Boston and started rehearsals again in late '93. I wouldn't show up from time to time because I had girl issues and ran late a lot, or I would cut out early to go home and deal with my nagging girlfriend who couldn't handle me being away on tour all the time. What else is new? Another problem was it was getting boring. We weren't writing anything new, we were just rehearsing the same songs over and over again. And when I would suggest that we write something, or that I had an idea, Stu would just shoot it down and tell me, "If you got ideas, why don't you go and start your own band?"

By the way, thanks for the advice, Stu! It's worked out pretty well so far.

Most of all, though, I hated Stu and his snobby, whiny ways. So it was a relief not to see him for days at a time. To be honest, I should've been there to support the project more, but I was having a rough time at home and my head wasn't in the right place anymore.

They gave me the bad news one day at rehearsal: "You're fired!"

Billy was the first to spit it out, and to this day I still respect him the most. I was fucking up and they wanted to carry on and felt like I was the problem, so they booted me. Fair enough! At least Billy had the balls to speak up and say what was on his mind, unlike Stu, who just hid behind everyone else. Actually, he was smart not to say much because I probably would've slapped him around like the half-a-sissy that he was. Billy was different—I respected him and Tim as musicians, so as bad as that blow was to me, I understood and moved on out.

Shortly after that I found out that I hadn't been the only problem. I learned that eventually Billy had enough of Stu and quit the band himself. When Billy broke the news to Stu in the rehearsal room, Stu pointed at Tim and said, "So what the fuck? You're gonna leave me with *him?*" Real smart, Stu! Tim told him to fuck off and he quit, too. End of story, end of band.

CHAPTER 17

DEAD BEAT

After Strip Mind, things got weird for me. I was struggling badly. I had no band, no job, no money, and my girlfriend, Betty, and I weren't doing well because I was slipping into a depression about being fired from Strip Mind. I sat on the couch all day, drifting away from the world, trying to figure out what I was going to do. I was having a hard time dealing with the fact that all those years of hard work and dedication to my music had finally paid off, had landed me a record deal and sent me on my way to becoming a successful musician, and then in a blink of an eye had all been torn away. What was I going to do now? On top of that, I had no dough to help Betty with the bills, so she kicked me out. So now I had no place to live. Great!

Even Bill DeMonaco (who I loved like a brother) gave me shit about getting my life together, telling me to quit the dream and get a real job. Boy did that fucking piss me off. Here's a dude who was in the trenches with me, grinding away every day and dreaming the same dream. And just

*With Maria and
Mom at Maria's
house in 1993*

because he decided to bail out and become some musclehead plumber, he thought he had the right to lecture me like my father. This one's for you, brother...(insert middle finger here).

My sister Maria was kind enough to help me out once again by letting me crash on the couch in her one-bedroom apartment in Methuen. I have to hand it to Maria; we had our differences, that's for sure, but she always helped me out whenever I was in real trouble.

After the drama of my breakup and mooching off of Maria for too many weeks, I decided it was time to get my shit together. I started to think that, despite being the only passion I had, maybe music was fucking up my whole life. I had sacrificed school, relationships, family, jobs, you name it, all for music. I was watching all my friends making money at their jobs, living in nice apartments, and driving nice cars.

Most importantly, they were able to pay their bills! I was feeling like a loser.

I had to admit, I had nothing going for myself. I fell real hard. But it was all because I'd thought I would get my break if I worked hard enough for it. Silly me, right? I'd been in all these bands that had always led to something a little bit better, and then it all slipped through my fingers before I knew what had hit me. I'd always heard that you usually only get one shot, and it felt like my shot had come and gone. So I decided I was done. I didn't want to play music anymore, I didn't want to be involved in a band. I just wanted to get a life.

What could I do in music anyway? I'd been in the last band in Boston to get a record deal and now the whole scene sucked. There was no one to play with. I knew I'd have to start a whole new band in order to get something going again, and I was just too depressed and discouraged to do that. I didn't want to start from the bottom again—I had toured the country and been on a major label record, and I just couldn't stand the thought of starting a band from scratch.

So in January of '94 I decided to get a job. I saw this ad in the *Lawrence Eagle-Tribune*: "Make $40,000 a year!" And I was like, all right! It was a job working for a collection agency in Lawrence called Capital Credit. And since there was no experience needed, I was hired on the spot.

For a while, things felt pretty good. I wasn't thinking about music at all. I was doing really well with this new job, making around $2,000 a month. I'd never had a dime, so it was awesome. It was a perfect job for me because I only needed to be street-smart to be good at collections—they look for attitude, not a college degree, and I had plenty of that.

In collections, you're basically bullshitting people into paying bills that they already know they owe; you just have to make the bills seem more urgent than they really are. I had no guilt about that—after all, the people owed the money! Everyone always used to say to me, "Oh, you're one of those pains in the ass who call on a Sunday while we're eating dinner to tell us our credit card bill is overdue, right?" And I would say, "Yes! That's me, I'm the guy asking you to pay your bills. The bills that you owe for money you took from a bank, remember? What, did you think that money was free? You borrowed it, now pay it back!" That was me, and I was enjoying it.

After working collections for a while, though, you lose all your compassion. You could care less about all the bullshit stories and excuses that people give you for not paying their bills. All you think about is getting their money in because you work on commission. Guilt isn't even an option anymore; the job becomes an addiction, and I got really good at it.

I got so serious about the job that I even cut my hair off. I figured, what the hell, it was always slicked back in a ponytail anyway. So I chopped it. Now I was a normal, short-haired person wearing a tie and going to work every morning.

I remember going over Fro's one night to surprise him and show him my new look. Anyone who had ever known me had only seen me with long-hair, so I figured I'd shock the shit out of him when he saw this, being the ultimate metal-head that he was. Well, shock was an understatement. Not only did he not look at me, but the son of a bitch even threw me out of his apartment that day. Bastard!

After working at Capital Credit for a few months and seeing what kind of money I could make, I decided to share the wealth with a friend. I called Muskrat, who was breaking his back working for a company that steam-cleaned carpets and cleaned out fire-damaged houses. I told him how easy it was at this place to make a ton of cash just sitting on your ass spinning numbers all day, so he came down for an interview and I got him into collections with me.

It all felt good again. I had my own money, I wasn't having anxiety attacks anymore, and most importantly, I didn't feel like a loser. My self-esteem went up again and I focused my sights on being as good as I could be at collections.

It came very naturally for me, and within no time I had become one of the best collectors in the office. I had no interest at all in going back on the road, or even being in a band. I was over it, and I was loving life.

With everything feeling so perfect, I couldn't imagine what could make me feel more complete. Then it happened. The new love of my life appeared right before my eyes, disguised as a collection agent. Here we go again!

Erin Roberts was so different from the psycho girlfriends I had before. She was wholesome, smart, loyal and beautiful. She was, like they say, "the girl next door." When Erin and I first met, she didn't like me very much. She thought I was this wise-ass bigmouth. (Okay, so she was right!)

When I finally got to talk with her at lunch one day, I couldn't help noticing how perfect her teeth were. So that's what came out of my mouth: "Did anyone ever tell you that you have really nice teeth?" That was my big pick-up line: "Nice teeth!" Nice job, Sully! Well, at least it was sincere and it got us talking.

Soon after that, we fell head over heels in love. She made me feel more like a man than any other girl I had been with. She showed me how to lead a better, more loyal life, and how to become a more trusting, faithful person without even knowing she was doing it—she just led by example. I felt better about myself when I was around her, and not so much like such a street punk. For the first time since Arlene, I felt that this could be the one for me. I wasn't thinking of music at all; I was completely focused on Erin and entering a turning point in my life. But I should've known better than to think that I was going to be satisfied with a "regular guy" life, or that music was something I wasn't going to be a part of anymore.

I wanted to shine for Erin. The more I fell in love with her, the more I wanted to show her what a wonderful and talented person I was. But I had no band, so I felt like I had nothing really exciting to offer her. I could only show her old Strip Mind videos and CDs. She was proud of that stuff and she'd show them off to her parents and all her friends, but that moment in time was over for me, so inside I felt like a has-been.

If you're a musician—I don't care how big you are—you always feel like you're only worth as much as what you're doing right now...and I was realizing that, money aside, I still wasn't *doing* anything. I felt empty again. I felt like I might be in danger of losing her because I didn't have any-thing to impress her with, and that maybe she would lose interest in me if I was just a regular guy. She nurtured me when I got depressed and tried to pick up my spirits, but that just made me feel sorry for myself, which came out in anger, so we'd get into arguments.

After a year of this, I thought to myself, "What the fuck am I doing? I need to play music!" I couldn't stand it any-more. Was I going to work at a collection agency forever? Had I spent my whole life mastering the art of drumming just so I could throw it all away and become a suit? No way! It was time to turn it on.

When the music bug came back to bite me I realized that

I just couldn't be anything else. Music wasn't ruining my life—
it *was* my life. I'm a musician from head to toe. It was inevitable that music would haunt me once again, and this time the
urge was stronger than ever. I had to get in a band, and soon.

The problem has always been that women and music are
my great passions in life, and for some reason, music always
seems to win. I think it's because I'm such a workaholic and
I'm so aggressive when I'm in it that I don't balance music
with the rest of my life. And I end up losing people who are
important to me. But at the same time, if I don't give music
everything, I won't get there. It's all or nothing.

Maybe that's why I needed to come back with a big bag
of I-told-you-so's for a lot of people, especially for Bill
DeMonaco and my father—they were two people who had
cut me down at one point and questioned my ability to make
it as a musician. It's not that I needed to be better than my
father as a musician; I just needed to prove him wrong about
making music my life. It's like I said at the beginning of this
book: things that happen to you in your childhood can drive
you for your whole life. So when I was a kid and my dad
told me that music should never be more than a hobby, that
lit a huge fire under my ass. And as you know by now, I love
a challenge!

I started writing songs completely on my own for the first
time. In the previous bands I was in, I just played what *they*
wrote. Or I'd help with arrangements, but it was more of a
collaboration; people throwing out ideas in the practice space.
I'd never actually sat down and written a song on my own.

I was also learning how to play some guitar—my friend
Barry Spielberg from Wargasm had showed me how to tune
a guitar in what's called "drop-D," which made it real easy to

play chords with just one finger. Soon I was putting together some progressions, and then I began fucking around with lyrics and melodies. Before I knew it, I had my first song written.

I found the inspiration for the lyrics through a terrible tragedy I had encountered through a friend of mine. Dave Delay was the guitarist of a band called Tin Pan Alley. They were a very cool Boston rock band—street punk kids who had a Skid Row kind of vibe to them.

One evening after him and his girlfriend had gotten into an argument at a party, Dave hung himself in his basement with a chain. He had gone through several years of drug abuse and had always threatened to commit suicide but never had gone through with it. I guess it was a case of the boy who cried wolf—no one believed he would actually do it.

Writing that song about Dave was the first time I felt overwhelming emotion while being creative, as an artist. As I sat on Erin's bedroom floor, I cried my eyes out writing those lyrics. I was putting myself in his shoes and thinking about how upset and alone he must have felt to actually go through with that. And the more I sang the lyrics with the melody, the more they fit together in a more powerful way than I ever imagined. Sometimes you sing some words and they connect with the music in a way that you can't really explain. That was hitting me for the first time and it hit me very hard. The song is called "Another Day"; maybe one day I'll record it and put it out as a single.

That song showed me the way to vent my emotions through my music. It made me realize how powerful a song can be if it's written from the heart.

I had learned something very important from my anxiety attacks: I had a difficult time expressing my feelings. I repressed everything, thinking that if I cried or talked to someone about

how I felt, I was weak. Wrong! Worst mistake you can make.
Get it out of your system when it first starts. Allowing it to
snowball can be devastating internally. Trust me, spending two
years in and out of hospitals for anxiety attacks is no fun. It
really helps to have a vehicle to vent through. If you're not a
musician, then try something else. For you it might be poetry,
or painting, or even kickboxing. But whatever it is, use the
tools that life gives you. They're your therapy. And finally,
through writing music, I'd found mine.

CHAPTER 18
THE SCAM

It all came together for me in February of 1995. One day I sat on Erin's living room couch and began to tell her how much I missed being in a band. The whole time I had been with her she had never seen me play. I poured my heart out about my longing to get back into music, and her response was very positive.

Then I told her I was thinking about starting a band from scratch and for once not just joining someone else's band. I wanted to write my own music and have control over the decisions, unlike the unorganized ways of Strip Mind or pretty much all the other bands I'd been in. I felt I had enough knowledge to be a bandleader and do it better than the other leaders I had watched in the past. She thought it was a great idea.

Even though I was bounced from Strip Mind, I still gained some valuable wisdom from those experiences. For one, I knew how important it was to be a lot more business-conscious. And little did those guys know that I'd been smart enough to keep a collection of all the contacts that we had made during our time signed to Warner Bros. Not only did I keep the numbers of booking agents, club owners, record label presidents and so on, but I also called them every so often to say hi, knowing that one day I might need their help.

Erin thought all of it was great, until I told her that I was also thinking about *singing* for the band this time instead of playing drums. That was the first time in the whole conversation that I saw a confused look cross her face. But in my mind, that was just the way it had to be; I was determined to be a leader. Besides, no one in the area sang the way I wanted. I wanted someone with a growl to their voice, not pretty and high—I didn't want any of that Stryper shit. So I figured I'd give it a go.

I wasn't really thinking about how much of a stretch it was going to be transitioning from drummer to singer, but what did I have to lose? You can't win if you don't gamble, right? You have to follow your instincts; you were born with them for a reason. So if you have a good feeling about something—even if some people don't think it's right for you— go with it. Not knowing is worse than failing.

So the hunt for a band began. My first objective was to find some musicians who could play at my level. I was definitely not going to the local music store to snatch a few names off the corkboard that displayed all the teenage kids in the area looking to start a garage band. I needed to find real good players in order for this to work. But it was slim pickings out there in New England. It wasn't really a happening place at that time. Boston has always been known for spitting out quality bands every few years—the J. Geils Band, Aerosmith, Boston, the Cars, 'Til Tuesday, etc.—but the music scene always came in waves. One minute there's a huge scene going on where you can pretty much go out any night of the week and catch a killer band that's packing in the clubs, and the next minute it's like a ghost town. And let's not forget that by this time the whole grunge thing had pretty much stripped away the last of the 80's hair bands and metal bands (*thank God!*).

The first person I called was Robbie Merrill, who was a good friend of my ex-girlfriend Betty's brother. I had met this cat a few times. He had long, scraggly brown hair and seemed to be a fairly quiet dude. He just worked his construction job, drank his Budweiser and played his bass. He was a regular Joe kind of guy.

I'd seen him play in the local bars, playing anything from Top 40 songs to country and reggae, but I remember even though I was bored out of my mind listening to some of the crap they played, he was killer at his instrument. Sure, he wore his bass guitar way too high around his neck and did the Methuen two-step when he danced his groove on stage, but I felt with a little work on lowering that bass down to a Sid Vicious-style altitude and educating him on writing and performing heavy rock music, this dude would be able to rip it up as my bass player.

I'll never forget Robbie's reaction when I called up to see if he was interested in getting together and starting a new project. He knew about my capabilities as a drummer and seen me play with Strip Mind, but when I dropped the bomb on him that I was going to sing instead, I think I heard the phone fall down every step in his house while the sound of laughter floated in the distance.

"I'm serious, dude!" I said to him. "I want to try fronting this project. I have a few ideas written already and I think it could work."

As we got deeper into the conversation, he told me he wasn't sure about this. Not because I was going to sing, but because he, too, had run himself into a rut with the music life and wasn't sure if he wanted to do it anymore. Although I shared the same feelings with him about not having anything to show for ourselves, the difference was, I was twenty-seven and he was thirty-two. He felt he was too old to go for it again, knowing how long it takes to get a new project on its feet. I felt like I still had a few years left in me before I came to that conclusion, so like they say in *The Godfather*, I made him an offer he couldn't refuse!

I said to him, "Let's not do this like we're used to it being done. Let's not get all caught up in the demands of being at rehearsal six days a week for ten hours a day. Let's just get together when we can, write some music and demo it off for fun."

I explained to him that through my days with Meliah Rage and Strip Mind, I'd made a lot of good contacts that could help us get our foot in the door a lot easier than most bands. I repeated my offer: "It'll be a low-key studio project that won't stress us out or interfere with our lives. Let's just give it one motherfucker of a go and try our best. I'll even make you a promise right now that by the time I celebrate my thirtieth birthday, if we haven't signed a record deal, I'll quit playing music with you forever!"

That's the promise that I made to Robbie, word for word, and I meant it!

Now that I had Robbie on board, we started to brainstorm about who would play guitar and drums. I could lay down the drum tracks in the studio so finding a drummer wasn't nearly as important as finding a lead guitarist. I was making good progress on guitar but I was definitely not capable of pulling off leads.

Robbie recommended we try out this dude Lee Richards. Lee was from North Andover, but he wasn't snooty like the rich kids from that town—he was a regular guy who made his living as a stonemason. He was a big, husky guy, and just great to hang out with. Lee had played in several different death metal bands and had sung for some of them, so I knew he was capable of playing at me and Robbie's level, and his capability to sing was just a bonus. Lee had a good chuckle when he heard I was going to sing, but we must have caught him at a good time because he jumped right on it. And just like that, we had a band!

Now we needed to start writing. We set up camp in the attic of the apartment building I was renting from my buddy Eric on Tower Hill in Lawrence and went to work. Our equipment was pretty lousy, but we managed. Lee had to borrow a beat-up Marshall amp because he didn't own any equipment, and I loaned him my $80.00 Cort guitar. What a piece of crap that thing was. I still have that guitar today; covered in stickers and always out of tune, this thing was far from a Les Paul Custom, but it birthed our first batch of songs. We would work on the songs as a band and then I'd take them home and come up with lyrics and melodies.

In April of '95, we did some recording at our friend Carmine DiMarcas' studio on the first floor of his house in Lawrence. Drums were no problem to bang out. I had plenty of studio experience by then, so in a few hours that part was history. Robbie and Lee followed, knocking out their parts just as fast. With the music out of the way, guess what was left to do? That's right, vocals! The only problem was, I had never sung before in my life. Sure, I wrote all the lyrics and melodies for the songs, but this was going to be the first time I'd actually gotten behind a microphone in a studio and sung.

Man, did I suck! I was so bad at singing in key when I first started that there was a point in the session where Robbie and I made eye contact through the glass and he just rolled his eyes and walked out of the building.

After several days and a lot of painful hours in the studio, I completed my tracks and our first demo was finished under the name, "The Scam."

We printed a bunch of cassettes to pass out to our friends and get a vibe for what they thought. The songs were so different from each other that nobody knew what to think. "Head" sounded like something Aerosmith could've written with its bluesy riffs and a horrible harmonica solo by yours truly. "Decisions" was really funky and actually had a horn section in it. "Here I Go" sounded like a bad Pearl Jam cover and "Homeward" was our dark acoustic ballad. We also had a song called "Voices" which you may recognize from our acoustic EP, *The Otherside*.

My roots were classic stuff like Aerosmith and Zeppelin but I was also starting to tune into the newer heavy music, like Helmet, Alice in Chains and Nine Inch Nails. "Seein' It Is Believing It" and "Eat the Sky" came out of those newer influences and people would always pick those songs out and say, "You guys should do more of that kind of music." So we did! We began building our catalogue off of heavier music.

I moved to a one-bedroom studio apartment in Methuen, where strangely I was right next door to the police station where many years prior I was locked up in for larceny of bread. We got a rehearsal room at a place called the Methuen Train Depot. It was a former train station owned by a man named Dan and his wife. That place became our second home for the next three years—so much for not rehearsing six days a week!

People were really digging our demo and we began to realize that we might have something here. It was evident that we weren't going to be just a studio band—the hunger had set in and I began obsessing about playing live. But we needed a drummer first.

I told Lee and Robbie about Tommy Stewart, the drummer I'd met when Strip Mind toured with Tommy's old band Lillian Axe. Anxiously, they encouraged me to call him in Houston and see if he was interested. The first thing I did was send him the six-song demo, followed by a phone call explaining that I had done the drum tracks on the tape. Tommy's reply was, "Cool! But why are you calling me?"

So I laid it on him: "I'm gonna sing for this band. That's me on the tape." Once again the laughter began. Ha fucking ha! Tommy had seen me play more than either Lee or Robbie had because we'd toured together and watched each other's show every night for months, so he got a huge kick out of this, but he said that he dug the demo and wanted to give it a shot. "Great!" I thought to myself. "We have a drummer—and a good one, too!"

Tommy packed his bags in Houston and moved up to Methuen. Robbie put him up until he got himself a job and a place of his own. He got a job working at UPS, throwing people's packages around all day. I think the poor guy is still cursed 'til this day with knowing every zip code in New England, but he eventually got himself a cool little apartment right near me and we were off and running.

Rehearsals became very demanding. We didn't follow any of the rules me and Robbie had agreed on when we started the thing. What was supposed to be a fun studio project, with no pressures about rehearsals, soon became five to six nights a week, six to eight hours a night. We really dug in and figured out what we were going to sound like. Lee was a writing machine and would come up with new riffs all the time. All we cared about was when we could book our first show.

After a few more songs came together, it was time to test out this material in front of an audience. Our first gig was at a place called the Rock Pile in Saugus, Mass., near Boston. This guy named Chris was running it at the time and he was nice enough to give us a chance opening for an old metal band called Death Angel.

I was very excited to invite not only my personal friends to the gig, but all my friends at Capital Credit. And of course I was the most excited about finally being able to perform in front of Erin.

The objective was to bring in as many people as we could so we could play in front of a large audience. About forty people showed up, including Mike, my old singer from Meliah Rage, and his girlfriend Nancy. I felt really weird about that because me and Mike were in such a powerful heavy metal band together, and here I am about to play basic hard rock, not the heavy, intricate metal that Meliah Rage played. I was shitting myself about going on stage for the first time as a singer. I remember thinking, "I have no drums to hide behind!" That's where my comfort zone was. In the past, if we played in front of an audience that didn't like us, I could always hide behind my drums and let the singer take the brunt of the abuse. But this time *I* was the singer. I thought, "What am I going to say to the crowd? And what am I supposed to do with my hands when I'm not singing? Ahhhhh! I'm fucked!"

Well, despite all the anxiety, we went on anyway. Funny thing is, once I hit the stage, I felt fine. Yeah, it was still a bit weird to perform as a singer, but it wasn't as bad as I thought it would be. I was in my world as a musician and I felt protected while I was there.

Still, I remember looking out at Mike and Nancy at one point as they shook their heads and walked out before our set was over. That wasn't good for the ego, but looking back now, I would've done the same. We had to find a definite direction and style—we had heavy songs, we had light songs, we even had that funky song with horns. We were fresh meat to be devoured if we didn't get our shit together real quick. And besides, I'm a perfectionist. I wanted this band to be perfect.

As months passed, we practiced all the time while we held down our day jobs. My buddy, Jim Mustapha, and the big boss at Capital Credit weren't getting along, so Jimmy went over to a different agency named Zwicker and Associates, which was a law firm collection agency based in Andover. He called me up and told me that the money was so much better there, and since it was a law firm, the collectors had more control over the debtors. So I jumped ship with him. I wanted to make killer money so I could have a nice car and a cool apartment like everyone else. Plus the boss at Zwicker, Joe Ormand (another person who helped get me where I am today), was extremely cool and much more laid back than the guys over at Capital Credit.

Things got real good for a while. I was making about $40,000 a year to yap on the phone—not too shabby for a high school dropout. I had a lot of fun working there, threatening people to pay their bills. (My alias was "Brad Sullivan," for those of you who might have gotten a call from me.)

Sometimes I think I had *too* much fun, because I know for a fact I drove my boss crazy at times. You see, I had a knack for this collections thing. I always found it easy to convince people to pay their bills and collect the money, and I never had a problem hitting my quota for the company. The only problem for Joe Ormand was, I would do it in half the time that a normal collector would. So halfway through the month when I reached my quota, I would just fuck off the rest of the time and either not come in or, when I did, just make phone calls for the band all day long, booking gigs.

Poor Joe—he really did like me, which was lucky for me, because most people would've been out on their asses for the shit I got away with. But Joe was cool.

I was quickly learning how to be a frontman in a band. You have to get in people's faces and take control—people sense fear, and they'll take advantage of that if you don't show them who's boss right from the get go. At first I didn't know how to do that. But the more gigs we played, the better I got at it. I also did my homework, studying the pros to get pointers.

I learned about how to show strength through watching the presence of James Hetfield and how to capture that mystique from watching Layne Staley. I paid close attention to the energy that Steven Tyler had in concert, commanding the audience with every breath and gesture. I was also learning about communicating with the audience better, and how important it is to be real with them. Keeping their attention is half the battle—being not just a singer, but an entertainer.

We all became very serious about the band. And throughout the months that passed, songs like "Time Bomb" and "Bad Religion" were born. We even took Paul Geary's advice to change the name. He felt that "The Scam" was a little dated-sounding and suggested that we look for another one. None of us was all that attached to it to begin with, so we took his advice. After scanning my CD collection one afternoon, we all decided on changing the name to Godsmack, which we found from an Alice in Chains song. Later we redefined the name to give it our own unique identity. I'll get to that in a minute.

The night that changed our whole perspective on the band and gave us the confidence to take it all the way was the first time we played at Axis under the name Godsmack. It was the night before Thanksgiving of 1995, and the club Avalon had a band by the name of Korn playing there that night. Although they were brand-new at the time, they were doing extremely well. They were a new metal band that had emerged into the limelight and was taking over the music scene. We were offered to headline next door at Axis, which was connected to Avalon; we'd start as soon as Korn finished. The deal was, whoever wanted to come into Axis after Korn was finished could get in for free with their ticket stub. So we took the gig and hoped for the best.

Korn was wrapping up their set around 10:00 that night, so around 9:45 I slipped downstairs from the dressing room to take one last peek into the hall to see if anyone was there. It was dark, quiet and empty. We were going to play to no one that night. Regardless, we still got dressed and decided that we'd take our $50.00 and play our set anyway.

Ten o'clock rolled around and we started walking downstairs from the dressing room. The closer we got to the stage, the more we could hear the murmuring of a crowd. We turned the corner and saw the club was jam-packed from front to back with about 400 people (which is about all Axis can hold) from the Korn show, all fired up and waiting to rock again. Instantly we snapped into this warrior-style attitude and shook off the discouragement we had felt just minutes before. We took the stage feeling really confident that we were going to rock this crowd, but we also were very aware that, except for a few close friends in the audience, not one of these people had ever seen or heard us before. It was going to be a crap shoot.

Three-quarters of the way through our set it hit us all at once: no one was leaving. We were actually holding the crowd there for the entire show. They were slammed up against the front of the stage cheering and raging through our entire set! Even the people in the back who prefer to be the critics and not hurl themselves into the depths of the pit were still reacting positively to us and genuinely enjoying themselves. That's when we really knew we had something. After we finished, we went back upstairs to the dressing room and looked at each other in amazement, all of us realizing the same thing—this band had played to an audience that had never seen or heard of us before, and not one person had left the room. Especially considering how tough a Boston crowd can be, we did fucking great!

About one year into the life of the band, in early '96, things started to feel really solid. But knowing how my life had always consisted of peaks and valleys, it shouldn't have surprised me when things went bad again. It seemed like whenever I was granted a new beginning, there was always a tree lurking around the corner waiting to fall on my head. In other words, things couldn't get better until they got worse.

Our reality slap came to us when Lee Richards was surprised by an ex-girlfriend who appeared one day and gave him the news that every man fears: "I have your child," she told him, and said she needed his financial help. That was that! Lee came to us with the worst look on his face I've ever seen. "It's time for me to move on," he said to us. "I have to do the right thing and support my child."

Even though the band was doing better and better, we still didn't get paid enough to try and convince him otherwise. We were all working full-time jobs to pay our bills and gigging when we could. Robbie had a job roofing and siding homes, Tommy was miserably slinging boxes for UPS and memorizing zip codes, and I was still working as a collection agent. Making money wasn't a possibility for us in the beginning—not that we cared about that. We just wanted to create a buzz and spread the word that there was a new band in town that was kicking ass. Sadly, but very honorably, Lee left the band to do the right thing by his newly-found child. At that point we had to take a step back, put the band on hold, and figure out who would fill the slot.

The search was on for a new guitarist. We went to shows, scoping out local talent, and dug through our phone books to see what kind of ex-band mates were available and qualified.

A band called the Crushed Tomatoes had been playing quite frequently in the Salem, New Hampshire area, about thirty minutes north of Boston. They were just a local cover band jamming on Alice in Chains, Stone Temple Pilots, Rage Against the Machine and stuff like that. Robbie had seen them a few times and began encouraging me to go check out this guitar player named Tony Rombola.

So one night in March of '96 we all got together to see

the Crushed Tomatoes at a little restaurant/bar called L.J.'s in the Rockingham Mall in Salem NH. I remember thinking, "What the fuck am I doing here? I'm not interested in anybody who plays covers." I wasn't even sure if I could fairly judge the creativity of someone who was playing covers. Then, to top it all off, they took the stage and I really was thrown for a loop: there was this guy Tony Rombola, dressed in balloon pants and a Gold's Gym muscle shirt, wearing his guitar so high around his neck that I was worried he might choke himself.

I collapsed my face into my hands and shook my head in disbelief. "Maybe I'm strange," I thought to myself. "Maybe *everyone* wears their damn guitars that high and I'm just out of touch with what's cool." But growing up watching people like Jimmy Page, Joe Perry and Sid Vicious, I felt that nothing could be cooler than hanging a Les Paul down to your knees and making noise rather than playing those "look at me!" leads. I didn't care about technique like some of these guys did. All I cared about was attitude. That's what works for me. Being a great player is helpful and all, but can you make a guitar feed back like Hendrix and look cool doing it?

Fortunately I was wrong about Tony's playing. They played songs that I knew very well so I got a real good idea of how killer this guy really was. It didn't take long for me to be convinced that this dude could play his instrument. His guitar solos were unbelievably accurate – and not only did he play them note for note, he played with conviction. I started thinking, "He definitely has a great ear for music, and if he can pull off covers this good, why would it be any different for him to learn our stuff?" All he had to do was lower that damn guitar—like, a couple of feet.

After the show, Robbie set up an audition for Tony and

passed him a six-song demo of our music. That was Tony's audition: "Play these songs great and you're in!" And he did! Note for note, he cranked out every single riff and played even better solos than Lee did. My eyes got real big, real quick. Tony even came up with the little funky wah-wah part in the verses of "Immune."

It was one of those times when you just knew after one or two songs that this was the guy. Tony was a nice, soft-spoken guy and he could play his ass off. We didn't have to look any further, and thank God for that, because we hated the thought of auditioning people. We just wanted to get the show rolling again.

The one deal we made with Tony about joining the band was he had to lower his guitar one inch a week.

"If you're gonna play a Les Paul," we told him, "you can't have it up around your chin, okay?"

With a great sense of humor, he accepted the challenge and went to bat for the team. Robbie had already lowered his bass down about a foot, so our band was getting a decent stage presence together.

Of course, no sooner did we fix one problem than the next obstacle slapped us in the face. We had only a handful of rehearsals with Tony before Tommy dropped the bomb on us: he'd decided to leave the band. Great! One fucking thing after another. It happened so close to Tony joining the band that I remember Tony asking me if *he* was the problem. But it had nothing to do with him. Tommy just felt that the band wasn't moving quickly enough and he was going through some personal problems, so he felt that rather than roll the dice with this band, he was going to move on and try something else. Fine! Tommy headed out to Los Angeles and we were back to a three-piece again.

Back to a three-piece:
outside the train depot,
1996

We sat around and talked about what we were going to do. Giving up was not an option. We had something brewing in this band that was too special to just give up on. So, once again, we decided to look for a drummer. In the meantime I would get back behind the kit and keep bashing out the tunes to build up our catalogue of music.

Over the next few months, songs like "Situation," "Stress," "Get Up, Get Out" and "Voodoo" developed, songs that we felt real good about. Now we needed to get back out into the clubs and keep the buzz going, but we had to find a drummer. It wasn't going to be easy. I won't bullshit you, I'm a really picky bastard when it comes to drummers—I'd been playing for twenty-five years by that time and I was not going to settle for just anyone. And besides, Tony, Robbie and I had this great chemistry when we wrote and recorded together, so they weren't going to accept anything less than great, either. But sometimes God has a weird sense of humor, and you have to be careful about what you wish for.

We began putting out the word that we needed a drummer and little by little, people started lining up for auditions.

But the few who auditioned were not that good. As a matter of fact, one dude drank so much beer before we even started that he forgot he was auditioning for a band. He was just there to party with us and play cover songs. Hell, he even did a drum solo for us.

Finally a guy named Joe Darco showed up. He had played with Tin Pan Alley, who had broken up shortly after my friend Dave Delay killed himself. We gave him the six-song demo and sent him off to learn it.

A week or so later he called saying he was ready to go for it. I set him up with my drum kit and one by one he began knocking down the songs with authority. Compared to the other nitwits we auditioned, he was definitely worth working with. So we prepped Joe for Godsmack's journey back to the club scene.

After a few months of long, hard rehearsals and yelling at Joe all the time to play the songs better, we finally got back into the club scene. I dug through my rolodex of contacts and finagled us some gigs that would be key to getting us in front of as many new people as possible.

We got gigs opening for Powerman 5000 (who were red hot in the Boston scene at the time) and Ronnie James Dio, compliments of Paul Geary from owning a new theatre in Rhode Island. Shit, we even opened for Ratt once. That was the most amusing gig we ever played.

It was 1996, but the whole theatre was swarming with 1980's poseurs who hadn't quite figured out yet that the hair band days had ended years ago. All the dudes looked like bad versions of Brett Michaels from Poison and all the chicks were living in denial, pretending that their Spandex pants could actually still hold in their fat asses. It looked more like ten pounds of cottage cheese stuffed in a five pound onion sack. It was funny as hell.

Halfway through what we felt was a great set, I thought I could hear the crowd starting to murmur "God... *Smack!* God... *Smack!*" But as it got louder and clearer I started to realize that it wasn't "Godsmack" they were chanting, it was "Ratt! Ratt! Ratt! Ratt!" I couldn't believe it! I just turned around and started laughing. How can you get upset over that?

Then I noticed this girl standing right in the front row doing her lipstick and fixing her hair. She wasn't paying any attention to the show or us; she was simply there to claim her piece of real estate so when Ratt came on she could attempt to catch the singer's eye by showing him her fried-egg tits and hopefully get pulled backstage to suck a cock or three.

It didn't offend me that she wasn't into our band. No, what offended me was that when I happened to glance down at her, she gave me this shitty look—then flipped me off in between fixing her lipstick and makeup! I leaned over to her and smiled ever so gently as she continued to look at me with that puss on her face, and as soon as she got her make-up exactly the way she wanted it and clicked her make-up case closed, I took all sixteen ounces of beer that I had in my cup and fired it right into her face. Oh man, it was awesome! She was horrified, makeup running down her face and her big hair all flattened out. She just looked up at me and yelled, "You fucking asshole!" then ran to the bathroom. Best laugh I'd had in a long time.

After playing some low paying gigs, we were able to save a few bucks and do some photos so we could make a better press kit for ourselves. It was at that photo shoot that we were able to redefine the name "Godsmack."

Now, I'm only going to tell you this once, so pay attention.

And stop asking us this stupid ass question about the name of the band. It's old. The only reason that I even decided to write this in the book is to hopefully shut up some of the religious critics that think we're some child sacrificing demon band.

One day, when the entire band was at our rehearsal room

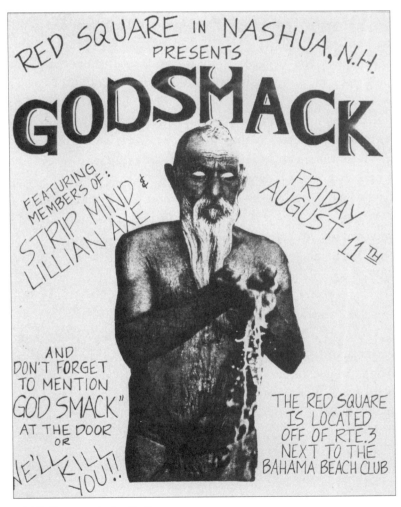

1995 flyer made by Sully

waiting to do this photo shoot, Joe was complaining miserably about this huge cold sore on his lip that he had gotten
the night before. The fucking thing was the size of a dime—
real gross! Being the wiseass that I am, I started breaking his
balls about it, saying shit like, "Well, that's what you get for
sucking other guys' dicks and kissing strange men."

I know it's cruel, but that's just my Lawrence boy sense
of humor.

Anyway, he begged us to try and reschedule the shoot
until the crater on his lip went away, but we couldn't because
we'd already paid for the photographer. Besides, we had to
get this done ASAP—we weren't signed yet and we needed
some good photos to shop to record labels and whatnot.

I continued to rag on Joe mercilessly all day, to the point
where even he was laughing about it after a while. The next
day when we all showed up to rehearsal, lo and behold, I
came walking into the practice room with this huge-ass cold
sore on my lip, same size, same spot.

Of course Joe was the first one to look at me and say,
"Oh shit! Sucking the same guy's dick, were ya?"

Then Tony looks over at me and says, "See? God just
smacked you for making fun of Joe yesterday."

And so our name took on a new meaning. I felt a lot
better about it after that. I'd always hated the thought of us
being pegged as an Alice in Chains cover band (which we
never were, by the way). So instant Karma redefined the name.
It was a much better representation of what we were about.
It's like making fun of someone for their hair falling out,
then *your* hair starts falling out. That's a Godsmack!

CHAPTER 19
PAIN IS CAUSED BY PLEASURE

There was a time when Erin and I were dancing on clouds together. We were inseparable for the longest time, and I can't *ever* remember loving anyone more than I loved her.

My day job was nicely secured which had brought my financial situation to a much better place, but unfortunately, the other parts of my life were about to become pretty unstable. And I was very unprepared for it.

Erin was a very honest and wholesome kind of person, but I was still all fucked up from all the other girls who had cheated on me or deceived me over and over again. And I struggled with trust issues, so we fought a lot about my insecurities. I was still a punk from Lawrence, and she was an angel from Salem, New Hampshire. There were times when I felt like I had no business being with someone so good. She glowed with innocence from being raised in much nicer surroundings. She didn't have the scars that I bore from my past.

Instead of just realizing that things were going good and

accepting the rewards that life was nourishing me with for all the hard times I'd gone through, I just took advantage of the fact that Erin was so loyal to me and I was able to get away with anything. I started hanging out with my friends and my band all the time, going to clubs until all hours of the night and drinking way too much.

On one of those evenings I ended up bumping into my crazy cokehead ex-girlfriend Lisa. Seeing her fucked me all up again. The split second I saw her, my heart hit the floor and I felt like my whole world was spinning out of focus. Here I was, four years later, and I was still feeling confused about why Lisa had left me. It sent me for a loop when she reappeared, and I was immediately drawn to her again.

I realize now that I really just needed to ask the question, "Why? Why did you bail on me? How could you just shut it off so fast with no regrets or no phone calls?" And to top it off, "How could you be such a cunt, to marry my friend and really twist the knife in my back?" I couldn't just walk away from Lisa—I wanted *answers!*

My past had caught up with me and I just had to confront it. My intentions were simply to get my answers, then tell her to fuck off and show her that I was through with her once and for all. But life has a sick sense of humor sometimes and the devil's claws grabbed hold of me once more. Before I knew it, she had turned on that charm and sweet smile, luring me right back into the gates of hell.

We started sneaking around behind her husband David's back (which wasn't a big deal to me since I'd already written him off as a friend). We'd go into Boston and hit the clubs, where neither David or Erin would ever go. And she would come over to my apartment a lot and stay the night. I was falling for Lisa in a big way all over again. She would tell me how bad she hated David and wanted out of their marriage, and I would lie to her and tell her that me and Erin were having our own problems and that I was having the same thoughts. So we began talking about getting a place together and becoming an item again. But I was stupid about it and didn't cover my tracks very well.

Erin was getting pretty insecure by this time because of all the distance and arguing. She became very suspicious and broke into my voicemail one day. That's when she heard this exact message from Lisa: "Hi, baby! I've been out looking for apartments for us and I found a few, call me back." Erin called me up and asked if I could come by her work and see her, so I did.

When I got there, I'll never forget the look on her face. As she came out of the building, she began to approach me and told me to come closer. I knew right away that she was upset about something by the heartbroken look on her face. I became very hesitant to approach her, but she insisted that I come closer. As I reluctantly got within arms reach, she completely lost her mind and began smacking me in the face, crying and yelling at me about what a fucking asshole I was for doing this to her. Not knowing at the time why she was upset, I was still a little confused. Then she let it rip: "I heard Lisa's messages on your fucking voicemail, so fuck you!"

She walked away and I was left there stunned. It hit me like a train. I had broken the heart of someone who was nothing but wonderful to me.

I ran back to my apartment, determined to get Lisa out of my life and to call Erin as soon as I could. But when I got home I found my apartment trashed. It shouldn't have been such a surprise, now that I think about it. My CD's were scattered all over the floor, pots and pans were everywhere, my whole house was rearranged. The funny thing is, even though my apartment was a mess, Erin is such a sweet girl that even in the midst of her rage, she was still nice enough not to break anything. She just messed shit up.

I wanted so bad at that point to be the boyfriend that she'd hoped for me to be, but it was no use. The damage was done and she was gone. I called and called and called, but she wasn't answering. I went to her apartment that night to see her, but she wouldn't open the door. I crawled up on her balcony and went in through the sliding door. I entered her apartment and saw her sitting on the floor with a bunch of candles, listening to her Alanis Morrissette CD in the dark and crying like her best friend had just died. The best friend who died was me. What a weird feeling that is, seeing your own funeral. That's what it felt like.

I went to her and hunched over her back, crying with her and apologizing in every way I could. I couldn't even imagine trying to lie to her. I just had to face the music and hope that she would forgive me. Then the strangest thing happened.

She stood up, grabbed me by my hands and asked me to slow-dance with her. I looked at her as tears rolled down her face, wondering what she was talking about.

She pulled me closer and asked me again, "Dance with me please". I became a little freaked, thinking that maybe she was going to stab me or something when she put her arms around me. I knew she was that hurt. It felt like something out of that movie *Fatal Attraction*. I was very nervous and didn't quite understand why she was asking me to dance with her when seconds ago she wouldn't even talk to me. So I started to plead with her.

"Erin, Please! What are you talking about? You're freaking me out here!"

Again she just looked at me very gently and asked, "Will you please just dance with me? In all the time that we've been a couple, you have never asked me to slow dance".

I approached her very slowly and wrapped my arms around her. I began to cry and tell her over and over again how sorry I was for doing this to her, that I didn't love Lisa, I loved her. But she didn't respond.

She rested her head gently on my shoulder and danced with me until the song was over, then she kissed me softly on my lips, said goodbye and showed me to the door. That was the last of my true love.

To this day I have never felt as much guilt and pain as I felt that night with Erin. I was a man reduced to a scumbag. I had deeply hurt someone who had done nothing but love me and care for me like no one had ever done before. I carried that cross uphill for a long time.

Until that door had closed behind me, I had never stopped to think about how much better my life had become because of her. That was a big turning point in my life.

The whole time she was teaching me through example, yet I never learned. Things like trust, family values and un-conditional love all seem so important to me now, but all a little too late for Erin and me.

I've never been one of those people who really wishes I could change my past. Making mistakes is how we learn and grow. Still, if I could do it differently, I would. Not so much because we'd still be together, but more because I truly never wanted to hurt Erin. She didn't deserve that.

Throughout the years I saw Erin from time to time when she would show up at a Godsmack show to see how we'd evolved since the club days. Or maybe we'd bump into each other at a bar and say hello. We've both grown up and have let the past be the past, and I believe that she's finally forgiven me for the painful memories I left her with. Or at least I hope she has. I try to remember only the beautiful times we had together, and my memories of her will always be some of the best. Losing her was painful, but I realize now that I brought that pain on myself. She really did make me a little bit more of a man than I was before, and for that I'm forever grateful.

I was now in the darkest hole of my life. My grandparents on my mother's side, the ones I was closest to, had passed away, and the love of my life was gone for good. My drinking became insane. I was hurting beyond hurting. For a guy who's only 130 pounds, a bottle of Jack Daniels *and* a twelve pack of beer every night can't be very healthy. I got so wasted one night that I drove up to my grandmother's grave and sat there staring at her tombstone, crying over my pathetic life. I finally fell asleep on the ground in the middle of my drunken stupor.

I was woken up the next morning by the local police. The sunlight shone in my face as if I was entering the gates of heaven, although my body felt more like it was in the fifth ring of hell. As I focused my sights on the uniformed officers, I heard them say, "Are you okay, son?"

I somehow pulled myself up into a sitting position and answered, "Am I still alive?"

"Yes," they replied.

So I said, "Well, then I'm not okay."

They offered me a ride, but I shooed them off and found my own way home.

After that I found myself spending a lot of time at home, hiding my feelings once again from my band-mates and friends. I was too embarrassed to talk about my fuck-ups, so I hid them the best I could while I was in front of them, never letting them see me hurt. I would spend my spare time drinking, eating Clonapins for anxiety and lying around my house wondering why I do the stupid things I do.

I curled into a shell. I didn't feel like anyone wanted to hear my bullshit and I didn't feel like I ought to bother anyone with it. I just felt like I needed to punish myself— the more pain, the better. After hurting someone like that, why shouldn't I make my own life as painful as possible?

Sometimes I thought maybe getting drunk would snap me out of the mood I was in and I would be able to go out and party with my friends. But it just made me feel worse once I was wasted. Then I just got tired of crying and feeling shitty about it, so I'd eat the pills to go to sleep.

That went on for a while and it just never seemed like it was going to get better. But I was committed to this band and I had to pick myself up and get myself to rehearsal every day. I would make a big show of being mopey, but whenever they'd ask about it, I'd go, "Oh, it's nothing, it's cool." I would never say what was bothering me because I didn't want to have to relive it. I just buried it.

When I did go to rehearsal, I'd do what I had to do, then get right out of there as soon as possible. If we had practice from 7:00 to 11:00, I'd be there at 7:00 on the nose and start walking out the door at 10:59. There were times when I couldn't even stand to be in that room—I felt like I had to get back to my apartment, to be alone, so I could figure things out. I thought I could figure out a way to make it up to Erin and get back together. But of course that could never happen, so I just continued to endure the pain until I finally accepted that that was the way it was going to be.

The only good thing about the pain I went through was that Erin became the inspiration behind some songs that are very dear to my heart. Most of the first Godsmack record was written during the time she and I were breaking up.

Before Erin, I'd been writing lyrics that weren't as real. They had some venting and dealing with feelings, but they were nowhere near as intense as what was came out of me at that point. The other guys in the band were like, "Whoa, this is pretty heavy."

That's how songs like "Now or Never" were born, inspired by how I felt at the time, being confused about Lisa coming back into my life and me forgetting about myself: "Can't remember my name, can't remember at all/ Finding you from past times I think, how did we ever fall?" "Keep Away," also inspired by Lisa, was geared more towards the desperation of wanting her out of my life, feeling numb to everything and a hint of that moment when she socked me one in her Jeep. "Twisting everything around that you say/ Smack me in my mouth 200 times every other day." All my frustration was funneled into lines like, "Breathing life into your lungs, are you immune to me?" which was my way of saying, "I'm trying to help you, but you won't accept it."

Then there's "Moon Baby," completely inspired by Erin. The whole second verse was about my episode in the graveyard. "Let's take a trip to the stars far away/ Where were you when I was down, staring into the dead?" "Situation" is another attempt at sympathy. "How can I feel if I can't breathe? What we once had will never be again."

I found myself writing more and more about the situations I was involved in. Not because I thought it would make great music, but because it's the only thing that was going through my mind at the time. I started writing everything down like it was a journal. Some of those entries grew to become songs, and some just remained journal entries. But what I did notice was that it felt a little bit better every time I was able to vent my frustration or anger, or depression. It was, once again, my source of natural healing.

I also didn't care about trying to mask my lyrics, or get all creative and artsy with fancy words. If I needed to say "fuck you," I'd say "fuck you." If I had to say "fuck me," I'd say "fuck me." I couldn't disguise that kind of stuff with intellect; I just wrote it as I felt it. Whether it was right or wrong wasn't the point. It was genuine.

They always say you should write about what you know. And that's exactly what I did. My source of inspiration was my own life, the events I was actually living through. It was a terrible time for me, but I look back now and feel very proud of what came out of me, considering how unmotivated I was at the time. Even though the lyrics were dark, they were still beautiful to me. It was a reflection of my life.

That's when I noticed that music had become more important to me than ever. I didn't even think that was possible. It was revealing a new face to me. It wasn't just art or passion anymore, or a way to express emotion. It became a healing vehicle for me. It was my light at the end of the tunnel.

I think most people underestimate how powerful music is. Did you ever sit down and actually think about why music affects you? Or how it changes your mood? Some may say it's the lyrical content and how they relate to the story in relevance to their own situations. Maybe some of that is true.

But I think that's just a small part of it. I think the lyrics are just amplified by the music's emotion. Let me clarify that a little better.

Why is it that an instrumental can make you feel happy or sad, sexy or angry? There's no words there; it's just music you're hearing, right? That's where most people are wrong! You don't hear music; you feel it with your soul. That's where it stems from.

Think about it. You're able to feel emotion in your body from someone just playing an acoustic guitar or a piano. They're not singing, there's no words, it's just a collection of different chords and sound waves. But it can make you feel happy or sad. Why? Well, this much I know...music is made of notes, and notes are made from frequencies, and frequencies are nothing more than vibrations. And for some reason, when your soul hears those frequencies, your body responds with emotion. Why do our bodies recognize this chord as happy or that chord as sad? Well, if you can answer that, there's a good chance you could be God. It's just another one of the great mysteries of the human body. Music is a universal language. It's a miracle.

CHAPTER 20
GODSMACK'S ANGELS

Song after song just started pouring out of me, and the band was digging everything they heard. Soon everyone was getting really excited again—we were making killer music that fit in with what was happening in the music scene at that time.

I began to immerse myself in everything the band needed: getting T-shirts made, copyrighting our music, booking the gigs, getting photos done, making flyers, work, work, and more work! Every single gig we booked was a big deal for us. We would play anywhere, anytime, for anything. We played backyard cookouts for a case of beer at a motorcycle club called the Talons in New Hampshire. We'd play a biker's ball convention thrown by the Hell's Angels just to get in front of people and try to expand our fan base. Some shows were great, others were terrible, but the good always outweighed the bad—our love for the music kept us going. That adrenaline rush that you get when you're on stage watching people appreciate and react to music that you wrote from your soul is better than any drug you could ever take.

We'd been introduced to the Hell's Angels through my friend T.C., who became friends with them while he was vice-president of the Talons. We actually became pretty popular with the bikers for a while. They were our first real audience in the beginning, although those weren't always the best gigs for us. Bikers can be a tough crowd—if you suck they won't hesitate for a second to let you know. We were a hard rock band and most bikers are big fans of classic rock or southern rock, so it was a little bit of a drag to be up there trying to knock 'em dead with our music when most of them were chanting "Freebird" or "House of the Rising Sun." But they always respected us and at least we never got booed off the stage. As time went on, we became friends with a lot of them and they became regulars at our shows.

There are good and bad sides to having bikers like your band. Obviously, the good is, who's gonna fuck with you when you've got Hell's Angels surrounding you? The bad is, they can get rowdy real quick. Think about it: mixing Godsmack with the Hell's Angels is like drinking Red Bull and gasoline. The fortunate part was, the buzz was getting around and we were attracting more and more people— including girls. We were finally getting some hot chicks to like our band.

Unfortunately, all the bikers were knocking out their boyfriends at our shows. Silly things would happen, like some Hell's Angels dude would pinch some chick's ass and the boyfriend felt brave enough to chest up to the biker, which inevitably resulted in that guy getting knocked the fuck out! That had to stop.

On the New Year's Eve before '97 we played a party in Lawrence, and again, some dude stepped out of line with the boys and got fucked up real bad. A fight broke out, and this kid who had already got his ass kicked was being carried outside over this biker's shoulder while a couple other bikers were still elbowing the dude in the face like it was target practice or something. All the girls got spooked and began to file out one by one, taking their boyfriends with them, until the place was completely empty. At the stroke of midnight we were playing to less than a handful of people. Happy fuckin' New Year!

Then there was the time at the Tank in Revere when one of the biker guys was complaining about the air conditioning being too cold and asked for the owner to turn it off. When the owner refused to accommodate him, the dude pulled out a gun and shot the air conditioner. Well, that did it for me. I had to put an end to this downward spiral. I hadn't spent my whole life building my career, reputation and fan base just to see these unnecessary events tear it all down.

My first phone call was to T.C.—I explained to him that things were becoming so crazy that people were afraid to go to our shows. I couldn't blame the people. They were just trying to go out and have a good time and enjoy some rock 'n' roll. I'm not so sure I would go to see a band if I knew it was always going to be a hassle either.

The only way I could think of stopping this madness and allowing our band to grow was to confront the leaders of those causing the problems. But that meant a confrontation with the Hell's Angels, and I was shitting myself thinking of having to take on that responsibility. I mean, I love my band and all, but was I willing to get my head bashed in over it? I was just hoping that they'd respect me for being honest and understand that we were just trying to make a career for ourselves, and that we didn't want to become known as the band that always had trouble at its shows. So I asked T.C. to talk to the guys and ask if they could not wear their colors at our shows anymore.

Now, if you know anything about bike clubs, you know that asking a biker to take off his colors is something you just don't do. You would have better luck trying to milk a dog. But it was the only way to make things right again. Don't get me wrong, just about all the bikers I know are good people, but just like in any large crowd, there's always a few bad with the good. Unfortunately, when bikers wear their colors in large groups it intimidates people, especially young little college girls.

After several meetings and phone calls with the clubs, they finally did right by the band and respected our request to back off and let us get on with our career. I really believe that this happened only because they appreciated my honesty, and because I treated them with total respect. Therefore, the respect was returned. To this day we're good friends with a lot of Hell's Angels and they continue to show their appreciation for our music, and I'm glad they have been a part of our story and our success.

CHAPTER 21

SO YOU WANNA BE A
ROCK SUPERSTAR?

Like the guys in Cypress Hill said, "So you wanna be a rock superstar and live large?" Well, here's the kind of shit you might have to go through to accomplish those dreams.

Right around the time we hired Joe Darco as the new drummer, our friend Eric was talking to us about recording a CD. Muskrat and myself had been hanging with this dude for a couple of years by this time and the both of us rented a second floor apartment from him in Lawrence. Eric became very close to the band. He began helping us pay for things like renting extra lights so we could do something a little bit cooler for the show than most bands were able to do, or helping us decorate for a Halloween bash. He'd always say to me, "I want to help you guys out because I want to see you guys get signed. I love music, I just don't know anything about it except for listening to it. Since I can't play an instrument to save my life, I want to learn more about the business; maybe I'll invest in a small record label or something."

Although we were good friends, Eric was nothing like us. We were all from the streets and had always struggled to earn a buck here and there; he was raised by a good family, got a good education and built up a great business for himself. But there's a saying that goes, "Rich people stay rich because they're greedy and cheap!" Eric was the type of person who wouldn't bat an eyelash at spending hundreds of dollars on a party to make himself look good, but God forbid you asked him for five bucks to get a pack of smokes. He'd come up with every excuse in the book why he couldn't afford it. And this is a guy who owns his own land surveying company and makes $100,000 a year.

Cassette tapes were quickly becoming extinct and CD's were becoming very cheap to manufacture. So everyone began recording their own CD's and people were starting indie labels all over the place so they could put out their own demos. But we didn't have the money for a CD—we were struggling just to scrape up a few hundred dollars to make a hundred t-shirts to sell at our gigs. Eric claimed that when he came to our gigs he'd hear people in the audience saying, "If these guys had a CD I would buy it."

One day in early 1997 Eric asked me what I thought it would cost for us to record a full-length CD. I asked him why, and he responded, "If it's not too expensive, I'm thinking about lending you the money to get one done. You can pay me back by selling the CD's."

He even added this, word for word: "If I make my money back that's cool, but if I don't, I don't even care. I just want to learn about the business. It will be an investment for me to learn about something I'm really interested in."

Then he went on: "Maybe I'll start my own label and we can sell the CD's ourselves until you guys sign a record deal, then I can say that I helped you guys get there. And in the meantime I'll get to learn a bit more about the biz."

I hadn't a clue what it would cost, but I told him I'd poke around and ask some people I knew from my Strip Mind days what they could do for us. Then Eric really blew me away. "If you can get it done for under $5,000, here's what I'll do. I'll lend you the money, but I take a hundred percent of the sales profits until my five grand is paid back. We'll take the cost money and put that back into making more CD's. After I get my $5,000 back, I'll take ten percent of the profits and you guys can take the rest."

I was so grateful to know that someone was actually going to step up and help us that I told him I would gladly take that offer, and made it clear that if we ended up getting a record deal because of him helping us, not only would he have made his $5,000 back and probably some extra from the 10%, but we'd even throw him an extra $25,000 or something out of our record advance to say thanks for being the guy who stepped up for us.

That was the deal. It sounded great to us because we benefited by having a CD to shop around to labels and radio stations. Once we signed a record deal, we would give each other a big hug and kiss and he would let this small-time city band go and grow up. And he'd get the glory of knowing that he was the hidden hero behind it all, the guy who gave us our break. It was a perfect friendship deal.

The first person I called was Andrew Murdock, the engineer who recorded Strip Mind's pre-production at New Alliance studios. I told him we had eleven or twelve songs we wanted to track and that we could do it extremely quick, possibly even over a weekend. We knew that tracking and mixing twelve songs in a three-day period was a little unrealistic, but we were well rehearsed and we worked fast in the studio. He agreed to take on the challenge and quoted us about $2,500. Then I called Super-Dupes, a CD printing manufacturer out of Wilmington, Mass., who quoted me about $1,500 to print 1,000 CD's. That was all well within our budget. As long as we tracked the songs in a three-day period, we were in good shape.

The only thing left was the CD artwork. Luckily we knew this local photographer named Susan Slater. I'd met her one night at the Rathskellar in Boston. She approached me and told me she was a student photographer and she really liked our band and wanted to shoot us live, for free. How could we refuse? It fit right into our budget.

Later that day I called Eric back and gave him the quote on the project. He gave the go-ahead to start recording, but said he wanted to have his attorney draw up a small contract stating the arrangements we had agreed upon. We told him that wouldn't be a problem because we wanted him to feel confident about us paying back his money, and since we were all such great friends, we trusted him to do the right thing in the contract.

Man, we were so excited that February day when we starting recording our first album. I was really hyper and anxious to get our gear set up at New Alliance and get the show on the road. Andrew and myself had recently patched things up about our first little scuffle in Strip Mind, so working together again was really pleasurable. He knew about the buzz we were creating in the New England area and felt this was a long shot he was willing to gamble on. Boy, was he right!

We loaded in very early in the morning, set up all our gear and got all our sounds together by mid afternoon. With me on the drum kit and Robbie and Tony across from me with their rigs cranked to 11, we began tracking every song we had. From "Moon Baby" to "Voodoo," we went right down the list, bashing out song after song after song. For the time frame we had to work in, we were the best threesome we could have been.

By the end of the third day, we'd tracked every song we knew. Then we spent another two days with Andrew working our asses off mixing. We worked ten or twelve hours a day to get it done. I started feeling bad about having Andrew work so hard and go beyond his call of duty by giving us the extra days to mix, but I'm very grateful to him for doing it and not bitching about it, or even charging us more dough. He obviously believed in what he was hearing and that's what kept him excited about working on this project. It's amazing that the mixes sound as good as they do, considering the limited amount of gear we had to work with and how rushed we were. We finally left there six days later with a complete set of songs ready for the press.

Our photographer friend Susan shot our first show back with Joe as our new drummer at the Axis club in Boston. A small crowd showed up that night, but the photos looked great and we used them in the CD insert; Susan also shot everything else on that disc including the inside band photo and the cover photo.

Don't ask me what we were thinking when we came up with the idea for the CD cover. It sounded like a good idea at the time, but looking back at it now, it wasn't very cool at all. (I'm talking about the CD cover that was on the self-released CD, not the version with the girl with all the piercings—that one came out after we signed to Republic/Universal.) We used our friend Christine Coleman as the model. She's sitting in front of a stereo system as if she's listening to music. The cassette tape is shooting out of the tape player, wrapping her all up as if she is being consumed by the music. Her hair is sticking straight up in the air and smoking as if she got zapped when the tape attacked her, and we caked a horrendous amount of makeup on her to make it look like she was someone who had no clue about fashion, real exaggerated. It was so bad. But it's what gave us the title of the CD, *All Wound Up*.

For the first run we printed one thousand copies, which was all we could afford with the money from Eric's loan. We'd sell some to get Eric his money back and to print more copies, and give away some to record labels, radio stations and press.

We were so pumped when we got that call from the manufacturer to come pick up those CD's. We couldn't wait to get them in our hands. We'd worked so hard writing and recording these twelve tracks, and we were really proud of them and couldn't wait to let everyone hear them.

Me and Robbie jumped in his van and raced to the manufacturer. We loaded up all one thousand CD's and drove right to rehearsal to meet the other guys. Even though Joe didn't play on the CD, we had still wanted to do the right thing and have his photo in there as the drummer, so that's what we did, and that's why he was just as excited to get a copy for himself. We all stood around and tore a case open to see the new shrink-wrapped professional-looking CD we had created. We ripped open the plastic, flung open the CD tray, grabbed the insert from the tray and lo and behold, there it was, our first batch of CD's, hot off the presses! And not a one of them was right.

As Murphy's Law teaches us, what can go wrong, *will* go

wrong. Every single CD had Joe listed as Tony and Tony listed as Tony, so we had two Tony's in our band, and a lot of the lyrics were either missing or incorrect. Oh boy!

So our first batch wasn't perfect; that sure as hell wasn't going to stop us from doing what we had to do with them. I immediately got to work sending CD's to every radio station in New England and every record company I could think of that I had made any kind of connection with during my Strip Mind days. Even if I didn't know people at a particular radio station, I still sent them a copy, hoping that someone would give it a listen.

The first stations to get the CD were WAAF in Worcester, Massachusetts, WBCN in Boston, WHEB in Portsmouth, New Hampshire, WHJY in Providence, Rhode Island, and WGIR in Manchester, New Hampshire. With most of those stations I went in on pure luck, without knowing anyone there. The only station I knew some people at was WBCN, but they never showed us any love in the beginning. Their first response to our fans calling up and requesting a song was, "Godsmack *who?* Yeah, we'll play that—at three in the morning. *Click!*"

As I went to the post office one day to mail out some CD's, I bumped into Frank, Meliah Rage's attorney. He asked me what I was up to, so I told him we had a new CD out and we were shopping it for a deal. He asked me for a copy. Of course I gave him one, figuring that he had more connections in the industry than I did.

A day or two later, my phone rings. Frank starts telling me how much he loves the CD and wants to work as our attorney and possibly our manager to shop our demo and help us get signed. With no other connections in sight, I ran to the guys in the band and bragged to them about meeting with Frank, and how well he was connected in the industry; he could help us get our foot in the door. They trusted my judgment and agreed to meet with him. So I set the meeting at a restaurant within a mile or two of all of us.

We all sat at this little Mexican joint in Derry, New Hampshire, with our best game faces on, pretending we knew what the hell we were doing, but knowing damn well that we hadn't a clue.

By the end of the meeting we all knew without even saying a word that we were going to work with old Frankie-boy. Even though we weren't sure what we had just got ourselves into, we signed a year contract with him, figuring that it couldn't hurt to let someone else help us, and if within one year he couldn't get us a deal, we had the choice to re-up the contract with him or boot him.

In the meantime, Eric had come to us with his contract. All three of us sat at the table in our buddy Rick Poulin's house (where Robbie and I lived at the time) and listened to the next bullshit pitch from our friend who'd had his own crackerjack attorney draw up the next piece of crap.

Now, I didn't know my ass from my elbow when it came to contracts and legal stuff, but what I did know was that Eric was a very close friend of both Robbie and me, and we trusted him completely. I even remember Robbie saying to Eric right there at that table, "Dude, I don't know all this legal crap, just tell me it says we'll pay you your money back. Once you're reimbursed, you'll take ten percent of our profits until we sign a deal, then you shake our hands and walk away, right?"

Eric replied, "That's exactly it! I don't want anything more from you guys than what I put in plus ten percent, and if I can be the guy that helps you get a deal, cool for me!" We signed it, shook hands and walked away.

A few months went by and we were back in the club scene. Eric and Robbie's brother Todd (who you may know as Fester from the *Smack This* DVD) would sell our CD's at the shows as best they could, but we never sold more than five or ten at a time. We just continued to inch our way through the streets of Boston, Manchester, New Hampshire, and Rhode Island, sweating blood and tears and collecting fans one by one.

Here's another piece of advice I'd like to share with you if you're starting a band: stick to a certain area when playing the club scene. Don't travel too far out of a 50-60 mile radius. Every 2 to 3 months or so, make another lap through those towns. Make as much noise as you can in one area so you attract as many people as possible. It will also attract the attention of industry people to you. Don't feel like you have to be in New York or Los Angeles to get a deal. That's bullshit! Just create as much of a buzz as you can in one area and you'll eventually draw the right people to you.

I was working day and night thinking of ways we could make more progress. We started a fan club and used our rehearsal space as our return address. We made our own t-shirts and printed up one hundred of them with the money we'd saved from gigs. We even set up a business account at the local bank so we would look more professional when we had to write a check for something. Without really knowing it, we were creating our own business and doing it right.

I eventually went down to a place in Boston called Newbury Comics, which is a pretty cool New England-area chain of stores, sort of like Hot Topic. I'd always been blessed with the gift of gab, so I figured maybe I could bullshit my way through convincing someone there to take our CD and sell it. A lady named Beth Dube, who was the product manager for all of the Newbury Comics stores, became another one of the hidden heroes in the success story of Godsmack. I thought I'd have to beg and grovel around to get her to take our CD, but instead, she gladly offered to take ten at a time on consignment and see how they sold. I'd had no idea stores would take CD's on consignment—that's how much I knew. I didn't even know what the word "consignment" meant.

I was so excited I almost jumped right out of my skin. "A real record store is going to sell our CD! Woo-hoo!" At that time, Newbury Comics had about seventeen stores. If we could get CD's moving in all those stores, we would definitely get a much bigger buzz going. I knew this was a good thing for us. Beth told me she would send us a check for the ten CD's once they sold and then re-order more. Good enough for me. Now we could just tell people where to buy the CD rather than try and sell them solely at our shows. Plus, now we could send out mailers to everyone on our mailing list, telling them that the album was available at Newbury Comics.

Not too long ago, the band went to do an interview that turned out to be right next door to that same Newbury Comics that started us out. As we pulled up, I recognized the building. I reminded the guys about Beth and told them we should go in and say hi to her, and that it would probably freak her out. So we walked in the building and were greeted by some warehouse dude. We asked for Beth and he said, "Hang on a second, I'll get her for you."

Soon she came to the door with a little baby in her arms. We all greeted her and told her that we just wanted to drop by and say hi and thank her again for everything she did for us in the beginning.

She stood there looking surprised. "This is so bizarre! How did you guys know I was here?"

"I recognized the building," I said. "This is where we did our business right?"

"Yeah, but what's freaking me out is I retired when I had my baby about a year ago and I just came in today for the first time to visit everyone and say hi myself."

So there you have it—fate works in mysterious ways.

At rehearsal one afternoon, the phone in the studio rang. We all just looked at it for a second because no one ever called that number. I picked it up and hesitantly said hello. A voice on the other end said, "Hey Sully, this is Rocko from WAAF. I finally listened to your CD and I love it. If you don't mind, I would like to spin 'Keep Away' on the night program."

I said, "Yeah, whatever dude, who the fuck is this for real?"

After he convinced me that it was really him, I hung up the phone and looked at the guys and said, "Holy shit! That was fucking Rocko from WAAF. He wants to play 'Keep Away' on his show. Fuck *yeah!*"

We were so psyched we could've shit ourselves. Sure enough, that night we all tuned in to the radio and heard Rocko announce our first whiff of fame on WAAF.

"*Here's some new music from some local boys out of Methuen, Mass for ya. Off their new demo titled* All Wound Up, *which you can buy at your local Newbury Comics store, this one is called 'Keep Away' from Godsmack on the only station that really rocks, 107 point 3 W-A-A-F!*"

POW, motherfucker! It's on! Every one of us was calling

the next guy, "Dude, it's on! Did you hear it? Turn on your radio!"

We rambled on to each other like a bunch of high school girls talking about giving their first blowjob.

A year later Rocko was still spinning this song three to four times a day and creating a buzz for us that we didn't know was possible. It was the first time we started to realize what radio could do for you. The more he played the song, the more people came to our shows. The more people came to our shows, the more the record sold at Newbury Comics. The more the record sold, the more people requested it on WAAF. On and on it went, snowballing until we couldn't keep up with it anymore.

What started out at ten CDs a month for Newbury Comics quickly turned into 100 a month, then 500 a month. They were selling as fast as we could have them made. We paid back Eric's loan in three months! By late '97 it got to the point where we were selling 1,000 CDs a week out of the Newbury Comics chain. We were outselling Metallica and all the other national rock bands. We even became the #2 best-selling CD in New England through that chain of stores. We were so busy trying to keep up with it that we didn't realize it was finally starting to happen for us.

The only mistake we really made through out that time was when we saved up some gig money and financed a trip for ourselves out to L.A. to showcase for some record labels. The trip cost us a bunch of money and we got nothing out of it—except some bad news that we found out a little sooner than we might have.

Our old drummer Tommy's ex-girlfriend Gayle lived out in Los Angeles, where she worked for Korn's management company. Gayle tried to hook us up with some showcases but we only did two shows and didn't play in front of anyone but Gayle, her new boyfriend and the bartenders. Not a single person showed up. And we opened for Tommy's new band, which was weird, too. I know it made Joe feel uncomfortable, but Tommy was real cool with him and we ended up having a good time. It also reminded us of how much better Tommy was than Joe, and Tommy realized that he missed playing with us.

On the plane ride home we discovered a major problem. Joe was sitting about five or six rows behind Tony, Robbie and myself. I kept noticing him twitching and being extra fidgety, and his eyes would roll back in his head like he was convulsing or something. At first we all were like, "Dude, check out Joe, he's stuck in the middle seat between two fat guys and he's freaking out."

We'd laugh about it a little and randomly keep looking back to check out what he was doing. He would stand up and walk around the plane looking insane, then he would go back to his seat when the flight attendant would tell him to, and within seconds fall right back into the tweaking thing.

Every time he'd see us looking back at him, he'd snap out of it for a second, then the eyes would start rolling around again the second we looked away. That's when I stopped laughing and started realizing that he was going through some kind of drug withdrawal. I started thinking back to all the rehearsals when he'd come in and look real grey and wired, and when we would break for dinner, he would just tell us that all he ate were Sugar Babies and Tootsie Rolls. That should have been a dead giveaway right there. All the signs of a junkie were right there in front of me. I'd been around drugs my whole life and I didn't even realize that our own drummer was jacked on heroin.

After confirming it with some of his close friends, I decided that this was not a place I was willing to go back to. I didn't want to have anything to do with anyone who was on drugs. We gave Joe several chances to clean up his act, but he just kept lying to us. It all came to a head when we played our first real showcase at CBGB in New York City.

We spread the word to all our New England fans that we were going to showcase in New York for a bunch of record labels that attorney Frank had supposedly set up for us. We sent out a mailer asking people to sign up for fifty bucks and come to New York with us to pack the club for the big gig. The money went towards paying for two buses to New York, and they all got a free t-shirt that we had specially made for this trip. It had a picture of us on the front and in big letters on the back it said, "*The day Boston fuckin' raped New York!*"

Even Rocko and our friend Ian Barrett, who was the producer for WAAF's "Real Rock TV show" (a local cable rock show that was televised throughout most of New England) came down with us, taped the show and aired it when they got back.

For the most part the trip was a success. We didn't get signed from that showcase but we had a really good time and we showed everyone from the world-famous CBGB what kind of pull we had in the Boston scene. We'd filled two Greyhound buses with the rowdiest bunch of Godsmack fans we could muster, and together we were rocking the house. Everything felt great. We were cranking out song after song and everyone was jumping and cheering for us through the whole set.

Then we got to "Moon Baby" and Joe fucking blew it completely. I'm not sure if he was wasted or just really nervous about the show, but we were right at the end of the song and he drew a blank and forgot where he was; for whatever reason he just would not end the song. Now, that's not such a big deal, we all do it sometimes, but Joe was forgetting songs all the time these days. We would rehearse every day for weeks before a show, get everything perfect, then he would get on stage and just forget it all.

So we're onstage at CBGB and it was like the CD was skipping, but it was live. Several times I turned back at him and gently gestured for him to end the song. But he'd just look at me with this panicked look on his face and continue playing, so after what felt like a lifetime of looping the same part over and over again, I turned to him and yelled, "End the fucking song, Joe!"

Then Robbie came over and yelled the same thing, "Joe! Fucking end it!" Finally Joe put the brakes on and we got out of it alive. Phew! It felt like forever.

That's when I knew we had to get a new drummer. Joe was just not in the same headspace as us. We were so focused and hungry for success and he just didn't seem to care enough to want to sober up and put out the effort we needed.

In January of '98 I finally made the decision to let Joe go. When we got back from the trip to New York we all met up at the railroad station to load in our gear. Before Joe got there, I sprung it on Tony and Robbie that I'd had enough. Those guys used to be pretty quiet and rarely spoke up about anything, but to my surprise they strongly agreed that it was time to find a new guy. We were growing fast and Joe wasn't able to keep up with us. I know it broke his heart at first, but I think he's come to terms with the fact that he had plenty of chances to turn things around for himself, but just chose to ignore our pleas. So that was it, Joe was out.

So there we were again, back to a three-piece with no

drummer and wondering where to go from there. Quitting wasn't an option. We had a really strong buzz going on in New England, so that thought never even crossed our minds. Things weren't bad; we just needed to find another drummer, and quick!

Then one day I was in my bedroom in the basement of Rick Poulin's house, sitting at my computer working on leads for a new drummer when my phone rang. I heard a man say, "Can I speak with Sully Erna please?"

"This is Sully!"

"Hey Sully, my name is Avery Lipman from Republic Records."

I think I said, "Yeah, sure it is, Eric! Quit fucking around!"

"No, seriously. We've been noticing how well you're doing in the New England area through the Soundscan reports that we monitor from Newbury Comics, and we want to sign you to our label and distribute your music nationally."

I *knew* my friends didn't know that kind of music business terminology—this guy was for real! I can't even remember what I said after that. I was in shock, standing there in my room as if someone had shot me up with a stiff dose of Thorazine.

When I came to my senses, I thought, "Fuck this, Paul Geary is taking this band. I can't handle this anymore. We can't even keep up with the amount of CD's that we're selling on a weekly basis, and now this? We need a manager!"

I knew that Paul was a big reason that Extreme was so successful—he pretty much co-managed the band throughout their career. He's very smart and he's a self-made guy from the streets, just like me. And like the best people in my life, Paul had earned my trust over a long period of time.

In the past, I'd begged Paul to manage the band, but he

always gently declined, claiming he had too much going on. But this time he wasn't getting off the hook so easy. He'd started managing a couple of acts that hadn't panned out so well for him, then he opened up the Strand Theatre in Providence, Rhode Island for a while, but eventually that didn't work out either. So the stars lined up; he seemed desperate for success as a manager, and we were desperate for success as musicians.

I called him up. "Paul? You've got to take another look at our band, dude. We're doing as good as we can do in the area, and I'm afraid that if we don't get something soon, this thing is going to eventually just fizzle away. Now I've got fucking record labels calling me in my bedroom offering me deals. Help!"

I went over his house and showed him the business we were doing, and we talked and talked. He suggested a meeting with the rest of the band. He was very grateful for my offer, but I was thinking, "Why is this guy thanking me? Doesn't he realize that he's the one helping us?" Little did we know that we would be the reason for each other's success. Godsmack got the help we needed from an honest and trustworthy person to help us grow to the next level, and Paul got himself a rock band that kicked ass and helped his management company grow.

Paul has not only proven himself a great manager, but more importantly, we've been able to maintain our friendship exactly as it was the day we were hanging out in his basement ten years ago, polishing off a few bottles of Dom Perignon while we played Road Rash on Sega until three in the morning. Those were the days.

When the band got to Paul's house I'd already briefed them about Paul and how good he could be for us, so they already knew he was going to be the guy for the job. Of course they wanted to meet him. After several hours of conversation, we all stood up and happily shook hands, congratulating each other that we finally had a manager. This project really had a shot at going somewhere.

CHAPTER 22
GREEDY LITTLE BABY!

The first thing I did when I got home was call Eric and tell him all the good news. I was extremely excited, rambling on and on about how great this was going to be, and how we were finally going to get a record deal and have a manager and go on tour. I assumed that Eric would be just as excited as me, but the more I bragged about shit, the more evasive and standoffish he seemed.

I took a step back. "Don't you get it, dude? Republic is going to sign us and we'll be able to throw you a decent check to say thanks for all you've done for us. I'm not sure how much they'll give us yet, but if it's something like $300,000 or so, we'll flip you $25,000 just for helping us out."

"What about my ten percent after that?" he said.

I was stunned. "What do you mean ten percent? Ten percent of what?"

"Your record sales."

"What the fuck are you talking about? We agreed on ten percent of profits while we were selling the CD ourselves, then if we got signed you would cut us free. We're offering you a check out of the goodness of our hearts to show you that we are truly grateful to you for helping us out. *So what the fuck are you talking about?*"

"Dude, I can take a lot more than ten percent of CD's if I want to be a real dick and stick to the contract," Eric said. "I can take ten percent of *everything!*"

All of a sudden, I got real worried. "Oh shit," I thought to myself. "What the hell did we sign when we signed that contract with him?" I needed to get off the phone to buy myself some time to call someone, and have them look at this thing for us.

At that point I immediately stopped being argumentative and switched to a nicer, more agreeable tone. "You know what, Eric? You're right. You deserve to be a part of this. I'm sure we'll work things out. Let me talk to Paul about how we include you into this deal and I'll call you back."

I sat there with steam shooting out of my ears. The thought of this little son of a bitch trying to cash in on something that I worked for my entire life was enough to make me nauseated.

I should've known better. People like that don't get embarrassed. They don't even realize how ridiculous they look when they're acting that way. They become obsessed with the whole money thing and they forget about loyalty and ethics. They forget how to be a decent human being and treat everyone around them like shit. Bad mistake: *never* sign anything without clearing it with your attorney first. There's too many ways of twisting words around that can seriously fuck you later. But like I said, we trusted Eric like our own brother.

Unfortunately you don't think people will ever do something to you. I mean, even his ex-girlfriends would mention to me about how much of a real tight-ass he was with his money and stuff like that, but I didn't ever think he would pull any crap with *us*. All the signs were there and none of us caught them in time. Sometimes people show their true colors right away, but if we don't pay attention to it and realize that those aren't the people we should have around us, we only set ourselves up for pain somewhere down the road. That's the lesson I learned from Eric: listen very seriously to your first instincts about people.

This was the first time in that whole three-year grind that I felt like I'd really fucked something up. Whenever I'd taken control in the past, the results had paid off. But this time I felt like I had let down the team, like I'd been caught in a lie—the lie that I knew what I was doing.

Well, I wasn't going to let this happen. I called Paul Geary, frantically explaining to him that we might have trouble and told him all about my phone call with Eric.

None of us had thought to get an attorney to look at these documents before we signed them, and now we desperately needed to know exactly what this piece of paper said. Paul told me to come by and drop off the contract so he could have a look at it and then pass it on to an attorney.

The next day my phone rang with the news from hell: "Sully, we have a problem here," Paul said. "This guy can really fuck you guys if he wants to. This contract is worded so vaguely that he could not only take ten percent of all record sales, but if he knows what he's doing, he could take ten percent of all your merchandise, publishing, concert income and tour support all the way through the year 2004, everything."

After I picked the phone up off the floor, I asked Paul what we should do. He said, "Let's be real careful how we handle this, kid. We need him out of the picture as soon as possible before the band makes any kind of real money. Otherwise, we may never get rid of him." Remember that old saying, "Keep your friends close but your enemies closer?" Well, that was our new mission.

It was the most painful thing we'd had to deal with yet. I tried everything to snap Eric out of it and let him see the bigger and better picture. I sat down with him several times as a friend and tried to reason with him.

"Eric, we're friends, dude," I said, "What are you doing throwing this all away for a paycheck? You can seriously come out of this with some extra cash and more importantly, you'll be the hero behind the whole success of Godsmack if we make it. Think about it. You'll be the guy in all the articles that we'll say helped us out when no one else would. I can tell the whole world you fronted us some money to get us started, and because of the demo we were able to make with that money, we were finally able to land a record deal. Isn't that more important than trying to suck us dry and never being friends again? You've got to let us go and grow up as a band. We have to get away from the local scene in order to accomplish that and none of us have the capability of doing that unless we have the help of a real manager and a real record label. So let us go, man!"

Nothing worked. And believe me, I was sincere at first in trying to salvage the relationship, despite what he was trying to do to us. He showed no interest in that at all. He heard nothing I was trying to say, or maybe he didn't want to.

Eric was obviously not budging and was going to create a problem with us signing our deal, so at that point I had to tell the band what was up. When I approached the guys, their jaws hit the floor. They asked me if I tried this, and if I tried that, and all I could say was, "I've tried everything. He's being a prick!"

Finally Robbie blew up and revealed that the whole time

I had been arguing with Eric, he had been at Eric's house building him a brand new deck. Robbie was very handy with construction, so Eric went to Robbie and asked Robbie to save him some money and build him a big deck with a hot tub in the backyard of his new home. Robbie, being the good guy that he is and not knowing that his so-called buddy Eric was being a scumbag, not only agreed to do it for him, but built Eric a $15,000 deck and only charged him $5,000.

Now *my* jaw was on the floor. Robbie was so pissed off, I could see his face getting beet-red to the point where I thought he was going to burst right in front of me. Eric had reached a new low. It was one thing to just be a greedy little bastard, but now here was Robbie, who's a real honest hardworking guy, building this beautiful patio and cutting him a great deal on it while Eric was ripping him off behind his back.

This went on for almost a year. Robbie finally confronted Eric and asked him what the hell he was thinking, figuring he could get through to him because they'd known each other since high school. But all Eric could see was dollar signs.

"Why shouldn't I collect on this?" Eric said. "The way I see it is, this was a smart business investment."

Well, I have to give him that much. It really was a nice roll of the dice for him. I guess it all depends on your own values—if friends and family are less important than making a quick buck, and you're willing to burn the people who care about you to get it, then be my guest and go for it. As for me and the boys in my band, it's not our style. Loyalty is sacred to us.

Finally, we just had enough and decided to let Eric go as a friend and do what we had to do to protect our future. With the help of our newly appointed attorney, Elliot Groffman, we proposed to Eric exactly what we said we would do when we all made our so-called promises to each other.

After all the bullshit he put us through, we still offered him $25,000 to show our appreciation. He replied through his attorney, "No deal! I want $100,000 to sign out."

We politely replied with, "Fuck you, you fucking loser! That's a third of everything we're getting." The two attorneys and our newly appointed business manager Jeff Schwartz finally got him to agree on somewhere around $70,000. If we agreed, he would sign the new contract saying that he would be out of our lives and have no further ties with Godsmack or any one of us individually anymore. Our team advised us to take the deal and run.

They said, "We know it seems like a lot of money right now, but trust us, if you guys become successful, you're really going to be pissed when he's collecting millions." So we listened to reason and agreed to take the deal.

Between making back his initial $5,000 and the money he made off of the CD's we had sold on our own, Eric walked away with somewhere around $80,000. I guess that was the price we had to pay to get rid of a dishonest person and learn a valuable lesson.

I've wondered from time to time if he and his attorney realize how bad they screwed up that deal. Eric always claimed to be such a smart business man, but it looks like he wasn't so smart after all.

If he only knew what he could've made off of us if he didn't hire some low-budget lawyer to represent him. But like they say, you get what you pay for.

And it cost him irreplaceable friendships. Now that I think about it, we don't really wonder about him that much at all. He's not worth our thoughts.

To this day, none of us have ever spoken to Eric again. But it sure is nice to have the last laugh. Cha-ching!

CHAPTER 23

...AND IN THE 1998TH YEAR, GOD CREATED SMACK!

In early '98, after the Eric nightmare was over, Paul was working to get our record deal in place and it was time to get back to playing the clubs. But we still needed a strong, solid drummer. My first call was to my old friend Shannon Larkin. I always knew in my heart that Shannon would be the perfect drummer for this band, but when I reached him on the phone, he said he couldn't do it because he had just started a band called Amen. I understood right away and I really didn't try to lure him away. I know Shannon, and he's a very loyal person. When he joins a band, he is there until the death of it. It's not about the money or the success for him. He's there to sink or swim with the people he dedicates himself to.

We held auditions but all we got was a bunch of meatheads. There was nothing out there. So I brought up the idea of bringing Tommy back. Robbie wasn't really down with it—Tommy always used to butt heads with us, and that made it tough to be in a band with him. But I pointed out that at least Tommy was solid and had a lot of experience; maybe it would just work out, especially since things would be a lot easier now that we had a deal in the works. Robbie reluctantly went along with it.

We called Tommy and told him what was going on. At first he seemed hesitant. He'd been spending the last couple of years getting certified as a physical trainer while working as a bar-back at a nightclub in LA. But after an hour or two of conversation, he decided that he would come back and give it a shot with us. By this time we practically had the record deal waiting for him on a silver platter. Paul had been closely in touch with Republic/Universal and they were still very eager to get our band on their label.

Tommy arrived in April and we got right to work rehearsing every day. We needed to play some gigs right away so we could tighten up our live show—that way if the label wanted to see us live, we would have our shit together.

We'd been bragging to Tommy about how good the band was doing now and how we were packing every place we played, so to prove it we set up a gig through Rocko from WAAF at Worcester State College in Massachusetts. There was no way this gig wouldn't pack them in. For one, it was in Worcester, which is where WAAF was located at the time, and we were booming on that station. And for two, it was a college. How could it miss?

We were surprised to find that the room we were playing in wasn't even close to a being a nightclub. With its narrow rectangular shape, white walls and velvet curtains it looked more like a funeral parlor. On top of that, maybe twenty people showed up. Tommy sat there looking at us as if to say, "Are you sure you guys are selling out around here?" But we did the gig and reassured Tommy that it wasn't usually like this.

After that we booked a series of shows at cookouts and different events outside of the Boston area (maybe too far out), but I guess we weren't popular that far outside of Boston yet. Everything was looking lame for us. We couldn't figure it out. We'd been kicking ass everywhere we went, but now all of a sudden it was as if no one had heard of us before.

Maybe we should've stuck to playing the places we knew we were packing in. But at the time we felt like we needed to space those shows months apart in order to keep the live attendance steady. Sometimes playing one place or one area too much can backfire as well.

We had a show coming up at the good old Tank on Revere Beach (this was the same place where the biker pulled out a gun and shot the air conditioner for being too cold). We never really felt safe playing there because of the bikers, but we needed to keep the buzz going in the Boston area.

Although, the last time we had played a gig at the Tank, I had found myself true love once again. My good friend Dawn Pothier dragged her sister Dee down there to see our band play. I had met Dawn through two girls that the band had crowned the "Original Smacketts," Sonja Courcey and Carrie Donovan. I think they came to almost every show we ever played for the first two years. Sonja and Carrie were more involved in recruiting people to our shows and making them fans than we were. They were our Godsmack Warriors!

Anyway, as soon as I saw Dee I practically fell off my seat. I remember being in the dressing room, peeking like some kind of creep through the one-way mirror that overlooked the club. Dee was sitting right below the window and I was pulling all the guys in my band over one by one to check out the blonde beauty!

Dee was wild, funny, hyper and extremely smart. Rock

music was not really her thing at the time, but even though she found herself way out of her element hanging at the scummy Tank, we still found a way to fall in love and for years had some of the best laughs together.

There wasn't any major catastrophe that ended our relationship. It was simply the fact that she was a very laid-back kind of person — the limelight thing didn't impress her. (Can't say I blame her either—it's way overrated.) She likes to kick back with her family, take nature walks, go up north kayaking, smoke a little weed with her sis on the couch while watching their favorite television shows and run Stomp, her American bulldog, around the park—the kinds of things we should all remember to do once in a while. Then there's me, the Tasmanian Devil. The fast-paced lifestyle that I lived, and still live, just seemed to eat away at her. If me and Dee had stayed together, she'd probably be gray and insane by now. But she sure was a blast to be around, and I enjoy the memories that she's given me.

Back to the Tank. Paul Geary let us know that Republic/Universal was going to come down there to see us play live. At first, all we were thinking was, "Just perfect. Bring them down to hell so we can lose this record deal." Then we thought it might be good after all. The club only holds about 200 people, tops, and we could easily put those kinds of numbers in that room and look great for the label. So that's what we planned to do. We sent out flyers and spread word of mouth to every friend and fan that we could think of to make sure that the room was packed!

So there we were at the Tank. It was Saturday night and we were right in the heart of our biggest market. Paul showed up with Avery Lipman, the general manager of Republic

Records, his brother Monte Lipman who was the general manager of Universal Records, and Arma Andon (Paul Geary's partner at the time).

Paul walks this entire crew backstage and introduces us to all of them. Actually the dressing room of the Tank was the kitchen, so it was tight back there, and to make things even worse our ex-attorney, Frank, comes barging in with a half-glass of whiskey because he'd spilled the other half all over himself, yelling and stumbling around. We had no clue what he was doing there, but he was so fucking drunk and obnoxious that it was embarrassing. The label guys were all looking at him as if to say, "Who the fuck is this guy? Is he with the band?" I was mortified, but we were able to shake it off because we knew that in a matter of minutes, we would hit that stage, light it up and forget all about any of this.

The only problem was, *nobody showed up!*

I couldn't believe it. Out of all the places that we knew we could pack, the Tank was a no-brainer. But there were maybe thirty people there. We were dying. I'm sitting in the empty dressing room with my head in my hands and I'm thinking, "We're so dead! There goes our record deal. We're in the worst club on the east coast, our ex-attorney decides to show up and cash in on the work that me and Paul had done and is hammered out of his mind embarrassing us, and worse than any of that, no one is here! We're dead!"

Sure, Paul Geary had assured us it was a done deal with Republic/Universal, but we just didn't believe it. I'd had the rug pulled out from under me before with Strip Mind, and we had believed so many liars in the past that all of us were in denial until we signed the dotted line. So all we could think about was how all the hard work we had put into this band for the last three years was about to get flushed right down the

In concert with
Godsmack in 1998

shitter. The chances of getting a label to fly in from New York to see you play to begin with are slim to none, so how the hell were we ever going to get them to come back again?

We took the stage, and I was determined to just block out the whole pathetic scene and rip it up the best I could. The whole band had the same attitude: "Let's just fucking do this!"

And we did. There was only a handful of people there, but they heard us rock one of the best performances we've ever played. We killed them.

And wouldn't ya know it? That night in that shit-ass club we signed a three-record deal for half a million dollars.

Later we found out that all the big-wigs from Universal like Doug Morris and Mel Lewinter had been hounding Monte and Avery about us. Doug Morris (the Godfather of the music industry) had noticed how many CDs we were selling in New England and called them from his private jet to say, "Don't let this Boston band get away. Make sure you sign them."

We also heard years later that right around the time they signed us, Avery and Monte were being considered for promotions, but higher-ups first wanted to see what they could do with the next band they signed. Guess who their next band was?

With Godsmack's success, Monte and Avery became presidents of their labels. And we have continued a respectful and loyal relationship with them and the entire Universal/Republic staff throughout the years, never taking our friendships for granted.

In June of 1998 we signed with Republic/Universal Records and Godsmack was officially on the scene with our first single, "Whatever." The demo *All Wound Up* that we'd recorded over a three-day period back in February of '97 for a measly $2,600 had sold more than 20,000 copies independently by the time we signed our deal. It was never re-recorded. It went on the shelves with new artwork six weeks later and to date has sold over five million copies.

EPILOGUE

Not long ago when I was cruising my old 'hood in Lawrence, I happened to drive by the old house I lived in for my first seventeen years. I noticed that some children were playing in the front yard while their elders watched over them from the porch. The house was really rundown, even worse than when I lived there. And the neighborhood was in terrible shape: trash covering the streets, groups of under-aged kids standing on the corner drinking liquor out of paper bags and clocking whoever drove by—you get the picture.

As I sat there, parked on the side of the road, I thought to myself, "Holy shit. That was me! I used to be those kids." I found myself wondering, "Do they feel as trapped as I did once? Do they think this is their destiny, to always struggle and live a life of poverty and crime?"

I wanted to go over and talk to those kids about their dream and goals, and to tell their parents not to give up on their own dreams. I ended up doing what I felt was the next best thing: I wrote this book.

I guess I could've written the typical rock autobiography about sleeping with lots of girls and stumbling around drunk on tour. Instead I wrote about the stories that paved the way to all the good things I have today. Maybe they will even help you face your own challenges.

Don't think that success can never happen to you. It *can* happen, and it does. You just have to want something so bad that you'll go through anything to get it. At one point or another I've sacrificed everything for my music: education, relationships, jobs, family, friends, you name it. But music is also what got me off the streets as a kid and gave me the emotional outlet I needed when I was older. I believe it saved my life, and I thank God for it every day.

Maybe you want to look at this book as just a bunch of crazy stories to read. If so, I hope you enjoyed it.

Just recently, during another stressful time, I decided to get a reading done by a respected astrologer named Karen Thorne. She told me, "You're at a crossroad right now. If you choose to go left, you'll face demons. If you choose to go right, you'll be guided by angels. But both roads will lead you to heaven."

Whoa! That message knocked me off my feet. It reminded me not to worry so much. Some paths we choose will be harder than others, but they will all bring us where we need to be.

I'm no Karen Thorne when it comes to predicting the future, but I can tell you my own recipe for success:

Be conscious of your decisions. More importantly, take responsibility for the consequences they bring. When struggling with your passions and goals, be patient and *never* bail out! You'll eventually get your shot. Remember that only the strong will survive.

Be willing to sacrifice things you love to achieve your dream. Expect disappointments, because they will happen over and over again. Just never forget that there is definitely a pot of gold at the end of that rainbow—it's just a son-of-a-bitch getting there!

My life has been a series of crossroads, and each choice I've made has led me in a new direction.

These days I spend a lot of time traveling around the world with my boys in Godsmack, doing what I love most: playing music for all of you. And I continue to find new challenges and dreams to pursue. Some will work out, and some will not. But the paths will always be there to choose from.

As for the rest, my friends…well, maybe someday I'll tell you about it.

AFTERWORD

LESS THAN ONE PERCENT

I must say how grateful and blessed I am to still be going strong—even right at this moment—with Godsmack. Even more amazing to me is that we have not only done as well as we have, but that we are still very relevant in today's music scene. If that does not seem so extraordinary to you, you may not fully appreciate how difficult it is just to get a record deal, let alone survive this long. I've learned a lot about the odds that bands like us face to be successful, and it humbles me when I realize that it's nearly impossible nowadays to maintain a career in this wild, fast-paced industry. I probably can't fully explain, but let me put it to you this way...

My drummer Shannon Larkin has a tattoo on his hand of an arrow pointing downward, and inside the arrow is the symbol "1%." Which stands for "*Less than one percent.*" It's my favorite tattoo of his, and I'm getting one somewhere on me soon. When I do, I will proudly wear it like a badge of honor. It represents that we are now in the company of a very elite group of people based on what we have accomplished. Allow me to explain exactly what all that means.

Out of the hundreds of thousands of bands that hustle their asses off every year, hoping for a record deal, *less than one percent* of those bands ever get signed. *Less than one percent* of the bands that *do* get signed ever get the opportunity to release a second album. And *less than one percent* of those bands that actually get the chance to do a second album will ever receive a Gold Record (500,000 units sold). And those are the facts, Jack!

So to have the opportunity to be able to do what I *love* to do for work *and* beat those odds is something just shy of a miracle. And as you know by now, I've beaten a lot of the odds that were not in my favor, battling most of my life to get to where I am today.

And what a ride it's been! I don't want to be a tease here. I would love to have you walk with me, right now, down the path of my life in Godsmack. The only problem is that I don't know how that story ends yet, because I'm still living it!

There have been so many...how should I say, "interesting" events and experiences I have encountered throughout my years with this band that I wouldn't even know where to begin. After all, I've been traveling and touring now for almost 20 years! And when I tell you, *"I've seen it all and walked it tall,"* that's just an understatement. And one day, for sure, I will bring you with me when me and the boys decide to write *that* tale.

You can look at it like this. I sat down one night recently with my girl Joanna, chit-chatting about life over some wine as we usually do. Knowing what a crazy adventure we had to go through just for us to be together—I mean *Crazy Story*—we both realized that out of all the things that we've learned in our lives, the one thing we know for sure is: *We really don't know anything*! There are just too many unpredictable things that life throws at you every day that alter your course.

I know we all like to think that we're in control most of the time, but things just happen, and they constantly turn and twist our realities into new directions that we have to try and figure out and adapt to.

From the time I was growing up as a young punk, to figuring out a way to use all that anger and fear to become a successful musician, to becoming a father, and now crossing into another chapter in my life where the clouds have finally parted, I see life differently, better, more colorful and hopeful. Who would've ever known this is where I'd be?

Even the style of music I've chosen to pursue at this point has expanded. As I've grown from a boy to a man, I feel and see things differently. And over the years I felt this yearning to get out on my own and explore this new transition I was feeling.

It wasn't even so much that I wanted to not be a part of Godsmack, because I truly love my band brothers, and we really have worked so hard to get over the mountain of addictions and egos over the years, which I'm more proud of than anything. And we're tighter now than we've ever been by overcoming those challenges. But that's another story for later.

This was more about needing to fill a void. And I will never forget the first time I walked on stage without them. It was in Buffalo, New York at a small theatre called the Bears Den. Lights went down, intro played out, and it was... Show-time! All I could remember thinking was, "OH MY GOD!! I'm about to walk out on stage by myself? Are you kidding me? How the hell am I going to entertain this audience for

90 minutes? And what the hell am I going to talk about?"
My heart was pounding and my hands were trembling to
the point that I feared clunking on the guitar and making
a fool of myself. Because when you go solo, and there's no
band or *anyone* on stage backing you up to fill the music;
when you clunk, it's *very* obvious!

But once I got past the first song, I was home free.
Everything became very natural and fun again, and I truly
fell in love with doing *that* kind of performance immediately.
I knew right then and there that not only did I love this,
but it was vital to me to continue exploring this path.

Like my latest project *Avalon*. This debut solo album that
I chose to record was so important to me at this point in my
life. Now that I think of it, it was crucial for me to release
this work as well. All my life I had stuffed down the pain and
challenges that left me with so many scars. And now I've been
able to release those demons and forgive myself and others for
so many things through this very real and vulnerable album.
It was my opportunity to really get honest with myself.

It actually all started back on Godsmack's 4th album. As
soon as I wrote the melody for a song called "Hollow," I knew
that I wanted to use a female's voice to create a duet. I immediately thought of a dear, long-time friend of mine, Lisa
Guyer, who I've always admired as one of the best female blues
singers around. I called her and she agreed to work with me.

And after hearing the result on that song, I had realized
how well our voices worked together.

So years later when I decided to write a new album, I
called Lisa up and told her that I was interested in starting
something fresh, with a new sound. Over the years, I had
been inspired by bands like Dead Can Dance and Vas, and
amazingly, around that time Dead Can Dance, who hadn't

toured in many, many years, had decided to do a limited amount of dates in the U.S. I invited Lisa to come see the show with me at the Boston Orphium Theatre. She was blown away, hypnotized and inspired by how deep and powerful music like that could be. And it was at that show that I met percussionist Niall Gregory, who surprisingly had been a fan of Godsmack as well.

A few months or so later I got Niall and Lisa on the phone to discuss our trying to form something that was unpredictable, earthly, but modern. We weren't sure what is was going to be or sound like, but we knew that if we could take all of our musical influences and blend them together like a salad, we had a good chance of creating something really special and unique.

From there it all happened very organically. Lisa brought in a musician she knew and worked with named Chris Lester, who brought in a guitarist named Tim Theriault, who brought in the keyboardist Chris Decato, and so on it went.

We had discovered Irina Chirkova, our cello player, through my friends Leo Mellace and Steve Catizone. Leo and Steve owned Sanctum Sound Studios in Boston, which is where we recorded *Avalon*.

Irina had been teaching at colleges in the Boston area for over ten years after moving here from Bulgaria and graduating as a classically trained musician. And after hearing her play for literally less than one minute, I knew she was a perfect fit for this project.

Between all of us, one riff lead to another and melodies just started flowing. And the more we wrote, the more honest and vulnerable it became. I didn't try to control it or sensor it; I just let my body vomit it up, and piece by piece I carved it and arranged it.

I didn't even realize what we had until I was mixing the tracks in the studio with my producer/engineer Andrew Murdock, who you may remember from earlier in this book. And it was then that I sat back as these songs sang themselves back to me and realized, "Wow! This is really good!" And not only was it good, it was a complete departure from anything I had ever done previously with *any* band I had been a part of.

Put it this way: I've now learned that Godsmack is one side of me, Sully Erna is the other side and I need both for balance. Period! If you eat vanilla ice cream all the time, you eventually crave chocolate. Well, this was more like a huge bowl of rocky road! Just tons of textures and flavors. Yummy!

The title track "Avalon" refers to a place that certain faiths believe they go to when they pass on. Some religions don't have concepts of Heaven or Hell. They believe they go to a place of wheat fields and apple trees, blues skies and running rivers (The word "Avalon" actually means "the land of apples.") One well-known Avalon is from the legend of King Arthur, the island where he sails after his final battle to seek peace and healing. And so the song is about the feelings and thoughts that you experience while being under a meditative state of mind. It's an audio journey, but one that also takes you through a visual experience of colors and places. And I felt the album should begin with this track because it's so hypnotic that it sucks you in and sets the tone for the album. Beautiful!

"My Light" is a love song, the first I had ever written to my daughter Skylar. It's my promise to her as a father to always be there for her.

"Eyes of a Child" I had written about the anger and sadness I had felt once while watching a news special about young children who were dying of AIDS, and how unfair life can be sometimes.

"Sinner's Prayer" was a really fun treat for me. That one came unexpectedly through a great friend of mine, Paul Harb. Paul used to be Godsmack's video director and had moved on to work with Sly Stallone as a film editor. He had called me one day after speaking with Sly about me when Sly was looking for some new music for the movie *The Expendables*. It was one of my "Holy Shit!" moments.

I'll never forget when I walked into Stallone's office. The hallways were decorated with giant posters from all his past movies: *Rambo*, *Rocky*, *Cobra*, etc. I remember thinking how cool it is to be a movie star. But it wasn't until he actually walked into the room and introduced himself to me that I thought, "Holy fucking shit! It's Rocky Balboa!" I mean this guy is not just a star, but probably *the* biggest action hero of *all time*! And what an unbelievably cool guy he was. You can still find the song on the Director's Cut of *The Expendables* DVD in the opening scene of the movie. Thanks for that opportunity, Sly! I'll cherish it forever.

"7 Years" was an interesting track to develop. Because as we completed the music, I remember thinking, "This is a nine minute epic; what the hell am I going to write this song about?" But then it hit me. And it turned out to be the perfect topic to write about for a long song. "7 Years" became the title, because I had just ended a 7 year relationship with Jen, Skylar's mom. But our relationship was only part of it. The song became more about the people and paths we cross in our lives, and how we grow and learn from them. Not to dwell and punish ourselves for the mistakes we make, but to cherish the moments, and honor the experiences. "Life is but the memories we've created. For others to remember you in your life!"

And of course, "Broken Road," the most vulnerable and heartfelt song I have ever crossed paths with so far. Knowing that I was in a place and time that I wasn't meant to be in anymore, and trying to figure out how to pick up the pieces and start over again, it was truly a reflection of a very difficult moment in my life.

We all have moments of "Where the fuck do I go, and how do I begin again?" One of my favorite expressions of this is Alanis Morrisette's "Not As We." Check it out if you can. Very powerful lyrics.

I've been so happy with the results of *Avalon*. For a debut solo record, it has done extremely well. People have even compared it to Pink Floyd's *Dark Side Of The Moon*, which is such an honor because it's probably my favorite album of all time. But by no means am I, or anyone saying that it rises to the level of Pink Floyd's masterpiece. That would be blasphemy in rock 'n roll. I think it was more of the critics trying to explain *Avalon* as being a very powerful and visual album that paints unique pictures for you as you listen to each song.

And the logo, which many people have asked about, is simply three crescent moons and a star that make up my initials, SE.

There was a time when I felt I regretted coming from Lawrence and being subjected to the life I had. Deep down inside I think I was embarrassed to admit to people that I was a ghetto kid. But I don't feel that way anymore. I really am proud to be from Lawrence, Massachusetts. It taught me certain things about life that are priceless to me now. Things that not many people can understand unless you've lived in that life and came out of the trenches okay. Things like strength, survival, integrity and compassion. It made me the person I am today. And I wouldn't change that for anything in this world. That's the reason, in "Broken Road," I wrote the lyric "I don't know if I could say I've been through everything, but I've walked this earth alone with bare feet broken in the snow." It's a metaphor for saying, I'm not sure I've been through it all yet, but I sure as hell know what it feels like to push through life in pain. I've been through war, and have the scars to prove it.

Even in the song "My Light" when I tell my daughter, "Here I am, and I never thought I'd say, if ever I could live my life again, I'd live it your *way*," I'm trying to tell her, "Learn through my mistakes, baby, that sometimes the better way to live your life is through innocence and simplicity."

I wish I could tell you where I go from here and what I'll do next, but like I said before, life is just too unpredictable. And we can only hope that our dreams and wishes come true. But we've been gifted with an imagination and the power of prayer. So I say, close your eyes and make a wish. Imagine your life *exactly* the way you want it. You may be surprised that the fairy tale that you've always hoped for isn't so far away after all.

I sure as hell don't know where this new chapter in my life is going to take me, and it's scary as hell sometimes to think about it. But something in my gut tells me that after all I've been through, and after being led to where I am today, it's all going to have a really great ending someday.